Iran Auto

Since the revolution of 1979, scholars have portrayed the Islamic State's industrial development capacity in a negative light. Global isolation, incoherent economic planning, and predatory Islamic institutions are often cited as the reasons for lackluster development. In *Iran Auto: Building a Global Industry in an Islamic State*, Darius Mehri shows how this characterization is misguided. Today, Iran has one of the world's largest automobile industries with national technical capacity. Previous studies ignore the consequences of three decades of Iran's capacity for successful industrialization and changes in global technology transfer that allow countries, even ones isolated from formal global institutions, to build an automobile industry. Mehri shows how industrial nationalists in Iran constructed a network of politically effective relationships to open up space for successful local industrial development and then tapped into a set of important global linkages to create an industry with high local manufacturing content. This book will open up a new line of inquiry into how countries in the global south can develop a successful national automobile industry without the need to conform to global economic institutions.

Darius Mehri holds a Ph.D. in Sociology from the University of California, Berkeley. Before becoming a sociologist, he worked as an automobile engineer in the United States and Japan. His publications have appeared in the *Socio-Economic Review, Studies in Comparative International Development*, and the *Academy of Management Review*. His book on the Toyota production system titled *Notes from Toyota-Land: An American Engineer in Japan* was published in 2005. He currently works as a Risk Analyst at the New York City Department of Buildings.

Structural Analysis in the Social Sciences

Mark Granovetter, editor

The series *Structural Analysis in the Social Sciences* presents studies that analyze social behavior and institutions by reference to relations among such concrete social entities as persons, organizations, and nations. Relational analysis contrasts on the one hand with reductionist methodological individualism and on the other with macro-level determinism, whether based on technology, material conditions, economic conflict, adaptive evolution, or functional imperatives. In this more intellectually flexible structural middle ground, analysts situate actors and their relations in a variety of contexts. Since the series began in 1987, its authors have variously focused on small groups, history, culture, politics, kinship, aesthetics, economics, and complex organizations, creatively theorizing how these shape and in turn are shaped by social relations. Their style and methods have ranged widely, from intense, long-term ethnographic observation to highly abstract mathematical models. Their disciplinary affiliations have included history, anthropology, sociology, political science, business, economics, mathematics, and computer science. Some have made explicit use of social network analysis, including many of the cutting-edge and standard works of that approach, whereas others have kept formal analysis in the background and used "networks" as a fruitful orienting metaphor. All have in common a sophisticated and revealing approach that forcefully illuminates our complex social world.

Recent Books in the Series

Iran Auto

Building a Global Industry in an
Islamic State

DARIUS MEHRI

CAMBRIDGE
UNIVERSITY PRESS

CAMBRIDGE
UNIVERSITY PRESS

University Printing House, Cambridge CB2 8BS, United Kingdom

One Liberty Plaza, 20th Floor, New York, NY 10006, USA

477 Williamstown Road, Port Melbourne, VIC 3207, Australia

4843/24, 2nd Floor, Ansari Road, Daryaganj, Delhi – 110002, India

79 Anson Road, #06–04/06, Singapore 079906

Cambridge University Press is part of the University of Cambridge.

It furthers the University's mission by disseminating knowledge in the pursuit of education, learning, and research at the highest international levels of excellence.

www.cambridge.org
Information on this title: www.cambridge.org/9781107171671
DOI: 10.1017/9781316761564

© Darius Mehri 2017

First published 2017

Printed in the United Kingdom by Clays, St Ives plc

A catalogue record for this publication is available from the British Library.

Library of Congress Cataloging-in-Publication Data
Names: Mehri, Darius, author.
Title: Iran auto : building a global industry in an Islamic state / Darius Mehri.
Description: New York : Cambridge University Press, 2017. | Series: Structural analysis in the social sciences
Identifiers: LCCN 2017029158 | ISBN 9781107171671 (hardback)
Subjects: LCSH: Automobile industry and trade – Iran.
Classification: LCC HD9710.I73 .M44 2017 | DDC 338.4/76292220955–dc23
LC record available at https://lccn.loc.gov/2017029158

ISBN 978-1-107-17167-1 Hardback

To my parents, for endowing me with the intellectual capacity and courage to pursue higher education.
And to my twin boys, Adrian and Emil, who bring constant joy to my life.

Contents

Figures

Tables

Acknowledgments

I am indebted to a number of people for their help and support. Peter Evans for his inspiration to take on the project of Iranian automobile development. His scholarly advice was instrumental in understanding the complexities and nuances of industrialization in the global south. Neil Fligstein for introducing me to social field theory and how it can be used to analyze positive development outcomes in intermediate states. Heather Havemen for her inspiration to appreciate and apply mixed methods in social science research. Robert Cole for his many conversations about the global automobile industry and his myriad suggestions to improve the manuscript. Taghi Azadarmarki of the University of Tehran for educating me about Iranian politics and industrialization.

I would also like to thank the reviewers who provided excellent advice to shape the manuscript and to improve its theoretical framing. In addition, a number of scholars provided valuable feedback by reading chapters of the book or during conference presentations. These scholars include Josh Whitford, Clemente Ruiz Duran, Danny Breznitz, Andrew Schrank, Sean O'Riain, Kevan Harris, and Peter Moore.

Without the assistance of local Iranians, fieldwork would not have been possible. I would like to thank Hossein Bahrainy for his valuable research assistance and for his contacts at the University of Tehran. Aref Vakili was instrumental in making contacts in the automobile industry, in setting up interviews, and for archival research. Ali Dadgar assisted in finding valuable archival data at government development agencies. Hossein Mirazi for teaching me about how to interact with government and Islamic institutions and setting up interviews with managers at automobile companies. Others who were very important include Yadollah Dadgar, Ali Heidarnia, Noushin Sayar, and Samira Kazempour.

I would also like to thank Roberta Scholz for her excellent editing work and Gloria Chun for teaching me how to write more clearly. I am grateful to Ali Sadegh, my former engineering teacher at the City College of

New York, who was the first to inform me about the existence of Iran's automobile industry. Thanks to Mike Ross of CGI International, who taught me how engineering consultancies develop automobile industries in the global south.

I would not have been able to complete my dissertation without loving support from my family. Without the child care support from my mother-in-law, Socorro Gomez Ching, I would not have been able to conduct fieldwork in Iran. Socorro, I will always be indebted to you for being a wonderful and loving grandmother to my children. My wife, Meilin, for her support and encouragement throughout the years, even during the tough times of pursuing a Ph.D. in sociology. To my twin boys, Adrian and Emil, who have always brought me great joy, especially when my dissertation began to form into this book. In loving memory of my mother who gave me tremendous love and affection as a child and young adult. Many thanks to my father for his intellectual and emotional support to pursue a Ph.D. Also, in loving memory of Mahin Afzal, my aunt who provided a place to stay in Tehran for this research, and who provided my family with many years of loving support, especially during my mother's illness.

Finally, I would like to thank my former mentors and friends at the University of Hartford, where as a young adult I learned the importance of scholarly work. Barbara Streitfeld, my first semester psychology teacher and advisor, has been a great friend for many years and encouraged me to seek higher education. Howard Mayer who taught me the basics of good writing and the value of being a great writer. And David Goldenberg who has been a fan of my work over the years.

Introduction

Automobile industries have historically played an important role as case studies in understanding the success and failure of economic development. Countries that have attempted to build a national automobile industry have often chosen to do so as part of a larger project of promoting modernity through industrial development and the accrued benefits of long-term economic growth. In the automobile industry, these benefits include backward linkages to automotive parts suppliers who in turn support the plastics, rubber, and steel industries. Since automobiles are expensive, when exported abroad they provide a country with capital. Automobiles also transform society through the implementation of new manufacturing techniques (Kronish & Mericle, 1984; Biggart & Guillen, 1999). It has recently been estimated by the International Labor Organization that in 2004, 8.4 million people across the globe worked in automobile production.[1]

In the post–World War II era, many countries in the global south have attempted to take advantage of the economic benefits of automobile manufacturing by developing a local automobile industry with national brands. Only Japan and South Korea have been successful in this endeavor.[2] Since the 1980s, China, Malaysia, and India have attempted to emulate their success. An unlikely, and surprisingly successful, addition to the group is Iran, which in 2011 successfully produced 1.4 million vehicles a year and became the world's eleventh-largest producer of passenger cars, the fourth largest in the global south, and the largest in the Middle East.[3] Thousands of research and development engineers currently design national vehicles, while approximately 400 tier-one parts suppliers produce 70 percent of the local manufacturing content.

---

[1] www.ilo.org/wow/Articles/lang–en/WCMS_115469/index.htm. This does not include the jobs related to the sales and service of automobiles.

[2] Countries that have not succeeded include Indonesia, Thailand, the Philippines, Mexico, Brazil, Peru, Argentina, and Turkey.

[3] http://oica.net/category/production-statistics.

1

With $20 billion in revenues and an average annual growth rate of 29 percent since 2000, the automobile industry is the second-largest industry in Iran outside of oil.

This book focuses on the post-revolution success of the Iranian automobile industry. Despite enjoying a near monopoly and various subsidies, it stands out as the only industry in Iran where large enterprises have well-developed backward linkages to small and medium-sized enterprises (UNIDO, 2003). These linkages have created an industry that is Iran's largest source of employment (currently, over 100,000 direct employees and 500,000 to 1 million indirect employees).[4] Furthermore, it has been relatively successful on international markets – exporting over $500 million worth of completely built-up automobiles and parts to regional markets in 2011.[5] The post-revolutionary rise of the industry offers stark contrast to its less successful earlier performance: despite 15 years of development under the Shah, the Iranian auto industry by 1979 had only a low volume of assembly operations.

Given the commonly cited requisites for the development of a successful auto industry, Iran should not have been able to develop one. A remarkable characteristic of automobile industrial development in Iran is that it accomplished its goal of building a national industry despite decades of US economic sanctions and isolation from global economic institutions. According to the Economist Intelligence Unit, of sixty nations surveyed Iran was ranked fifty-ninth in overall openness to the world economy (Amuzegar, 2005). Iran is not a member of the World Trade Organization or the World Bank and has not allowed direct foreign investment to influence industrial strategy.[6] This book will show how there are more ways to tap into global linkages to build an industry than the conventional policy of conformity to global institutions, and it does so in a very interesting way with general implications about the role of engineering consultancies in building indigenous technical capacity. In this way, it is a novel contribution to the network-centered development literature that argues globalization has created new opportunities for industrial development (O'Riain, 2004; Wong, 2005; Whitford & Potter, 2007; Block, 2008; Breznitz & Murphree, 2011; Schrank & Whitford, 2011).

---

[4] Iran Statistical Yearbook (2005–2006), Statistical Center of Iran.
[5] Besides oil, rugs, and pistachios, the automobile and the related machine tool industries are Iran's largest exporters. The automobile industry has close to ten times the export revenue of the electronics industry. From World Trade Organization: www.wto.org/english/res_e/statis_e/statis_e.htm.
[6] Since the revolution, the amount of FDI entering Iran has been low compared to that of other developing countries. In 2000, the amount of FDI in Iran amounted to US $1.35 per capita compared to $12 in Turkey, $31 in China, and $68 in Malaysia. (From *Strategy Document to Enhance the Contribution of an Efficient and Competitive Small- and Medium-Sized Enterprise Sector in Iran*, United Nations Industrial Development Organization, February 2003, p. xxiv.)

In addition, the broad consensus within the sociology of development literature is that states shape development. Scholars argue that state structures have important implications for positive development outcomes and, more broadly, for economic growth and social provision. They further argue that successful development requires high state capacity, whereby development agencies are autonomous but embedded in society to coordinate development activities (Evans, 1995; Kohli, 2004; Chibber, 2006). The scholarship analyzing Iran's economic development since the revolution, however, portrays a negative view of Iran's state capacity. It is argued that political factionalism in post-revolutionary Iran has led to entrenched, institutionalized disagreements about which economic policies are best to adopt (Siavoshi, 1992; Baktiari, 1996; Moslem, 2002). Factionalism has resulted in a diminution of state autonomy, resulting in incoherent economic planning that in turn has led to industrial and agricultural decline (Amirahmadi, 1990; Schirazi, 1993; Amuzegar, 1997b). Islamic institutions and foundations that own large industrial organizations are implicated in transforming Iran into a rent-seeking predatory state (Maloney, 2000; Saeidi, 2004). Furthermore, self-interested actors in government bureaucracies have created import monopolies undermining local industrial development (Keshavarzian, 2009).

Economic dependence on resource-based exports should have further undermined the capacity of the state to develop an automobile industry (Karl, 1997). Instead of creating an economy that is accountable through taxation, oil-rich countries rely on oil as the primary resource for state revenues. This resource dependency has a large impact on a state's institutional development and its ability to direct the activities of private interests. The state – and not the private sector – becomes the center of accumulation, and hence institutions are structured around state actors who live off the teat of oil revenue. This arrangement leads to the hyper-control of development through high rates of patrimony and centralization, and industries eventually fail due to inefficiencies and incompetence.[7]

The influence of Islamic laws and institutions on industrial development should also have undermined Iran's ability to develop an automobile industry. In clerical establishments, typically characterized by traditional authority and age-old principles, appointments of staff members into positions of power are based on patrimony over merit (Weber, 2013). In addition, Islamic states tend to have "despotic" regimes that undermine protection of property rights and embrace laws that diminish the ease of opening private businesses to support economic development (La Porta,

---

[7] Karl's analysis should be distinguished from more strictly economic theories of "Dutch disease," a process in which export revenues distort prices in such a way as to discourage industrialization and agricultural development.

Lopez-de-Salinas, Shleifer, & Vishny, 1998, 1999). We would therefore expect that a modern industrial development project in an Islamic state would fail.

The anomaly of Iran's automobile industry raises a number of important questions as to why Iran, a country with many factors that should impede industrial development, stands out as one of the few countries in the postwar era to develop a large automobile industry with national brands and indigenous technical capacity. Where did the state capacity come from for automobile industrial development? What roles did agency and the stabilization of the political and industrial fields play in transforming institutions to open up space for development? In the face of its isolation from formal global institutions and further exacerbated by US sanctions, how did Iran obtain the technology to develop an industry with domestic technical capacity? Why didn't the dominant political role of the clerics and the "resource curse" undercut the ability to construct an industry?

In this book, I will show that insulation of the Iranian automobile industry from a key set of organizations and from other parts of the state apparatus created a successful "mini-developmental state" for the automotive sector. I will also contend that origins of state capacity were contingent upon key actors constructing a network of politically effective relationships at key historical time periods to push forward a nationalist agenda. The Iranian auto industry, however, operates at the intersection of two fields: the political field and the industrial field. Institutions and strategic actors operating at this intersection were key to both constraining and making possible the necessary autonomy for successful industrial development. Once industry autonomy was established, the industrialists established infant industry protection. Then, despite isolation from formal global institutions and capital as well as the presence of US sanctions, they were able to tap into a set of important global linkages with engineering consulting firms, parts suppliers, and peripheral multinational automobile producers – all of which created an industry with high local manufacturing content. The engineering consulting firms, whose role goes largely unrecognized in the scholarly literature, were particularly important in transferring the necessary knowledge and technology to Iran so that industrialists could develop national brands with indigenous local capacity.

This book will make three major contributions to the industrial development and globalization literature. First, it will build on a subset of state capacity literature that studies intermediate states, which have a state apparatus that exists on the continuum between the predatory and developmental ideals. More specifically, it will argue that developing countries can achieve successful development outcomes by carving out a "pocket of efficiency" within a larger state apparatus that is otherwise not conducive to successful industrial development (Geddes, 1990; Cheng, Haggard, & Kang, 1998; Evans, 1998; Hout, 2007; Hertog, 2010). According to these studies, a pocket of efficiency is created largely through a top-down approach: a ranking state actor creates and protects the development organization from social groups seeking to undermine it for their own gain. Considering that scholarship, this research takes a different approach. Building on the social field and balance of power literature (Waldner, 1999; Moore, 2001; Khan, 2004; Doner, Ritchie, & Slater, 2005; Slater, 2010; Saylor, 2012; Hau, 2013) it shows that the construction of a pocket of efficiency in a politically fractious state relies on a higher degree of *agency* by mid-level industrialists to create and sustain a coalition to support industrialization.

The second contribution is the concept of sequencing. The dynamics of how states evolve through different levels of efficiency is not well studied. The importance of sequencing is much easier to understand when focusing on a sector rather than the evolution of the state as a whole. The sequence of constructing a "pocket of efficiency" in Iran's auto industry was a dynamic process: causality went from conflicts between industrial-nationalists and neoliberals and the left, to elite business-state alliances, to a pocket of efficiency lodged in the development agencies. My analysis of this process builds on the idea that a stable political field and elite coherence are important for building state capacity; it differs from studies emphasizing top-down processes by showing how pockets of efficiency can be formed through a middle-up lobbying process. I will argue, however, that a pocket of efficiency is fragile because a development agency's autonomy is directly related to state officials' ability to support and maintain the agency, protecting it from strong outside social forces that oppose or undermine development over time (Geddes, 1990; Evans, 1998). This shifts the focus away from associating state capacity with type of state (weak or strong, predatory or developmentalist) to an evolving sequence of developing agencies on the part of social groups with a shared agenda and the resources to realize it.

Third, this book will build on recent network-centered development theories arguing that the reconfiguration of industrial production has created new opportunities for industrial development (Gereffi & Korzeniewicz, 1994; O'Riain, 2004; Whittaker, Zhu, Sturgeon, Tsai, & Okita, 2010; Block & Keller, 2011; Breznitz & Murphree, 2011; Keller & Block, 2012). By building on current theories, it will introduce engineering consulting firms as important global network actors in transferring technology for the development of an automobile industry. The concept of global technology "networks" is important because local ties to engineering consulting firms enable countries to develop automobile industries with greater local indigenous technical capacity and to design and produce products with a greater degree of independence and autonomy from global automobile assemblers.

The role of engineering consulting firms in national automobile industrial development offers a completely different model, compared to more standard works on the auto industry, which privilege relations between global firms that dominate the end market for final products and national industries in less developed countries (Kronish & Mericle, 1984; Jenkins, 1987; Doner, 1991; D'Costa, 1995; Harwit, 1995; Biggart & Guillen, 1999; Thun, 2006).

This model, therefore, has a number of important implications for industrial development. First, despite the inability or denial of some national efforts to comply with political rules governing global economic relations instituted under the neoliberal order, there is still space for less developed countries to access technology via global corporate networks. This contradicts studies claiming that neoliberalism undermines national industrial development (Chang, 2002; Wade, 2003). Second, despite a country's isolation from global institutions and centers of economic power (i.e., the United States), it can still develop an industry with high technology if it establishes ties to engineering consultancies. Third, global corporate networks should not be treated as homogeneous. Different sorts of global corporate networks have very different properties and very different implications for national industrial development. Last, the positive potential for networks building around control of technology, without control of capacity, to compete in final product markets has been insufficiently acknowledged in the existing literature.

The arguments proposed in this book require theorizing to explain how state capacity was established in a politically fractious, incoherent state apparatus with predatory tendencies. The theoretical frame will include an explanation of social and institutional changes leading to the formation of state capacity. In addition, the theory will explain how, in the current globally integrated economy, isolated countries can construct a strategy to transfer the technology required to build an industry with high local technical capacity. The following sections will review the sociology of development literature and current institutional theory applicable to the case of the Iranian automobile industry as well as provide a brief explanation of the book's findings and arguments.

State of the Literature

The Global Reconfiguration of Industrial Production

The postwar development of automobile industries was associated with a late development strategy whereby developing countries absorbed knowledge and technology created in already developed countries.

Development strategy incorporated a step-by-step process of industrial upgrading: from assembly operations, to the manufacturing of vehicle parts, and finally the creation of research and design laboratories. One advantage of late development was the ability to borrow or license technology from the "technological shelf" created by already developed countries (Gerschenkron, 1962; Amsden, 1989; Whittaker et al., 2010). During the manufacturing stage developing countries could rely on reverse engineering to deepen technical capacity, taking advantage of developed countries being more lax in the enforcement of intellectual property rights (Kim, 2004). Manufacturing enterprises were vertically integrated, and the large manufacturing companies owned or tightly controlled their parts suppliers. If a developing country therefore established a tie to one or more large vehicle manufacturers, it could obtain the assembly and parts technology to manufacture vehicles.

Some scholars posit that the global reconfiguration of industrial production and rapid innovation have undermined late development strategies (Breznitz, 2007; Whittaker et al., 2010; Breznitz & Murphree, 2011). Industrial reconfiguration is associated with two major changes in global production – industrial "fragmentation" and the rise of global value chains (Gereffi & Korzeniewicz, 1994; Arndt & Kierzkowski, 2001; Sturgeon, 2002; Whitford & Potter, 2007; Sturgeon, Biesebroeck, & Gereffi, 2008). Industrial fragmentation began with the outsourcing movement of the 1990s when the large manufacturers spun off their parts supplier companies. The outsourcing strategies allowed parts suppliers to establish independent supplier relationships outside their traditional assembler-supplier network. In addition to this policy change, large automobile companies expanded into emerging markets in the 1990s – outsourcing the production of parts to a supply chain in regions where they had established assembly operations. These new policies delinked innovation, design, and marketing from production and thus created large, independent global parts suppliers with increased scope and scale of operations.

Along with the increase in fragmentation, the automobile industry is now a globally integrated industry where modular components and parts, made in several worldwide locations, are produced and supplied by global automobile parts suppliers to the lead automobile assemblers. The rise of global value chains has resulted in a given country's ability to develop a niche in design or production of automobile components at a particular stage in production – and to market those components via a global supply chain.

Rapid innovation has also undermined late development strategies. Highly integrated advanced electronics have replaced many of the simpler mechanical components in most contemporary vehicles. The most important of these new technologies are in advanced engine design and electronic control units that are key components in meeting stricter global environmental standards. These changes have weakened the ability for developing countries to rely on reverse engineering to develop local technical capacity during the early stages of product development (Block, 2008).

A less well understood impact of the reconfiguration of industrial production is that it has opened up a space for engineering consulting firms to play a critical role as key network actors to assist in building greater local, indigenous technical capacity for automobile industrial development. Engineering consulting firms achieve two goals. First, they transfer higher, value-added technology and knowledge as well as their own intellectual property rights to local firms. In this way, developing countries can move up the automobile global value chain by acquiring rapidly innovating technology without the need to depend on multinational automobile assemblers. Second, consulting firms use their own network of ties to global parts suppliers to help developing countries create local industries with independent, national brands. This is accomplished when they link local parts suppliers to a network of global parts suppliers to license and manufacture parts locally.

Many of the most prominent engineering consulting firms were founded prior to the mid-twentieth century. Their core business through the 1980s existed mainly among large automobile assemblers in Europe and America. Starting in the early 1990s, the firms began to expand their client base when automobile companies started to outsource their engineering research and design work (Turner, 1996; Robinson, 1998). This policy increased the engineering knowledge and technical capacity of the firms, making them more important players as "knowledge and technology brokers" (Bessant & Rush, 1995; Hargadon & Sutton, 1997). The engineering consulting firms are now multinational corporations with offices in Europe and the United States and in developing countries that are active in developing national automobile brands. Technology transfer through engineering consultancies is most important for isolated countries, such as Iran, that do not have as much access to conventional technology as countries that are more globally integrated.

The reconfiguration of industrial production, therefore, has created new opportunities for industrial development not available to countries prior to globalization. Countries, however, need to engage in a network-centered strategy whereby they establish links to multiple actors. These actors include ties to multinational assemblers of finished automobiles, multinational parts suppliers, and – if they are developing national brands – engineering consulting firms. The industrialization process in the current global economy, however, requires a state to have sufficient capacity to coordinate industrial activities. The next section will discuss the role of state capacity and how it has changed due to the reconfiguration of industrial production.

Developmental and Neo-Developmental State Theory

Since the 1980s, the coordination of successful industrial development has been attributed to the concept of the developmental state (Johnson, 1982; Wade, 2004). A prominent subset of the development state scholarship is the work on state capacity. According to state capacity theorists, states can be divided into two ideal types: developmental states that enable industrial development and predatory states that undermine development (Evans, 1995; Kohli, 2004). Developmental states tend to have coherent Weberian bureaucracies that are autonomous but embedded within society. Autonomous bureaucracies allow state actors to implement a development project without political influence or capture from social groups or classes. They are characterized by individuals driven by collective goals and tied to state agencies as well as their constituents. A bureaucracy's *esprit de corps* allows it to transcend individual interests in order to achieve national goals, and its embeddedness allows the state to negotiate goals, monitor activities, and receive feedback to ensure the success of a development project. An important point here is that states that are high in "state autonomy" are more likely to form the embedded autonomy structure that leads to positive development outcomes. In predatory states, state autonomy is low – so development does not take hold because individual incumbents are allowed to pursue their own goals and ties to society are forged through individuals or social groups who divert a development project's resources to themselves and their constituents.

The study of state capacity offers scholars a predictive model for the success or failure of automobile industrial development. What would this development look like in the two extremes of state capacity? In ideal-typical developmental states, the bureaucracy functions as a nodal agency to coordinate and maintain coherent industrial policies leading to the development of successful industries (Johnson, 1982; Amsden, 1989; Wade, 2004; Chibber, 2006). In these states, the industrial development bureaucracies, the industrial elite, and the state are in agreement regarding which development policies to implement. Important development state policies include protection of domestic industries through high tariffs on foreign imports, guiding investments into priority sectors, and promotion of joint public/private research organizations to build indigenous technical capacity. Our understanding of state capacity would predict that an automobile industrial development project in a predatory state would be doomed to failure. State actors in government agencies would plunder the finances allotted for the industry for personal gain.

Recent scholarship on state capacity adds important insights into the factors leading to coherent policies in developmental states. Chibber (2002, 2006) argues that states with autonomous development bureaucracies embedded within society will not sufficiently achieve successful industrial development. Instead, development organizations must have significant "institutional power" to discipline agencies within the state apparatus to develop coherent industrial policies. A strong nodal organization leads to a growth-oriented alliance between state and capital. He argues that if a capitalist business class significantly weakens the power of the "nodal" development bureaucracy, a country will not have the capacity to become a developmental state. For instance, lack of institutional power of India's Planning Commission industrial agency was predicated on the presence of strong business associations that undermined its autonomy. Due to various domestic and external factors, this capitalist check on autonomy was more or less absent in Korea. Kohli (2004) makes a similar claim but emphasizes the role of a strong executive branch that uses economic nationalism as a tool to exhort social groups to engage in economic advancement.

Most states, however, are not ideal-typical predatory or developmental states. Many can be considered "intermediate" because they exist on a continuum between the two ideal types. Evans originally argued that when these states engage in industrial development, the lack of a proper balance between autonomy and embeddedness will result in mixed industrial development outcomes. For instance, states with weakly embedded autonomous bureaucracies will not receive adequate feedback from business elites on how to correct policy mistakes. States without rational bureaucracies will fail due to close patrimonial ties to business elites who will create a rent-seeking industrial apparatus (Evans, 1995; Wright, 1996).

Subsequent studies, however, show that industrial development can succeed in intermediate states – or, in more extreme cases, where the state apparatus is dominated by predatory behavior. These states have industries where key actors in the state apparatus have carved out an "island" or pocket of bureaucratic efficiency (Geddes, 1990; Cheng et al., 1998; Evans, 1998). A pocket of efficiency refers to a development bureaucracy intentionally created to be independent of state bureaucratic control; hence it is insulated from clientelistic pressures within the state apparatus and social groups that can undermine industrial development. This arrangement allows development agencies or firms to control their own financial and human resources, thereby leading to a greater probability of achieving successful industrial development. A pocket of efficiency, however, is fragile because a development agency's autonomy is directly related to state officials' ability to support and maintain the agency from strong outside social forces that oppose or undermine development over time (Geddes, 1990; Evans, 1998).

Even if a country can create a pocket of efficiency for an industrial sector, it is broadly understood that since the early 1990s it has become more difficult for nations to implement developmental state policies. Developing countries are now incorporating a global economic integration strategy whereby they are conforming to rules put forward by the World Bank, the International Monetary Fund, and the World Trade Organization. These policy strategies typically include privatization of state-owned industries, reduction or elimination of trade barriers, and relaxation of state control over the markets through deregulation (Woods, 2006; Harvey, 2007). The aggregate of these organizations and the rules and laws they promote are what at times is referred to as the "neoliberal regime."

If global integration and policy conformity to global institutions represent the new paradigm for industrial development strategy, Iran's global economic isolation raises important theoretical questions as to how it was able to develop an industry with indigenous, local technical capacity. Current theoretical frameworks to address this question can be summarized in terms of three perspectives. First, successful industrial development can be achieved only with a nationalist developmentalist strategy (Chang, 2002; Wade, 2004; Kohli, 2010). According to this view, the neoliberal regime threatens industrial development by forcing counties in the global south to eliminate high tariffs on imported products. In addition, recent World Trade Organization rules are creating further multinational corporate control over technology by enforcing strict intellectual property laws on patented technology.[8] It is argued that this new policy limits the development of indigenous, local technical capacity by prohibiting the utilization of reverse engineering during the early stages of product development and by increasing multinational corporate domination over the higher value-added technology (Block, 2008).

A broad set of respected economists, however, claims the opposite: the more fully a country is integrated into global markets and conforms to global policy norms, the more successful its industrialization project will be (Bhagwati, 2004; Wolfe, 2005). The globalist scholars claim that relying on locally developed manufacturing technology will retard industrial development. Tariffs inevitably create "rental havens," where a lack of competition creates inefficient industries and reduces incentive for technology upgrades. Instead, their approach points to the benefits of full integration into the global economy and a highly reduced role of the

---

[8] These scholars often cite the World Trade Organization rules in the Agreement of Trade Related Aspects of Intellectual Property Rights (TRIPS), incorporated toward the end of the Uruguay round on the General Agreement on Tariffs and Trade in 1994.

state in development. Industrial development should be through foreign direct investment, joint ventures, and global competition in order to compel companies in a country to adopt new organizational techniques and technologies.

More recent scholarship on the "developmental network state" has posited a more nuanced theory of development. These scholars claim that global economic forces have transformed the ability to implement a nationalist developmentalist strategy. Rapid innovation, the reconfiguration of industrial production, and the neoliberal regime prohibit countries from relying on infant industry protection that favors large, national firms in transferring technology for industrial development (O'Riain, 2000; Breznitz, 2007; Block, 2008). According to this perspective, the state should be conceptualized as a facilitator and organizer of industrial development. For instance, the state should organize and facilitate the development project through joint ventures or foreign direct investment or by establishing R&D laboratories that enable high-level knowledge and technology acquisition. In addition, the state should help facilitate connecting a global network of innovation and organizational technology to local networks of learning among engineers, businesspeople, and government officials in order to generate industrial capacity. The state should also motivate the private sector to make long-term commitments to industrial development. The idea here is that the ties create new opportunities for industrialization because they facilitate the development of local business innovations that "bubble up from below" that can be marketed on a global supply chain (Negoita & Block, 2012).

Developmental network state scholars believe high state capacity leads to positive development outcomes but that the state cannot be conceptualized as a commander of industrial development. They claim that in the new global economy, state development organizations should be conceptualized as autonomous entities not beholden to social groups or special interests; they are embedded within the industry insofar as they facilitate and help establish ties between local industrial organizations and foreign firms. During this process, they monitor the project and receive feedback on the best industrial policies to pursue.

The Formation of State Capacity: Social Fields and Institutional Theory

Although state capacity allows us to understand the factors important for the success of a development project, it does not address two preconditions important for its implementation. The first is that political and industrial actors need to be aligned with the goals of the project. Conflicts within the political and industrial apparatus will likely lead to a depletion of state autonomy. These conflicts are often external to the development organizations but can have a negative impact on development outcomes. The second is that the ability to coordinate a development project largely depends on its legitimacy among key actors in the political field so the state can justify its long-term support. Financial and human resources need to be available on a continual basis so that entrepreneurs and development organizations can carry out the day-to-day coordination tasks. The key here is that an industrial project needs to be considered "legitimate" to the extent that the project will not be abandoned by the political or business elite.

Recent advancements in the field of neo-institutional theory provide the analytical tools to understand the preconditions important for embedded autonomy. These include the idea of a "field" and the idea of "social skill." A field in institutional theory is defined by Fligstein (2001) as containing preexisting societal practices, a unique set of rules, and actors that have cognitive structures that utilize cultural frames. Once in place, fields constrain and guide action and are generally considered domains of competition. Field theory is particularly useful in analyzing how state actors can change the rules to create stable fields leading to the rise of sectors in an economy (Fligstein & McAdam, 2011). In this case, the Iranian auto industry operates at the intersection of two fields: the political field and the industrial field. Understanding this intersection will be essential in explaining the differential success of the industry at different time periods.

Important to understanding transition in a field is Fligstein's theory of "social skill" that is based on the notion that participants in collective action need to be induced to act (Fligstein, 2001). Skilled strategic actors provide cultural frames for motivating others to engage in collective action, and they influence the field by creating a new order. In Iran two fields were important in shaping development outcomes: a political and an economic field. Within a political field, actors with social skill are "political entrepreneurs" who build political coalitions by finding ways to get disparate groups to cooperate by adopting an ideological frame that appeals to a large number of actors. Within an economic field, actors with social skill are "economic entrepeneurs" who use cultural frames and their political and economic ties to create or develop a market for their industry. I will argue that the "social skill" of key actors in the political and economic field played a critical role in the trajectory of the auto industry, especially during the years preceding the inflection point that began in 1992, when the industry's growth accelerated. The actors that were particularly effective were industrialists in the economic field who managed the large automobile companies. I will argue they were successful because they had two key components important to engage in political action: cohesive within-group relations and an advantageous structural position in the political field to achieve their goal of developing market for the automobile industry (Mizruchi, 1992).

If social skill is important in understanding changes in trajectories, "path dependence" must be given equal consideration. The idea of path dependence focuses on the way in which current possibilities for change are constrained by the structural legacies created by past political choices. The study of path dependence is particularly useful in offering explanations of the outcomes of institutions built on temporally ordered and causally connected events (Mahoney, 2000; Pierson, 2004). Path dependence constrains and guides action at critical junctures when actors make decisions on what policies to implement (Stark, 1991; Mahoney, 2001; Collier & Collier, 2002). The basic assumption is that during transitions new institutions are often built on the legacies of old institutions (Stark, 1991; Guthrie, 2001). The development path of the auto industry in Iran since the beginning of the 1990s has been constrained by the institutional structures created by the Iranian revolution – and even those created earlier by the Shah.

Biggart and Guillen (1999) have produced the most important case study on how institutions shape outcomes in automobile industrial development. They argue that automobile development depends on linking a country's historical pattern of social organization with opportunities made available by global markets. During the process of development, key actors in countries either can create a space for industries to develop or can undermine development by enacting laws that inhibit the growth of national industries. As a result, a variation for development exists, whereby countries can have a logic that favors large firms and the sale of products on the global market, small firms that sell parts on a global supply chain, or countries that are linked to the global economy through foreign ownership. These models interacted with actors and institutions in various ways, leading to the success or failure of state policies.

One of the key points to be gleaned from the Biggart and Guillen study is that historical accidents and junctures produce auto industries that policymakers may not have intended. A study of four auto industries – in South Korea, Taiwan, Spain, and Argentina – found that, at various points in time, the four states employed import-substitution and export-oriented policies that drew on mixtures of dependency or free market models (Biggart & Guillen, 1999). For instance, South Korea targeted the automobile industry for industrial development through an import-substitution policy that prohibited the imports of assembled cars but allowed tariff-free imports on components; as a result, domestic parts producers suffered. Consequently, South Korea has developed a strong assembly industry but a weak component industry and is now targeting emerging markets to expand its business. Spain also implemented import substitution to build an industry, but the outcomes were very different. In the 1950s import substitution choked private initiatives in auto assembly, and by the 1980s liberalization had led to the failure of many of the auto companies – leading to predominantly foreign ownership of the industry. Although Spain is now the sixth-largest producer of automobiles, the focus of the industry is on lower-end auto parts. In another example, Argentina opened its markets to the auto industry more than fifty years ago but allowed twenty-one different assemblers and auto parts firms to operate in an import-substitution economy that did not produce more than 200,000 vehicles a year. High costs and the mistake of requiring companies to localize content within five years – in a country without a parts market – drove the industry to ownership by foreign capital. In the case of Taiwan, foreign manufacturers were allowed to partner with local firms to build an industry. Weak local-content laws and a sudden shift to export-oriented production directed by an inept state management led to a dramatic reduction in auto production.

The Case of Iran Auto

History of Automobile Manufacturing

The Iran automobile industry was founded in the 1960s, when the Shah implemented import substitution industrialization and two large private companies were established: Iran Khodro and Saipa. The most successful vehicle produced, Iran Khodro's Peykan, was based on a knockdown kit supplied by Talbot of Britain. Citroën also established a presence in Iran through Saipa, and American Motors Corporation and General Motors had local assembly operations. Local content increased to 24 percent and

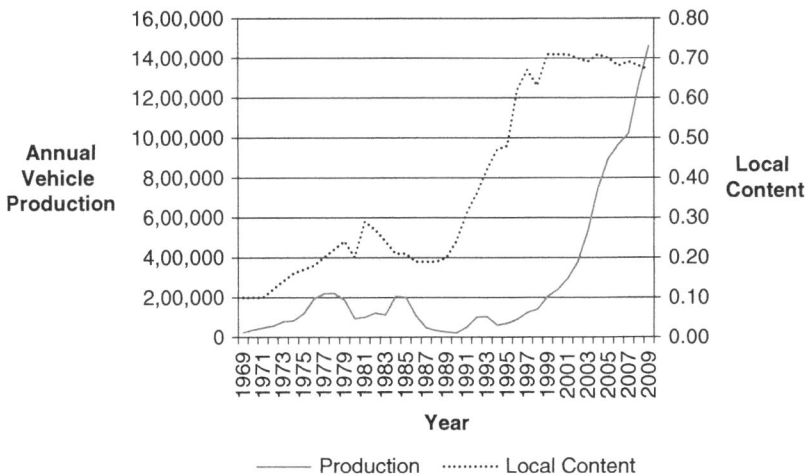

Figure 0.1 Automobile Production and Local Manufacturing Content, 1969–2009

annual production to 190,000 vehicles by the time of the 1979 revolution.[9] Figure 0.1 shows annual production and average local manufacturing content data from 1969 to 2009.

Between 1979 and 1990, the industry fell into decline. Iran severed its ties with most Western countries, and all foreign automobile companies except Talbot left Iran. During this time period, the capacity to engage in industrial development was hobbled by political factionalism, the Iran-Iraq War, and a leftist industrial policy that shifted production away from cars to the production of buses and trucks. In addition, foreign car imports were banned.[10] By 1990, the industry was on the edge of collapse: 24,000 vehicles a year were produced, and the average local content for all vehicles decreased to 20 percent.

One focus of this book is on the inflection point in 1992, when the industry began an exponential increase in local content and production, and will examine how it was able to maintain the increase in production over the years. For instance, by 2009 yearly production had increased to 1.4 million vehicles with 70 percent local content. Entrepreneurship in the industry also increased exponentially. The number of parts suppliers increased from thirty-four in 1988 to approximately 800 by 2009.

The corporations responsible for this increase were Iran Khodro and Saipa, the country's largest automotive manufacturers; together they produce 94 percent of all vehicles sold in Iran. Iran Khodro's flagship vehicles are the Samand, the Peugeot 405, and the Peugeot 206. Saipa's main production vehicles are the Kia Pride and the Kia Rio.

Organization of the Industry

Prior to the revolution, the automobile industry was privately held but highly protected by the Shah. After the revolution, automobile industrial

[9] Local content was calculated using a weighted average. (Data obtained for the time period before the revolution from Parvin Alizadeh's *The Process of Import Substitution Industrialization in Iran (1960–1978)*, unpublished dissertation, University of Sussex, 1984. Data obtained after the revolution from various documents and publications distributed by Iran's Ministry of Industry during field research 2010–2011.) Data are for four-wheel passenger cars and commercial vehicles, including buses, mini-buses, vans, pickup trucks, heavy-duty trucks, and jeep-type vehicles. Production of the Peykan, which was licensed from Talbot of England, reached a high of 40 percent local manufacturing content by 1979. Local content of all other vehicles, however, was considerably lower.

[10] In 1973, the Shah liberalized the economy, allowing imports of foreign automobiles. Imports peaked in 1979 to 65,548 a year, which represented 30 percent of the annual total number of cars sold in Iran. The ban on passenger cars after the revolution was lifted temporarily in 1992, leading to more than 33,950 vehicle imports. This represented 33 percent of the total number of vehicles sold in Iran at that time, but a currency crisis caused by vehicle imports subsequently led to the passing of the Automobile Law that prohibited imports. The ban on imports was lifted in 2005, but high tariffs have limited imports to approximately 30,000 vehicles a year. This number currently represents approximately 2 percent of vehicles sold annually in Iran.

development was facilitated and managed by two government organs. The Ministry of Industry and Mines, financed by the parliament, worked with the Industrial Development and Renovation Organization (IDRO) to facilitate and organize automobile development. During rapid growth that began in the early 1990s, responsibilities included project financing, favorable lending to entrepreneurs for establishing parts companies, facilitating interactions with multinational corporations for obtaining development resources, and transferring modern organizational and management techniques to the automobile companies.

Second, Iran Khodro and Saipa, key government organs, were responsible for the heavy lifting of industrial development: building organizational capacity for development, establishing R&D facilities, building factories, and transferring technology from multinational corporations in order to create local technical capacity. The private sector was largely responsible for producing parts assembled in the large Iran Khodro and Saipa factories.

Factors Influencing Production

Besides the increase in automobile production and local content, it is important to explore factors influencing production. The two most important are vehicle imports and a measure of the resource curse. Figure 0.2 is

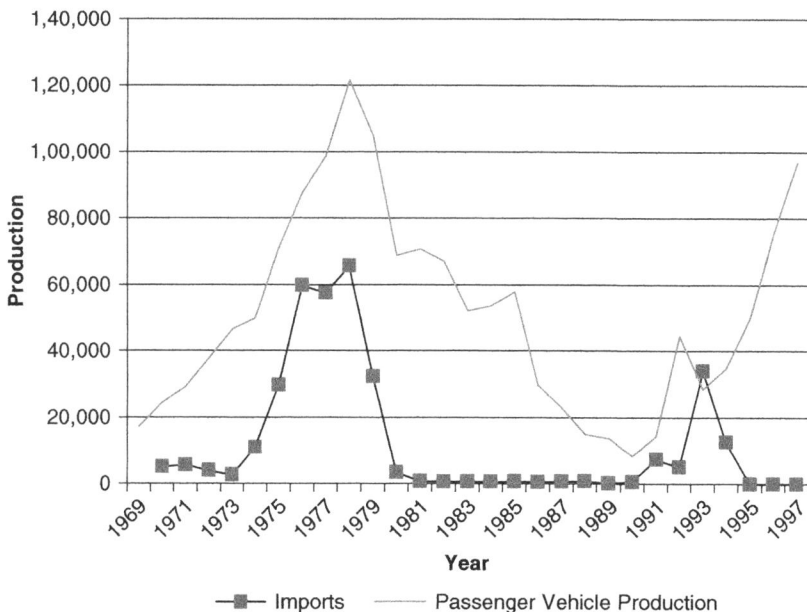

Figure 0.2 Passenger Vehicle Production versus Imports, 1969–2009

a time series graph of local vehicle production and imports. As seen in the graph, imports are insignificant except for two peaks in the late 1970s and early 1990s, when trade was liberalized. The late 1970s peak was followed by stagnation in local production due to problems related to the post-revolution depletion in state capacity. The early 1990s peak is the inflection point when infant industry protection was established that subsequently led to a rapid increase in local production.

A measure of whether the resource curse has influenced automobile industrial production is the price of oil versus the local manufacturing content of the vehicles produced in Iran. If the increase in the price of oil is associated with a diminution in the state's ability to build a local industry, we should see an association whereby the price of oil increases as local manufacturing decreases. A yearly time series graph of the price of oil and local manufacturing content is shown in Figure 0.3. The increasing price of oil is associated with an increase in local manufacturing content from 1969 to 1979. When the oil price decreases from 1980 through 1988, local content also decreases. The association exists because oil revenues were used to purchase vehicle kits and parts from Talbot to assemble the Peykan in Iran. However, after the implementation of infant industry protection in 1992, the industry became decoupled from the price of oil because there is no association between local content and oil revenues. When the price of oil decreased dramatically from $40 a barrel in 1990 to $17 a barrel in 2000, local content *increased* from 0.2 to 0.6. Conversely, when the price of oil tripled from 2000 to 2007, local content increased to 0.7.

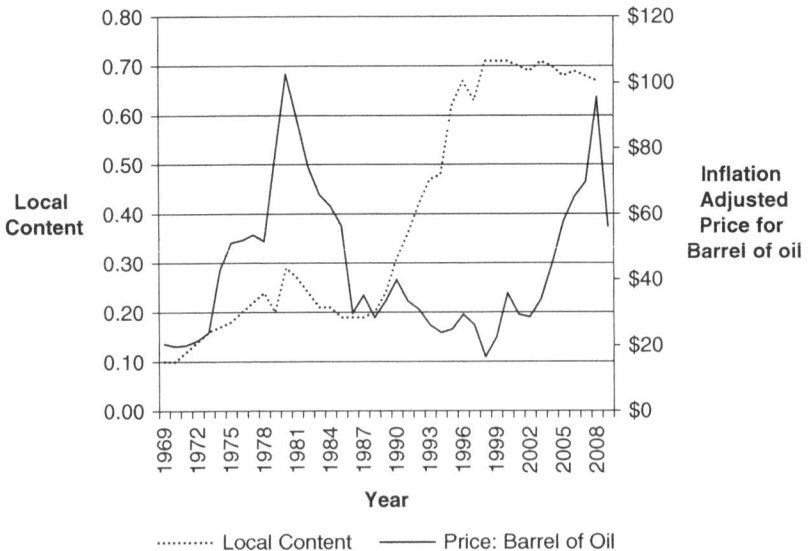

Figure 0.3 Oil Prices versus Local Manufacturing Content

The Puzzle of Iran Auto

For a country to successfully implement an industrial strategy, it is argued, the state must contain sufficient capacity to coordinate the activities for the project. If political factionalism has resulted in incoherent industrial development strategies or if Islamic institutions or the resource curse has created sufficient predatory behavior and rampant clientelism to undermine industrial development, where did the state capacity in Iran come from? Where did the required technical capacity come from to develop an industry with modern, indigenous technical capacity? Why didn't the political isolation of Iran vis-à-vis American sanctions and the global neoliberal political economy prevent it from building an industry that is normally considered a global industry? More specifically, does this case support those who argue for the necessity of escaping global neoliberal rules in order to industrialize?

I will argue that the analytical framework of embedded autonomy is important in analyzing positive development outcomes in the Iranian automobile industry. However, in a politically fractious country, it is important to build on embedded autonomy theory by incorporating the mechanisms behind its formation. This conceptualization is particularly important in analyzing Iran, a country where its post-revolutionary economy has been contested by three powerful, distinct, and fundamentally conflicting economic visions: those of nationalist industrialization, neoliberal commercialism, and left nationalist popular development. This book therefore will build on the concept that social fields are competitive spaces where the formation of state capacity is rooted in the balance of power between contending social groups. According to this perspective, the creation of a pocket of efficiency is possible when conflicting social groups settle their differences through a coalition in which each party enjoys gains without imposing significant costs on the other. The idea here is that the formation of a pocket of efficiency is a dynamic process where causality goes from conflicts to political coalitions to state capacity. This theorizing should also incorporate agency and social change outside the state development organizations and explain how the actions of strategic actors within the state and industrial organizations were shaped by institutions and their ties to social groups within society. These findings therefore show that in addition to the *balance* of embeddedness particular *qualities* of relationships are equally important for positive development outcomes.

The advantage of this study is that it focuses on a single industrial sector to show how state capacity can influence development of that sector over time. According to state capacity theorists, the optimal state structure is one in which autonomy and embeddedness are balanced: the development organization must have sufficient autonomy to coordinate industrial activity but also must maintain ties to society to correct or modify policy decisions. Building on this framework, in Chapter 1 I will show that in its early years, the development project lacked the balance between autonomy and embeddedness – leading to mixed development outcomes. For instance, prior to the revolution, state autonomy was established when the Shah used his relationship with the United States to suppress opposition to industrial development. Over time, however, the state became weakly embedded, resulting in poor economic planning and the eventual overthrow of the Shah (Skocpol, 1982; Gasiorowski, 1991). For these reasons, even though a nascent industry was created, domestic industrial development did not reach beyond assembly operations. After the revolution, the state apparatus became more embedded in Iranian society. However, autonomy declined when the leftist Islamic government implemented populist economic development policies and staffed development organizations with Islamic ideologues.

Chapter 2 will analyze the factors behind the formation of the state capacity and the subsequent creation of an opportunity to develop a "pocket of efficiency" for the automobile sector. Political factions in postwar Iran are important because they either undermined or enhanced state capacity, depending on whether they succeeded or failed at diverting development resources to their constituencies. Therefore, to understand how a pocket of efficiency was successfully created, the chapter unpacks the ideological orientation of the factions and shows how they were positioned in a political field and how they framed the debates over automobile industrial development.

This chapter then covers how in the early 1990s, in response to an economic crisis caused by the Iran-Iraq war, President Rafsanjani used his social skills in the political field to strengthen state capacity by reframing Islamic economics – moving away from radical, socialist-leaning populism to a pragmatic, pro-business economic agenda. However, his policies created a complex conflict between the left, the conservatives, and the industrial nationalists around the issues of neoliberalism and globalization. Ultimately, Rafsanjani's implementation of neoliberal policies led to an economic crisis opening up space for industrial nationalists to use their social skill in the economic field to successfully claim that localization of the automobile industry was in the nation's interest in order to avoid future economic crises. Strong lobbying ties to the political field were key in getting political leaders to accept their policy agenda. The ideological frame used by the industrialists to convince disparate social groups to support industrialization combined Rafsanjani's pro-business agenda with nationalist, developmentalist policies. By using this frame, the industrialists created a stable industrial field and a long-term pro-industry coalition with government officials and members of parliament.

Chapter 3 will cover how the political coalition of 1992 led to autonomous development organizations having significant institutional power to coordinate development activities and to implement coherent industrial policy. This era of coherence is characterized by policy alignment between the state apparatus and the industry. Infant industry protection, a key component of the industrial nationalist policies, led to rapid growth and a space for entrepreneurs to develop a local parts supply chain. In addition, the development of local manufacturing content was achieved through ties to selected multinationals that transferred the technology and knowledge to local Iranian companies. As a result of these policies, the industry became highly profitable – one that would contribute to economic stability. The chapter will build on research that shows that autonomy should be conceptualized as the ability of pro-industry technocrats to be united by a nationalist agenda but with sufficient power to protect it.

Chapter 4 will build on recent network-centered industrial theories that argue the reconfiguration of industrial production has created new opportunities for industrial development (Block, 2008; O'Riain, 2004; Whittaker et al., 2010; Block & Keller, 2011; Breznitz & Murphree, 2011; Keller & Block, 2012). By building on these current theories, this chapter will analyze engineering consulting firms as important global network actors in transferring technology for automobile industrial development. The concept of global technology "networks" is important because local ties to engineering consulting firms enable countries in the global south to develop automobile industries with greater local indigenous technical capacity and to design and produce products independently of multinational automobile assemblers.

Engineering consultancies were particularly important in Iran because by the late 1990s the industrialists reached an upper limit on technology transfer from large multinational automobile assemblers. This chapter reveals how Iran was able to get around these restrictions when it established ties to engineering consulting firms. It suggests that development of an automobile industry in the current global economy does not require reliance on multinational investment as a primary source of technology. In addition, by establishing ties to engineering consultancies, even countries isolated from global institutions can engage in more rapid technological learning and industrial upgrading when more conventional ties to sources of technology are unavailable.

Despite the industry's progress, by 2005 liberalization policies promoted by social groups and political factions in the political field threatened to undermine local manufacturing. Chapter 5 shows how the industrial nationalists used strategic action to insulate the industry from these policies that they saw as a significant threat to their national project of building an industry based on local technical capacities. I will argue that the industrial nationalists engaged in strategic action to protect the industry from those opposed to local manufacturing. They did so by deepening their political ties within the state apparatus and by gaining ownership control of Iran's largest automobile assemblers. By making these arguments, this chapter will make two contributions to the industrial development literature. First, I will argue that in intermediate states the concept of embeddedness needs to be refined to include ties to social groups or factions willing to support the industry in exchange for benefits to their constituents. The second contribution is to the literature on privatization. I will argue that an industry can be insulated from liberalization policies through a stakeholder model of privatization.

Finally, Chapter 6 will cover industry fragility, quality, and conflicts over globalization policy. While preceding chapters will show how specific state structures and field stabilization opened up space for industrial nationalists to become dominant players in the automobile industry, Chapter 6 evaluates the overall success of these policies and the debates around the future of the industry. The basic finding is that, although the Iranian automobile industry has generated high employment, the industry is currently facing a number of challenges related to vehicle quality, political instability, and sanctions. This chapter informs two theoretical perspectives of the book. First, it explores the "fragility" component of the pocket of efficiency argument. Second, it shows how social fields, path dependency, and institutions shaped the outcomes of Iranian automobile industrial development.

1

Setting the Stage: The Pre-Revolution Rise and the Post-Revolution Decline of the Automobile Industry

Introduction

This chapter will analyze state capacity in the early years of the Iranian automobile industry, a period defined by the founding and nascent development of the industry under the Shah (1965–1979) and by the post-revolutionary period of decline (1979–1988). Since the early 1990s, scholars have claimed that autonomous development organizations are important for industrial development (Amsden, 1989; Evans, 1995; Chibber, 2002; Kohli, 2004; Wade, 2004). A key variable important for autonomy is that the development organization must not be co-opted by social groups that divert resources to themselves and their constituencies. According to state capacity theorists, the optimal state structure is one in which autonomy and embeddedness are balanced: the development organization must have sufficient autonomy to coordinate industrial activity but also maintain ties to society to correct or modify policy decisions (Evans, 1995).

This study, however, advances state capacity scholarship by making a distinction between the autonomy of the state and the autonomy of the development organizations and their embeddedness within society. By doing so, this study claims that the location of influence in the political field necessary to create the state structures required for positive development outcomes can change over time. Before the revolution, the Shah established an absolutist monarchy in which the power over economic policy in the political field was centered with him, his cronies, and his close group of advisors. The Shah and his close group of cronies therefore greatly influenced the policy decisions that impacted development outcomes. After the revolution, however, economic power became more decentralized and diffused over various agencies and ministries. This political arrangement required political factions and social groups to maneuver within the political field to influence industrial policy.

Building on this framework, I will show that in its early years, the Iranian automobile development project lacked the balance between autonomy and embeddedness – leading to mixed development outcomes. With the Shah's postwar implementation of industrial development, state autonomy was undermined when landowners diverted resources to agricultural development and trade was liberalized. State autonomy was eventually established in 1960, when the Shah used his relationship with the United States to suppress opposition to industrial development. Subsequently, he implemented import substitution industrialization and established development organizations and agencies that founded the automobile industry. Over time, however, the state became weakly embedded in two ways. First, in his drive toward building a modern, industrial economy, the Shah alienated the rural poor, the traditional merchant class, and the religious leaders – important social groups that could have provided policy feedback to create a more balanced economy. Second, the Shah shifted economic power and decision making to a close group of insulated economic advisors, industrialists, and cronies who monopolized the Iranian economy (Skocpol, 1982; Gasiorowski, 1991). These policies resulted in poor economic planning. A case in point: in the early 1970s, the Shah undermined industrial development in all sectors when he abandoned import substitution industrialization and liberalized trade. For these reasons, even though a nascent automobile industry had been created in the 1960s, by the time of the revolution, the development of the industry did not reach beyond superficial assembly operations.

After the revolution, the power over economic development was shifted to the parliament, the industrial ministries, and their organizations. The state became more embedded within Iranian society when these organizations and agencies implemented populist economic development policies. However, the autonomy of these agencies declined as soon as the government staffed the ministries and development organizations with Islamic ideologues. In addition, the war with Iraq – largely supported by the Islamic leftists – diverted resources away from vehicles to buses, trucks, and munitions to support the war effort. Although these policies led to the near destruction of the industry, they also set the stage for its eventual rise in the 1990s.

From Incoherent Development to State Autonomy

Early industrial development in Iran was marked by uneven and incoherent development. At the turn of the twentieth century, three major social groups contributed to Iran's economy: merchants (*bazaaris*); landowners, who controlled the agricultural sector; and craftsmen and -women, who produced small-scale crafted items such as Persian carpets. The development of modern institutions in Iran began in 1925, when Reza Shah Pahlavi (1925–1941) overthrew the Qajar Dynasty to establish a modern parliamentary system and Western educational institutions. During this period, however, industrial development focused primarily on building the Trans-Iranian railway and constructing commodity industries such as cement and sugar plants. A more organized industrial development strategy was implemented under Reza Shah's son, Mohammad Reza Pahlavi (1945–1979), when he drafted the First Development Plan (1949–1955). The plan was the first to allocate resources according to a national and more comprehensive strategy of development – that encompassed agriculture, heavy industry and small craft industries. The plan fell far short of its goals when the landowners, who had strong ties to the Shah, convinced the Shah to shift 54 percent of the plan's financial resources to agricultural development. In addition, poor implementation of the development plan was partially caused by the 1953 CIA overthrow of the democratically elected nationalist government of Mohammed Mossadegh (Gasiorowski & Byrne, 2004).

After the coup, the Shah began working on the Second Development Plan, but like the first plan, it fell far short of its goals. Implemented in 1956, it differed from the First Plan in that projects were to be funded by oil revenues, based on an agreement between Iran and international oil companies. Also, in 1956, assembly of automobiles began with joint ventures with Jeep of the United States and Fiat of Italy. However, these companies agreed to assemble only knocked-down kits and would not agree to transfer technology for manufacturing. One contributing factor that led to the weakening of Iran's ability to develop automobile manufacturing was the lack of a coherent industrial strategy. In the 1950s the economic affairs of the country were organized into four separate organizations: the Industry of Mining, an Economic Planning Organization, and the Commerce and Customs Departments. Rivalries existed among the organizations leading to a lack of coordination. "There were many arguments among the heads of these departments. For example, the minister in charge of customs wanted to increase imports in Iran because he was making a lot of money and he wasn't interested in supporting local industrialization."[1]

Furthermore, as in the early 1950s, the landowners used their ties to the Shah to shift financial resources to projects from which they would benefit. The plan's main achievements were the construction of a large number of dams and other projects to increase agricultural productivity. The plan also benefited the merchant class by implementing liberal

---

[1] Interview with a high-ranking deputy of the Ministry of Economy in the 1960s, January 2010.

trade and lending policies. Many of the high-profile construction projects, however, failed due to corruption and incompetence. By 1960 the liberalization of the economy caused severe inflation, a large balance of payments, and an overexpansion of credit to the private sector.

This economic crisis provided the impetus for both Iran and the United States to establish closer ties. As a result, a patron-client relationship between the two countries was established: the United States provided technical and organizational expertise for the Iranian government to suppress political opposition to development, and in return the Shah served as a strong anti-Soviet ally in the region (Halliday, 1979; Gasiorowski, 1991). At this time, the Iranian state became autonomous from social groups that could potentially undermine industrial development: the rural poor, who supported agriculture over heavy industry; and the merchants, who had strong ties to the clerical establishment. Instead of building power-sharing coalitions with these groups, the Shah chose to suppress or crush them. The state therefore became weakly embedded within Iranian society because the Shah and his group of advisors did not receive feedback from a broader cross-section of that society to correct bad policy decisions (Skocpol, 1982; Gasiorowski, 1991).

The Founding of the Automobile Industry

The industrial development strategy implemented by the Shah in 1960 incorporated practices common during the time period, including import substitution industrialization, which placed high tariffs on imported products. To improve the success of these new industrial polices, the Shah sought to eliminate inter-agency rivalries by merging the Industry of Mining, the Economic Planning Organization, and the Commerce and Customs Departments into the Ministry of Economy. The goal was to improve coherence and coordination of development. The Ministry of Economy and the Plan and Budget Organization (an independent, American-influenced, state-funded organization that provided consultancy resources for development projects) became the two leading industrial development organizations (Abrahamian, 1982; Foran, 1993). Furthermore, the Shah relied on a mixed economic development strategy. He chose to assist the private sector in developing new industries when he was confident this could lead to successful development of an industry. But when doubts about the strength of private capital emerged, he relied on the state or quasi-state organizations to engage in industrial development.

The founding of the automobile industry exemplifies the state's role in assisting the private sector. Jeep and Fiat would not agree to manufacture vehicles under the newly adopted import substitution industrialization laws. By 1963, the Shah was not satisfied with these joint ventures and ordered one of his deputies who was a member of his Economic Council, Reza Niazmand, to begin automobile manufacturing; he threatened to terminate Niazmand's position if he could not start the process within six months. The major obstacle for those working on the development project was convincing the major auto companies that Iran had the capability to manufacture vehicles. Niazmand approached several European companies in an effort to optimize the chances of obtaining a reasonable contract. Mahmud Khayami, a machine shop owner and son of a wealthy landowner (Milani, 2008) who showed interest in auto manufacturing, was introduced to Niazmand through connections with the Shah. Niazmand explained how Khayami was used as a middleman between the Iranian government and the multinational corporations to obtain a contract:

> I heard about a German company called DKW that was going bankrupt, so I told Khayami to go to DKW and tell them that we would buy the company per unit weight and that we would pay the people to come to Iran to help us build the factory and train us how to use the machinery. He got the DKW contract, but I didn't want to build DKWs – they were out of business for a reason. So then I told him to go to Fiat and to show them the DKW contract, and within a short time he obtained a contract from Fiat. Fiat agreed to manufacture the body within the first year. Khayami asked me if we should accept the contract, but I told him I didn't want to manufacture Fiats because of their low quality. I wanted a contract with Talbot [formerly Roots] of England. They made very good taxicabs, and the cars had a very good engine. Khayami used the two contracts he had from Fiat and DKW as leverage and came back from England with a wonderful contract. They promised to give the design plans and the manufacturing tools to make the whole body of the car and to train people. In the contract it was agreed that within five years they would help us manufacture the engine in Iran.[2]

The government provided Khayami with preferable loans as well as a large influx of startup money to establish the factory. By 1965, manufacturing of the Peykan by Iran National, a company owned and managed by Khayami, began production.

---

[2] Ibid.

Pushing the Envelope of Industrialization: Streamlining State Organizations and Importing a Quasi-State Development Organizational Form from Italy

Despite the industrial development success that had started in 1960, the Shah by 1967 was dissatisfied with its speed. In addition, many older corporations founded in the 1950s and early 1960s were saddled with debt due to inefficiencies and incompetence. The Shah had grandiose visions that by the end of the century, Iran could achieve the economic might of any of the western European countries. He placed the blame for the slow rate of development on two obstacles: first, the inefficiency of state-owned enterprises; second, the lack of an entrepreneurial class to establish large industrial firms. Up until 1960, capitalist activity in Iran was based on commerce and centered in the bazaar (Halliday, 1979; Alizadeh, 1984; Keshavarzian, 2009). Iran lacked private investors to open large manufacturing organizations (such as those that had existed in Brazil in the nineteenth century) as well as an industrial middle class such as that which had emerged from the colonial system in India (Evans, 1979). The land reform policies implemented in 1960, requiring land-owners to distribute their land to peasants, were supposed to free up capital for industrial development but in fact fell far short of their goals (Keddie, 2003).

The Shah was searching for a solution when a manager from the Industrial Management Organization, a small Iranian management consultancy organization, informed him of the success of the Italian Institute for Industrial Reconstruction (IRI). Established as a quasi-state holding company in Italy in 1933, IRI was jointly owned by the government and the private sector. By the 1960s, IRI was gaining recognition as an effective model for economic state intervention in western Europe and Britain (Pozner & Woolf, 1967; Holland, 1972). It was heralded as being as efficient and dynamic as a private corporation but with its goals oriented toward government economic policy. The corporations under IRI's control essentially followed liberal market principles – hiring and firing staff and taking the initiative in developing new products and markets within a competitive open market. IRI controlled its companies through a system in which its six subsidiary financial holding companies owned (or partially owned) a majority interest in industrial companies in Italy. Any shares not owned by IRI or its financial holding companies were owned by the private sector.

The Shah sent Reza Niazmand to Italy to study IRI. On the basis of his report, the Shah established in 1967 the Industrial Development and Renovation Organization (IDRO), structured on the IRI model.

The goals of the organization and its autonomy are explained in government documents:

> The government has been accorded the right to create an independent organization named the Industrial Development and Renovation Organization in order to expand and modernize industries and mining [by] using scientific and technical research and managerial expertise [in] the creation of industrial, mining and services companies or [by] participation in the equity of existent companies and to give technical support to industrial and mining units ... The organization, together with its affiliated companies and units, is totally independent and is not subject to the rules, general articles, and general accountancy concerning governmental and pro-governmental organizations.[3]

What the Shah found particularly attractive about IDRO was its ability to hire and fire at will and to rid enterprises of inefficient regulations and rules so employees could "think" like entrepreneurs. The policy adopted by IDRO at the time was to renovate unprofitable existing corporations by making them profitable and then hand them back to the private sector by selling its equity in the corporations once profitability was established. Although IDRO was involved in renovating a number of companies in Iran, including those that had failed in the 1950s, in practice IDRO was more involved in founding industrial organizations and in training workers:

> When it was established, there was literally no modern industry in Iran; its industry was extremely traditional and out-of-date. IDRO was established to achieve great goals, and it has played a significant role in Iran's industry. It was intended to fulfill two functions: first, establishing industries in the country and second, the renovation of the existing ones. The organization started fulfilling the first objective by importing foreign industries and technologies. In fact, the organization founded 60% of our industrial development. What the organization was really good at was training specialists and industrial workers – building a worker society in Iran.[4]

The staff at IDRO were trained at American and British universities; Harvard University was used as the training ground for its management.[5] In the late 1960s, six large companies were founded,

---

[3] IDRO website: www.idro.org/enidro/About%20Idro/History.aspx, accessed 2011.
[4] Interview with engineer Hooshang Mokhlesi in *The Role of IDRO and Industrial Development in Iran*, 2000 (in Farsi).
[5] The Harvard Business School established a branch in Tehran in the 1970s, but it was closed after the revolution.

including a machine plant, tractor factory, aluminum plant, and ferti-lizer plant. Even though these companies were owned by the govern-ment, they were allowed to function as private corporations in making decisions in personnel, strategy, and other areas. The Shah, however, did not relinquish full control to IDRO or to the private sector. He established a fifteen-member council to advise and guide IDRO regard-ing which industries to develop and which companies to found. Four members of the council were government appointees, and eleven were from the private sector; the latter included a mixture of former politi-cians, lawyers, technocrats, and private-sector individuals with high-level connections to the Shah and the government. Despite the Shah's control, one benefit of the council was that it added the needed "legitimacy" to the young organization. By 1979, IDRO established more than ninety large industrial companies. None of the companies was profitable, and their shares remained largely in the hands of IDRO.

The Organization of Development

Figure 1.1 shows the organization of economic development during the Shah's era (1960s–1970s). Rectangles represent the government organizations and ovals the automobile industry. Dark lines represent strong ties and dashed lines weak ties. Strong ties are defined as ties where the Shah had direct control over the policies of the organiza-tion; weak ties mean the Shah had indirect control. Clearly, the Shah had direct ties to the Economic Council: his ministers and close advisors were on the Economic Council and were responsible for development strategy. The Economic Council had strong ties to the Plan and Budget Organization, which provided consulting advice to form economic strategy, and to the Ministry of Industry (formerly the Ministry of Economy). IDRO was, after all, a division of the Ministry of Industry. Ties from government organizations to parliament are weak (see dashed lines) because at the time it was a single-party, rubber-stamp legislature playing a minor role in economic development.

Ties from government organizations to the automobile industry are dashed lines because the automobile industry was privately owned and thus not controlled by government organizations. All private industries, however, were either protected or controlled by the Shah. Anyone want-ing to obtain an import license to engage in a joint venture with a foreign company or to import products needed the permission of the Shah. The Shah generally gave such rights to his cronies: those in his inner circle and family members (Katouzian, 1981).

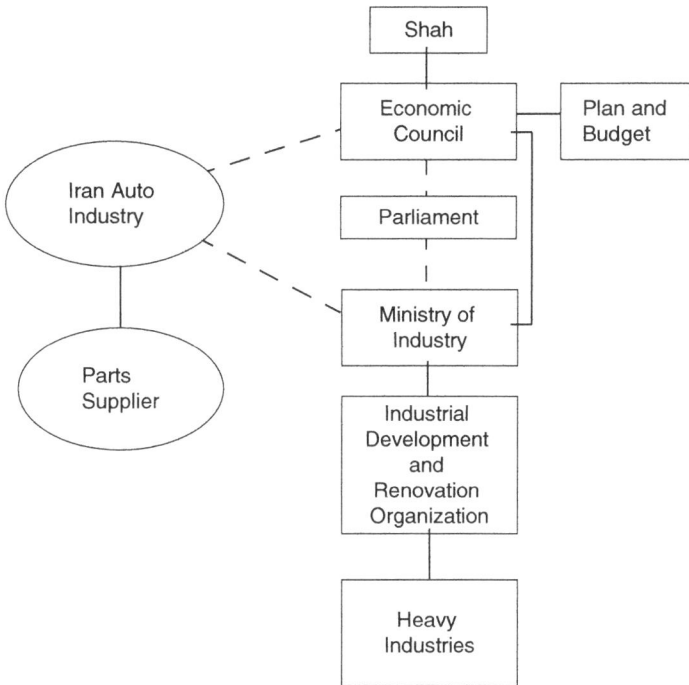

Figure 1.1 The Organization of Industrial Development under the Shah

Blunted Manufacturing and the Liberalization of the Industry, 1969–1979

The number of locally assembled automobiles versus the number of imports is shown in Figure 1.2. "British" refers to the Hillman Hunter (renamed the Peykan), the highest-selling automobile in the country. "French" autos were the Citroën Dyane and the Renault 5; "American" autos included the AMC Rambler, the Buick, the Chevy Nova, and the Cadillac. Imports came mainly from Western Europe and the USA. As seen in the graph, by the mid- to late 1970s the market was dominated by the Peykan and by imports. The increase in imports was a direct result of the Shah abandoning import substitution industrialization and liberalizing trade. Even though imports increased by more than 600 percent from 1973 to 1978, they do

Auto Production versus Imports

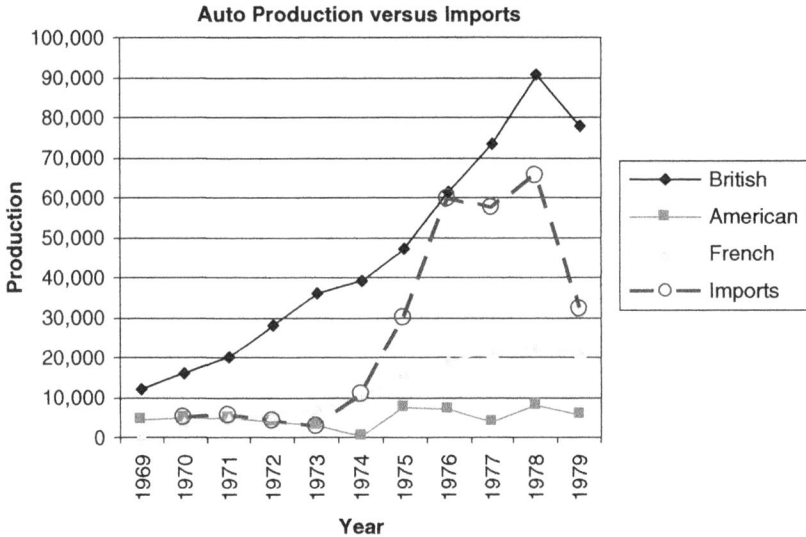

Figure 1.2 Automobile Production and Imports, 1969–1979

not seem to have had an impact on the assembly of autos in Iran in the years leading up to the revolution. One reason for this seeming inconsistency could be that imports were mostly luxury vehicles that appealed to Iran's upper classes, whereas the Peykan was a cheaper, low-end vehicle.

Turning to the issue of domestic manufacturing, achieving high local content was hardly a success – even though the Shah was successful at developing a nascent industry. The import substitution rules of the 1960s required auto companies to produce 49 percent locally; this was increased to 75 percent by 1978 with the planned establishment of engine manufacturing. Before the liberalization of trade in 1974, the incentive for local manufacturing was achieved by means of a 200 percent tariff on imports of finished cars and an average tariff of 30 percent for imported car parts. Iran National achieved a maximum of 45 percent local content for the entire vehicle (including the engine), whereas the other auto companies were assembling complete or semi-knockdown kits with no greater than 10 to 20 percent local content.[6] Of that proportion of the Peykan vehicle considered local content, 17 percent represents after-market or "hang-on" parts; these are considered the lowest value-added parts because they require the least sophisticated technology. They include tires, batteries, radiators, and oil filters. Another 10 percent of the value added came from assembling the complete knockdown parts of the vehicle – the parts imported from the country in which the

[6] All data in this section are taken from Tables 3.1 to 3.25 in Alizadeh, 1984. She obtained her data from the Ministry of Industry and the Industrial Development Bank.

vehicle is licensed. That left only 18 percent of the vehicle's local content for medium or high-tech parts (see breakdown to follow).

Although engine manufacturing (the highest value-added component) began in the early 1970s, local content of domestically produced engines remained very low, ranging from 3 to 8.2 percent of the contribution to the value of the vehicle. State-owned foundries for casting engine components were highly underutilized, since all casted parts were imported from abroad. Not only did the industry suffer from low local production of parts, but 90 percent of the raw material input for the auto industry was imported. The Iranian steel plant could not provide the complex mixture of alloys in the steel required for auto production.

Low local content resulted in a highly underdeveloped auto parts sector. However, founding of parts companies increased in the years before the revolution, indicating an increasing development trend. Thirty-four auto parts companies were founded before the revolution, nine of them in the late 1960s and the remaining twenty-five in the 1970s. Only three of these companies were founded after the economic liberalization of 1974, indicating that development dramatically slowed when companies were allowed to import parts without tariff restrictions. Forty-one percent of the companies were affiliated with Iran National, whereas the remaining 59 percent were independent companies or associated with other industrial groups (Salami, 2004). One possible argument for the low rate of parts development is the fact that, at the time, underdeveloped countries tended to produce parts at large auto plants instead of outsourcing to smaller parts suppliers – this because of low production numbers and the concentration of expertise in large organizations (Alizadeh, 1984). Table 1.1 shows a partial list of companies that existed before the revolution and the value added in what they produced.[7] The value added is designated *low* for after-market parts. The second category (*medium*) consists of mid-range parts that include more sophisticated

Table 1.1 *Number of Companies Producing Value-Added Parts in 1979*

Value Added	Number of Companies	Parts Produced
High	2	Pistons, ball bearings
Medium	5	Spark plugs, shock absorbers, alternators, auto glass, springs
Low	12	Batteries, radiators, mufflers, tires and tubes, etc.

[7] This is a "partial" list. According to the data gathered, it is, however, a good indicator that few companies in Iran produced high-tech parts before the revolution.

manufacturing and materials: the use of presses; moderate amounts of machining; and parts containing mixed components such as auto glass, door panels, spark plugs, and alternators. The parts with the *highest* value added are the mechanically moving parts requiring the most sophisticated manufacturing because of tight tolerances. These parts include pistons, crankshafts, ball bearings, and engine cylinder heads.

Despite the deficiencies in achieving high local content, the auto industry by 1976 was the highest value-added industry in the country after oil and more than double in dollars compared to basic metals and household appliances, the second- and third-largest value-added industries outside of rugs (Amuzegar, 1977).

Eleven assembly companies producing cars, trucks, engines, and buses were established before the revolution. Iran National, Saipa, and Pars Khodro were the largest auto assembly plants, but Iran National dominated the market by producing 68 percent of the cars, 88 percent of the buses, and 41 percent of the vans. Ownership of the assembly companies remained in the hands of Iranian nationals, but the auto parts companies were owned jointly by multinational corporations and state and local capital – depending on the value added of the parts produced. Lower-tech parts producers were typically joint stock companies funded by local capital and multinational corporations, with the dominant shares owned by Iranian entrepreneurs. The higher-technology, engine parts companies were joint ventures between multinational corporations (average 30 percent for all companies), the state (25 percent), and local capital (45 percent).

The Revolution Years and Incoherent Automobile Industrial Development, 1979–1990

Despite the increase in industrialization under the Shah, the country suffered from a number of economic problems such as inflation, infrastructural bottlenecks, and the decline of agriculture. The major source of inflation was the increase in the price of oil, which more than quadrupled the nation's budget. Corruption, oppression, and growing inequality contributed to political instability. The inner circle of the Shah's advisors and his family, who were involved in industrial development, were viewed as participating in crony capitalism – enriching themselves while excluding most citizens. Alienation of the Islamic clergy and the working class from the development project during the modernization process eventually led to the Iranian revolution of 1979 and the rise of the Islamic Republic.

When Ayatollah Khomeini became Iran's Supreme Leader, he was famously quoted as saying, "The revolution is about Islam and not the price of melons" (Amuzegar, 1997b, p. 17). Iran's Islamic movement in the early 1980s was an oppositional movement embracing anti-imperialist, anti-American sentiments. To resist foreign influence and achieve the heights of an Islamic state, its leaders adopted a policy of reducing consumption to the level of society's real needs by eliminating economic dependence on the West, eliminating unnecessary imports, and guiding domestic industry to achieve national economic goals. The culture of the times was a "marked antagonism toward bigness and business, interdependence with multi-national corporations, accumulated wealth by individuals, and unbridled private ownership" (ibid., p. 37). As a result of this radical shift in policy, the clerical and intellectual elite embraced socialist-leaning policies and all automobile imports for private consumption were banned.

When Ayatollah Khomeini came into power, he implemented a "neither East nor West" conception regarding the ownership of property. "East" meant the communists (in reference to the Soviet Union), who confiscated all private property, and "West" referred to those who promoted unbridled greed. Khomeini was steadfast in his position that Islam protected private property – but that it was a "divine gift from God" and, therefore, the state had a duty to enforce laws to protect it (Abrahamian, 1993). On the other hand, he posited, individuals were instinctively corrupt, greedy, and irrational – so as long as the government was "God's" government, the state's duty was to defend and oversee it. According to Article 44 of the constitution that was drafted in the early years, "The economy of the Islamic Republic of Iran is to consist of three sectors: state, cooperative, and private ... The state sector is to include all large-scale and mother industries." The private sector, however, would be concerned with industry and services that "supplement the economic activities of the state and cooperative sectors."[8] This article of the constitution is often cited as relegating the private sector to a subordinate role in the economy and establishing the state as the main actor in industrial development (Amirahmadi, 1990; Akhavi-pour, 1992; Keshavarzian, 2009). The post-revolution leftists were most responsible for drafting Article 44 because they intended to create a statist-oriented economy. However, they allowed enough space for the development of a substantial private sector. Iran's large automobile assemblers, considered large-scale industries, were transferred to IDRO; parts suppliers, categorized as small-scale industries, were allowed to remain private.

After the 1979 revolution, any organization owned by the Shah or his relatives was considered the spoils of war and was confiscated; ownership was placed into the hands of Islamic foundations (bonyads), which

---

[8] Article 44 of the constitution; www.iranchamber.com/government/laws/constitution_ch04.php

function as holding companies (Maloney, 2000; Saeidi, 2004).[9] As autonomous "parastatal" organizations, bonyads are neither privately owned nor government-owned and are accountable only to the Islamic leadership. Most industrial corporations were organized into the Foundation for the Oppressed and Self-sacrificers, which is currently the largest industrial bonyad in Iran. Since the auto industry was not owned by a member of the Shah's family and was considered sophisticated in its industrial output, ownership of the large auto companies was transferred to IDRO. The smaller auto parts companies, however, remained private.

The Organization of the State and the Development Project

When Khomeini established an Islamic state in Iran, he did not dismantle the institutions inherited from the Shah but instead made the existing modern institutions Islamic. The official state apparatus in post-revolutionary Iran is a system of "dual institutionalization" (see Figure 1.3). It is composed of modern government institutions and organizations inherited from the Shah on the one hand and an Islamic institutional apparatus created after the revolution on the other hand (Harris, 2010). The government is divided into the executive branch (headed by the president), the judiciary, and the parliament (with elected representatives). The ministry heads are elected by the parliament. Superimposed on the government is the Supreme Leader as "guardian" of the state – with the authority to dismiss the president, appoint military commanders, and declare war and peace. He also appointed leaders to the Guardian Council, responsible for ensuring that all laws passed by parliament conform to the sacred law as determined in the Koran. The Supreme Leader is also the head of the Supreme Leader's Office, which oversees the Islamic Economic Advisory Council, the Iran Revolutionary Guard Corps, and the Basij Paramilitary Forces.

The government and the Supreme Leader's Office manage their respective economic development organizations. With respect to the automobile industry, the government-owned Ministry of Industry and Mines and IDRO are the key organizations. The Ministry of Industry is financed by parliament and owns IDRO, which in turn owns the two largest automobile corporations – Iran Khodro and Saipa. Immediately after the revolution and into the late 1980s, the head

---

[9] From Article 49 of the constitution: "The government has the responsibility of confiscating all wealth accumulated through usury, usurpation, bribery, embezzlement, theft ... and restoring it to its legitimate owner; and if no such owner can be identified, it must be entrusted to the public treasury."

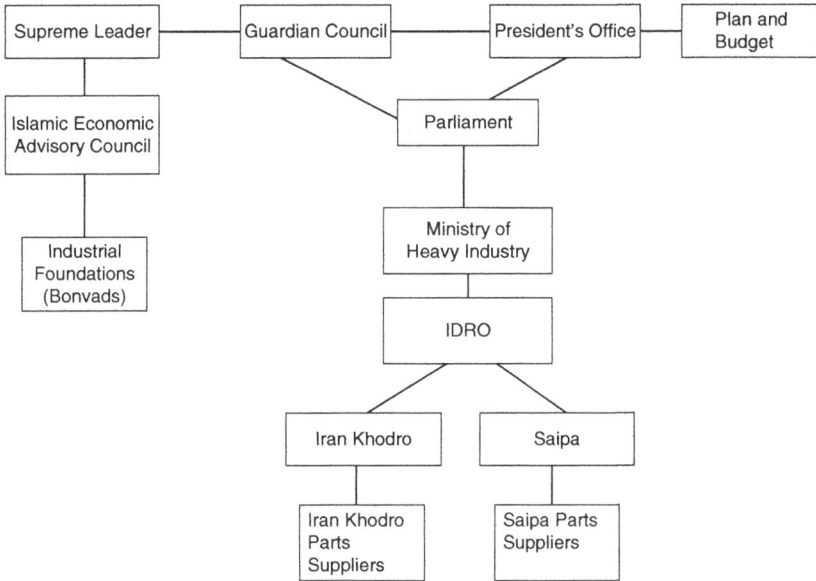

Figure 1.3 The Organization of Post-Revolution Industrial Development

of the Ministry of Industry was appointed by the president – however, before he could take office, he needed to receive approval by parliament. Compared to the organizational structure during the Shah's era, automobile industrial development is marked by two important differences. First, the large automobile assemblers in the post-revolution era are all state-owned enterprises. Second, the development project became more embedded in Iranian society – largely because the parliament became a more important organ of government, responsible for appointing ministers and for providing financial resources for development. In addition, the parliament became a politically pluralistic institution in which members, who belonged to various factions, voted according to whether the project supported their constituencies.

The Supreme Leader's Office is responsible for appointing managers to the bonyads involved in various sectors of the Iranian economy. The most important bonyad involved in industrial development is the Foundation for the Oppressed and Self-sacrificers. The official goals of the bonyads are to provide resources to the poor and disenfranchised. Although these organizations are important to Iran's economy, they are not major players in the automobile industry.

The Radicals and the Depletion of State Capacity

Although IDRO and the Ministry of Industry were staffed by well-educated managers with Western engineering degrees, state autonomy to implement development was hamstrung by incoherent strategies resulting from both radical Islamic socialist ideology and the war with Iraq.

A main obstacle in implementing state-led industrial development in support of Iran's auto industry was the domination of the policy agenda by Islamic radicals. In 1979, immediately following the revolution, the automobile industry was nationalized, coming under the management of IDRO. Implementing industrial policy became difficult when high-ranking managers within the auto industry embraced socialist-leaning, radical ideology and particularistic relations. In the following passage, a high-ranking government manager discusses the problems in reorienting the industry's managers and workers away from disrupting production:

> After the Islamic revolution, labor crises as well as disorder in companies soared. We had frequent reports of strikes. It would turn out, for instance, that the directors of many companies were leftists looking for a crisis. They said, "Burn these machines because they belong to landlords." There were several cases of setting companies on fire or other sabotage in the automotive industry. This led us to a crisis. At Iran Khodro, we spent hours talking to the workers. We said, "Gentlemen, if you want to slap the United States in the face, if you want to do something political, you have to work and produce more automobiles. Do not go on strike; instead, work more." These problems had crippled most industries. Most of the companies in the private sector were closed because the workers had occupied them and the owners could not even go to their companies.[10]

Within a few years of the revolution, Iran Khodro (previously named Iran National) went bankrupt, and ownership was shifted to IDRO. The radicals, however, embraced religious and revolutionary credentials over competency. Managers without much knowledge of the industry obtained positions on the basis of their connections with the religious establishment. "There was a company in my town where the director had no knowledge of the industry; he was completely incompetent. The employees tried to remove him, but he said he couldn't be fired because he was 'chosen by God' for the position."[11] Productivity declined at this company when many of the workers spent most of the day praying at

---

[10] Interview with engineer Mokhlesi in *The Role of IDRO in Industrial Development in Iran*, 2000.
[11] Interview with company manager, January 2010.

a mosque. In an interview, a manager at the Industrial Development Bank of Iran who had worked there both before and after the revolution discussed the transition from an emphasis on "scientific" decision making to decisions based on Islamic piety: "After the revolution, I had to go to the mosque to get approval for loans. But they weren't interested in using scientific methods to determine who should get the loans; the cleric would say, 'We don't need that.' He wanted me to give a loan to a person who he thought was a good guy, someone he knew that came to the mosque to pray five times a day."

As the 1980s progressed, the social upheaval of the revolution subsided, but the industrial development organizations suffered from a lack of financial support due to economic policies that shifted the development away from automobile production. A primary reason why auto production decreased was that left-wing ideologues saw automobiles as symbols of imperialism. An entrepreneur and owner of a parts company with more than 30 years of experience in the field explained how leftist ideology influenced automobile production:

> During that period, the revolutionary people were in charge – and they had responsibility for the industry. The radical thinking was that automobiles were symbols of imperialism, they were symbols of the capitalists. The radicals were interested in public transportation, so there was an emphasis on bus and truck production; we didn't have a good vision to guide us at that time.[12]

As a result of the lack of interest in automobile industrial development, IDRO lacked resources and entered a period of crisis management:

> After the Islamic Revolution, this trend [renovation and state-led development] broke down and the course fully changed, because prior to the revolution, IDRO was not supposed to manage the organizations. IDRO now was forced to manage nationalized, public corporations in a whole new fashion. This decade was a decade of "keeping," keeping what the government had granted. Due to the lack of resources and international sanctions, IDRO adopted crisis management to maintain the industries. It did a good job of crisis management but drifted off its mission.[13]

One reason for the lack of engagement in development was that IDRO's management was not interested in supporting any industrial development requiring financial support for large industrial corporations – such as

---

[12] Interview with ex-government official, June 2011.
[13] Interview with Reza Veyseh, former director of IDRO, in *The Role of IDRO and Industrial Development in Iran*, 2000 (in Farsi).

automobile companies. Rather, the radicals focused on small, cooperative enterprises. "The people in charge were not interested in industrial development. If someone came to IDRO and they were not pro-industry, nothing got done: they did not provide us with resources to carry out development."[14] Even if IDRO could have shifted from "crisis" to "development" mode, the Iranian constitution banned foreign direct investment. Furthermore, engaging in relations with meaningful technology transfer with Europe or the United States was essentially prohibited. This policy highly restricted the ability to develop a modern industry.

Another important cause was the costly war with Iraq, a war supported largely by the radicals. Production was diverted away from manufacturing automobiles to a centralized economy supporting war production. During the war, Khomeini declared that autos were an "ornamental luxury" item and should not be a priority for the country. Many factories were converted to manufacturing products important for the war effort: military equipment, buses, small pickup trucks, and large trucks. In 1985 Khomeini signed an order committing all industrial resources to the war; this dramatically reduced automobile production. At this time, the only way to obtain a new automobile was by participating in a lottery. Even if a person won the lottery, it was necessary to place a down payment on the vehicle and wait approximately two years to obtain it.

The war with Iraq was also an important factor in diverting human resources away from industrial development. Most highly skilled engineers and technocrats moved to working for the war department. One Harvard-educated technocrat explained why he left his job at IDRO to work for the war ministry: "Everyone wanted to work for the war department because the salaries were much higher; the war was the main reason I left IDRO."[15] By the end of the war, IDRO was reduced to a thirty-five-man operation located in a low-status area of Tehran.

Automobile Industrial Performance, 1979–1989

The production of automobiles and commercial vehicles decreased dramatically during the revolutionary years, as seen in Figure 1.4.[16] Automobiles are categorized as four-door sedans; commercial vehicles include buses, mini-buses, pickup trucks, and large trucks. The decrease in production from 1979 to 1980 was caused by the social upheaval of the early years of the revolution. A large increase in production of commercial vehicles in the mid-1980s resulted from the shift of auto production to

---

[14] Interview with retired high-level manager at IDRO, March 2011.
[15] Interview with manager at large parts supplier company, 2010.
[16] During the decade from 1980 to 1990, only 22,987 imports were allowed into the country.

**Auto and Commercial Vehicle Production
(1979–1990)**

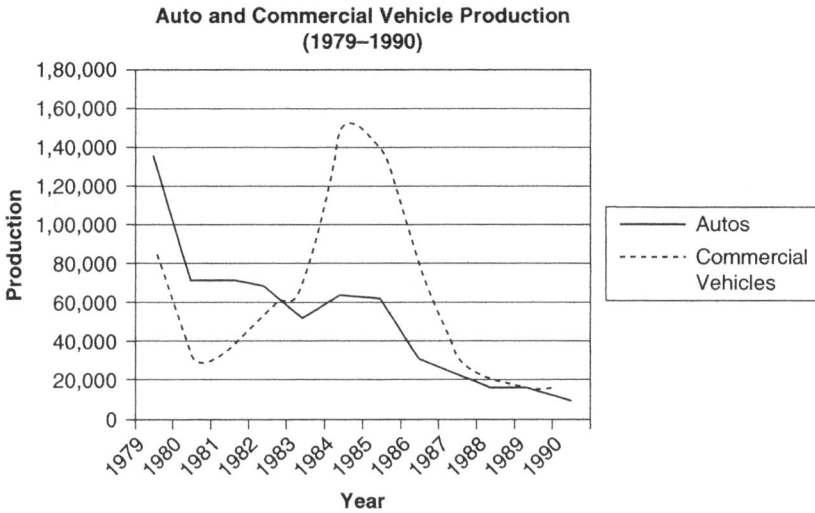

Figure 1.4 Automobile and Commercial Vehicle Production,
1979–1990

supporting the war economy. In 1984, during the peak of commercial vehicle production, pickup trucks represented the largest portion (61.8 percent) of total commercial vehicles produced; trucks were 29.7 percent, mini-buses 7.1 percent, and buses 1.4 percent. Auto production consisted mainly of the Peykan by Iran Khodro, the Citroën by Saipa, and a small number of American vehicles by Pars Khodro.

2

The Rise of the Industrial Nationalists: Postwar Conflict, Neoliberalism, and National Industrial Strategy

Introduction

Although embedded autonomy allows scholars to focus on studying which specific state structures lead to positive development outcomes, it does not address the causal mechanisms behind the formation of state structures. This chapter will use social field theory to analyze the preconditions leading to the formation of state structures important for the creation of a pocket of efficiency for the automobile sector.

The conceptual framing used here is that conflicts in the political field in Iran led to political coalitions and then to state capacity. This idea will build on studies that argue that industrial development can succeed in intermediate states – or, in more extreme cases, where the state apparatus is dominated by predatory behavior. These states have industries where key actors in the state apparatus have carved out a pocket of bureaucratic efficiency (Geddes, 1990; Cheng et al., 1998; Evans, 1998). A pocket of efficiency refers to a development bureaucracy that is insulated from clientelistic pressures within the state apparatus and social groups that can undermine industrial development. This arrangement allows development agencies or firms to control their own financial and human resources, thereby leading to a greater probability of achieving successful industrial development.

Scholarly research on intermediate states where pockets of efficiency are important for industrial development can be summarized according to three perspectives. The first emphasizes top-down construction of pockets of efficiency; the second focuses on the balance of power between contending social groups and their political organization. The third perspective, associated with the idea of the "developmental network state," claims that countries with fragmented development institutions and political forces opposing development can still have pockets of efficiency.

Scholars claiming that pockets of efficiency are created via a top-down process focus on how high-level state officials use their institutional power to create autonomous development agencies. For instance, the Brazilian Development Bank became a highly effective vehicle for industrial development when President Kubitschek in the late 1950s created funding sources for the bank outside of state control and staffed it with highly competent administrators (Geddes, 1994). According to these scholars, a pocket of efficiency is fragile because a development agency's autonomy is directly related to state officials' ability to support and maintain the agency against strong outside social forces or opposing political groups (Geddes, 1990; Evans, 1998).

Recent empirical research shows that even resource-dependent states (rentier states), countries with poorly performing industrial development projects (Karl, 1997; Hertog, 2010), can create pockets of efficiency resulting in positive development outcomes. Successful state-owned enterprises can become profit-oriented if management remains autonomously independent of interest groups within the state and society – and if they establish close ties to coherent groups of state officials who provide management with clear incentives to create market-oriented firms. For example, SABIC, a Saudi Arabian petrochemical and heavy industry established in the late 1970s, used its connections to Saudi royalty to insulate the firm financially from the state apparatus to hire competent personnel and become highly profitable, even during economic downturns. Hout (2007) claims that a state-owned enterprise can develop into a pocket of efficiency if the company director enjoys the power and legitimacy within the state apparatus to fend off attempts for control by political groups (i.e., a military regime) intent on using the firm for patronage. A state-owned enterprise can be further insulated if it is in a sector considered marginal to the dominance of other rent sources in the state apparatus (i.e., minerals instead of oil). Such independence allowed Suriname's largest oil company (Staatsolie) to build a corporate culture around organizational and technical capacity. A common characteristic of SABIC and Staatsolie is their profitability; thus the corporate leaders at each firm were able to acquire broad support within the state apparatus to sustain the company's claim to autonomy. These case studies contradict the negative portrayal of state-owned enterprises as burdened with non-profitable activities that become centers of political patronage (Waterbury, 1993).

The second theoretical perspective moves beyond the top-down approach, studying the political and ideological underpinnings of state agencies involved in positive development outcomes. Here, state capacity is rooted in the balance of power between contending social groups and the political organization of those relationships (Khan M., 2004; Jonathan & Putzel, 2009; Khan M. H., 2010; Saylor, 2012; Hau, 2013).

To these scholars, conflicts among social groups or political factions undermine state capacity. Conflicts arise when "a group believes that the underlying distribution of power has changed and the distribution of benefits is not reflecting it, or if changes in distributions of benefits do not reflect the perceived distribution of power" (Khan M. H., 2010, p. 7). The creation of a pocket of efficiency is possible when contending social groups settle their differences through an alliance in which each party enjoys gains without imposing significant costs on the other. Supporters argue that coalitions between political leaders and social groups are key factors in formation of pockets of efficiency in intermediate states (Doner et al., 2005), asserting that coalitions will be maintained with external social groups and will not undermine industrial development if they financially benefit from its success. They also argue that dominant coalitions and relationships within the coalitions impact the structure and performance of the state (North, Wallis, & Weingast, 2009; Hau, 2013).

Recent empirical work supports these arguments. Dan Slater shows that state capacity is directly related to the formation of business-state alliances, that these alliances are formed into a "protection pack" – where broad, elite coalitions are unified by shared support for heightened state power and function as "bulwarks against continued or renewed mass unrest" (Slater, 2010, p. 5). Protection packs are formed when elites perceive danger to their property and status due to endemic, contentious politics; for instance, business elites are willing to pay higher taxes if the state suppresses threats against their interests. This work builds on the idea that strong states have greater capacity to engage in meaningful development (Soifer & Hau, 2008) and that elite cohesion is important in the building of state capacity, whereas disunity and factionalism weaken it (Waldner, 1999). This work echoes Peter Moore's comparative work on the role of elite cohesion in strengthening state capacity in Jordan and Kuwait (Moore, 2001, 2004; Peters & Moore, 2009). He argues that elite business associations with strong ties to the state are important variables in creating coherent economic development policies. In particular, business associations with exclusive membership (instead of obligatory membership) tend to have stronger and more coherent leadership – and, therefore, enhanced lobbying capacity to participate in policy implementation. Such analysis of politics and ideology in the formation of state capacity is important: various post-revolution social groups and political factions in Iran have sought to undermine development projects in favor of gains for their group or faction.

The third theoretical perspective is the developmental network state: countries with fragmented development institutions and political forces opposing development can still have pockets of efficiency (O'Riain, 2000, 2004; Block, 2008; Block & Keller, 2011; Williams, 2014). Here, the rise of global value chains and fragmentation of production make it difficult for developing countries to create centralized development agencies to implement local development (Breznitz, 2007). Instead, developing countries need to link "local and global technology and business networks in ways that promote development" and sustain it through multiple pockets of state embeddedness in professionally led innovation networks and international capital (O'Riain, 2000, p. 158). Development network state theory is particularly important in explaining the success of development projects in intermediate states (such as Ireland, India, Brazil, Israel, and the United States) without a development state writ large and thus must rely on coordinating development through various loosely coupled state agencies.

Emergent coalitions can be important factors in the success of development network state projects. For instance, a federally funded developmental network state has emerged in the United States despite neoliberal economic policies in opposition to its very existence (Block, 2008). It came about through a business-state coalition whereby the state financed several development projects to achieve economic development goals while technology companies used the funding to innovate and then commercialize the technology. This began in 1980, when Congress passed a number of laws to maintain America's technological dominance vis-à-vis Japan. In theory, internal pressures from professional groups can result in regulatory agencies with autonomous authority to engage in development (Levi-Faur & Jordana, 2005).

Some key characteristics bind this scholarship. First, most development bureaucracies in intermediate states lack Weberian characteristics; therefore, these studies focus on how a pocket of efficiency is formed when development agencies achieve autonomy vis-à-vis the larger state apparatus. Autonomy is typically achieved through state financial support – independent of parliamentary control – or by creating firms independently financed through corporate profits. Second, a pocket of efficiency often forms after a crisis or a previous failure by political leaders to engage in effective economic development. This failure creates space for political leaders to garner support for establishing alternative "independent" development agencies. Third, coherent political leadership, including coalitions with social groups supporting industrialization, are important to produce a critical amount of state capacity for development.

This chapter builds on this literature in two important ways. First, the construction of a pocket of efficiency relies on a higher degree of agency in building a coalition to support industrialization. Iran's political field is more fractured than most other political contexts where pockets of efficiency have been described. Iran manifests three powerful, distinct, and fundamentally conflicting economic visions: those of nationalist industrialization, neoliberal commercialism, and left nationalist popular development. Thus the construction of a pocket of efficiency for the automobile industry could not be done merely within the state: building ties with external allies was much more important. Initially, these included lobbying ties between the industrial nationalist managers and the higher-level development bureaucracies and parliament in order to pass the protective Automobile Law. Its passage led to a coherent development strategy around a nationalist vision and the rise of local manufacturing.

In building on this theoretical concept, this chapter will borrow two concepts from organizational theory. First, it will be shown that it is possible for nationalists with a project of industrialization to decouple a key set of organizations sufficiently from other parts of the state apparatus to create an effective "mini-developmental state" within a specific industrial sector. Decoupling occurs when organizations connected to a larger social structure or political apparatus can implement policies independently from that structure or apparatus according to their own logic or interests (Perrow, 1984; White, 2008). Second, it will borrow from recent scholarship that argues that collective action through social movements can positively impact the emergence of new industries (Carroll & Swaminathan, 2000; Greve, Pozner, & Rao, 2006). However, an industry's success can create new grievances for other actors in society motivating them to form a counter-movement that opposes the development of the industry (Carlos, Sine, Lee, & Haveman, 2011).

A second characteristic is the concept of sequencing. The dynamics of how states evolve through different levels of efficiency is not well studied. The sequence of constructing a "pocket of efficiency" in Iran's auto industry was a dynamic process: causality went from conflicts between industrial nationalists, and neoliberals and the left, to elite business-state alliances and finally to a pocket of efficiency lodged in the development agencies. My analysis of this process builds on the idea that elite coherence is important for building state capacity; it differs from studies emphasizing top-down processes by showing how pockets of efficiency can be formed through a middle-up lobbying process. This shifts the focus away from associating state capacity primarily with the type of state (weak or strong, predatory or developmentalist) – to a sequence of developing agencies on the part of social groups with a shared agenda and the resources to realize it.

The *agency* and *sequencing* concepts developed in this chapter build on social field and neo-institutional theory. The idea here is that current state capacity scholarship lacks the theoretical power to explain how agency can change the political and industrial field leading to positive development outcomes. The analytical frame used in this analysis is social skill as agency within embedded autonomy. I will argue that the Iranian automobile industry entered a critical juncture during the reform years between 1988 and 1992. President Rafsanjani used his "social skill" to reframe Islamic economics in the Iranian political field away from leftist, socialist-leaning Islamic populism toward a pragmatic, pro-business economic agenda in response to the economic crisis caused by the Iran-Iraq war. While scholars have analyzed how political factions have reframed Islamic economics around a "Khomeinist" populist vision to appeal to a constituency and construct a policy agenda (Brumberg, 2001), this chapter will analyze how cultural frames were used to achieve specific policy goals for automobile industrial development.

During the early years of his presidency, Rafsanjani received support from both the radical left and conservatives who supported his postwar reconstruction effort. In the process of policy implementation, however, the political field interacted with the economic field in ways that caused conflict among political factions and thus shaped the outcome of the industry. This interaction was largely influenced by two events. The first was a threat to the state's autonomy in carrying out the project: left-wing radicals, whose constituency was with the rural poor and who therefore favored self-sufficient agricultural methods over automobile development, engaged in a protracted conflict with industrialists attempting to modernize the industry through ties to Western corporations. This conflict resulted in a compromise that led to localization of the industry but at the same time stalled higher value-added technical development. The second, and most significant, event was an alliance Rafsanjani built with the conservatives in which he agreed to liberalize trade and lifted the ban on imported automobiles. This policy brought about an economic crisis that was met by an elite counter-movement led by left-wing, high-level industrial managers of Iran's largest corporations: they succeeded in pushing through a nationalist agenda to develop a self-sufficient, modern, and more technically advanced automobile industry. After the crisis, Rafsanjani and his conservative followers lost their legitimacy and power over the industry. Instead, the industrial nationalists rose to dominate it. In doing so, they positioned themselves as national "reconstructors" by using their social skill to get disparate factions to support their policies by framing their objectives around Rafsanjani's pro-business agenda with the leftist policy of building a "self-sufficient" industry.

The key mechanism for success of the movement was embeddedness between the state and industrial managers established by Rafsanjani's Minister of Industry appointment. Close ties between the industrial ministers and managers of Iranian automobile corporations through the Automobile Committee allowed the managers to have a voice in pushing through a nationalist agenda. (An important measure of the unique success of the Iranian auto industry is that no other industry in Iran is protected through infant industry protection.) After the crisis, the political and industrial field became stable with the establishment of a new alliance between the industrial nationalists, government officials, and members of parliament – leading to the rapid growth of the industry.

This chapter will first present the two main ideological positions – the conservatives (the traditional right) and the radicals (the left) – in the political field in Iran as it existed in 1988. It will then discuss how President Rafsanjani attempted to reframe Islamic economics in the Iranian political field away from radical, socialist-leaning populism to a more pro-business and pragmatic economic agenda. This discussion will be followed by a description of how industrial nationalists reinvigorated the development of the industry in 1988. I will then discuss how embeddedness at the intersection between the political and industrial field led to compromises among social groups and the eventual rise of the industrial nationalists to implement infant industry protection. The chapter will end by analyzing industrial nationalist ideology and how it differs from the Rafsanjani pragmatist faction.

The Political Field in Iran

Since the revolution of 1979, the struggle for power in Iran has been a salient characteristic of the political field (Moslem, 2002; Siavoshi, 1992; Baktiari, 1996). Iran is officially a Shiite Islamic state; therefore, all economic decisions must be interpreted and legitimized through Islamic jurisprudence by scholars of the Koran (the *mujtaheed*). These precepts include such things as the definition of "social justice" and the role of the state in the economy. Important in understanding factionalism is "doctrinism": each faction claims that its interpretation of an Islamic state is authentic. The two most important factions in Iran since the revolution are described and compared in Table 2.1: the conservatives (the "traditional right") and the "radicals" (the "left"). The table illustrates the policy positions of the factions as they existed in the late 1980s. The conservatives historically had strong ties to the bazaar and the commercial class in Iran (the *bazaaris*) and therefore promoted economic policies supporting commerce. These ties go back several centuries and are the primary reason why a mosque is located in every bazaar in Iran. These policies include free markets, liberalized trade, and privatization of all enterprises. Conservatives support state initiatives to regulate and plan the economy but oppose state-led development and nationalization of industries. To them, the Koran was written in an era before modernization and therefore should not be used to interpret policy prescriptions on how the state should manage or control the economy. Social justice encompasses the need to lessen the gap between the rich and the poor, but a classless society is not achievable. Instead, hard work will lead to greater prosperity. The societal mechanism to care for the poor and needy is for citizens to be mindful of the poor and to distribute wealth through Islamic taxes (*zakat* and *khoms*). Conservatives, therefore, support strict

Table 2.1 *Factional Ideology, 1979–1988*[1]

Economic Action	Conservative (Traditional Right)	The Radicals (the Left)
Social justice and Islamic economic orientation	Social justice is achieved through liberalization of the economy – free trade, privatization, and rapid growth policies.	Social justice is achieved by supporting the "downtrodden" and "barefoot masses."
State role in economic development	State should be involved in offering fiscal incentives to private sector to take risks; it should introduce initiatives for development, such as planning and regulation.	High-level state institutions should be involved in development, but it should be guided along proper paths of social justice – such as supporting small business cooperatives and redistribution of wealth via subsidies and price controls.
Trade and infant industry protection	Modern economy is established through free trade and economic liberalization.	Self-reliance: Imports are banned and ties to MNCs are not allowed, eliminating need for infant industry protection
Ties to society	Maintain strong ties to the commercial class (*bazaaris*). These relationships were established and maintained over centuries.	Maintain ties to elite universities, Islamic foundations, clerical establishment, urban and rural poor.
Policy toward Western governments	Ties with Western governments are beneficial only if they related to trade; to avoid Western "cultural onslaught" against Islam, keep Iran closed to outside countries.	Western governments are seen as "imperialists," so reject all ties to Western governments and multinational corporations that could exploit the masses.
Corporate ownership	All corporations, whether large or small, should be privately held.	State should own all large industries to ensure that corporate policy maximizes redistribution of resources to the poor. Small and medium-sized firms should be privately held.

[1] Typology based on Moslem's *Factional Politics in Post-Khomeini Iran* (2002), Baktiari's *Parliamentary Politics in Revolutionary Iran: The Institutionalization of Factional Politics* (1996), and Siavoshi's "Factionalism and Iranian Politics: The Post-Khomeini Experience" (1992).

enforcement of Sharia law. Within this faction, some individuals support ties to the West in order to increase commerce and trade, whereas others are staunchly opposed to establishing such ties for fear of defiling Islamic culture.

The "radicals" of the left have an opposing perspective. They strongly support social justice but believe it should be implemented through policies that redistribute wealth to the "downtrodden and barefoot masses" and also through policies that eliminate "exploitation by the capitalists." Such policies include nationalization of large industries, price controls and subsidies for the poor, and support of small, local business cooperatives. According to this faction, development policies should focus on economic independence achieved through utilization of indigenous human, economic, and technical resources (Siavoshi, 1992, p. 31). Reliance on foreign capital and foreign technology is considered detrimental to the spirit of the revolution. The leftists, therefore, support banning foreign imports of industrial products and breaking ties to imperialist countries and their corporations.

An important question to pose is this: If either of these two factions had controlled automobile industrial policy, what would the likely outcome of the automobile development project have been? The conservatives would have supported liberal trade policies, resulting in imports of automobiles instead of local manufacturing. The self-reliant policies supported by the radicals – cutting off ties to Western governments and their corporations, for example – would have resulted, on the other hand, in complete failure of an industry or, at the very best, the survival of one with highly outdated technology. Neither of these two industrial policies, however, was implemented – Iran instead developed a large industry based on local manufacturing of modern automobiles. This outcome was made possible when a group of industrialists within the left faction emerged to defeat two other factions – the leftist agriculturalists and the conservative neoliberals – opposed to automobile industrial development. Once both groups had been defeated, they were largely excluded from participating in the localization of the industry. Instead, the industrialists with a nationalist policy agenda dominated the industry.

A Move toward Indigenizing Local Manufacturing, 1988–1989

By the end of the eight-year war with Iraq in 1988, the government made a move toward reinvigorating automobile industrial development and building an industry that was self-sufficient. The new strategy was based on opportunities made possible by the winding down of the war with Iraq, the restructuring of the global automobile industry, and the bankruptcy of a British automobile manufacturer. This section will discuss the beginnings of building local manufacturing. Later sections will discuss the opposition that it faced and the rise of industrial nationalists to gain control of the policy agenda.

When the war with Iraq ended, an estimated $210 billion worth of damage had been inflicted on Iran's machinery, buildings, equipment, and materials (Amirahmadi, 1990). In the later years of the war, the price of oil dropped from $99 a barrel in 1985 to $32 in 1989.[2] In addition, by 1989 the government, which had borrowed hundreds of millions of dollars to pay for the war, experienced difficulty in paying off the loans. In 1990, the official unemployment rate of 20 percent was the highest in Iran's history – but the unofficial rate was estimated to be 30 percent (Keshavarzian, 2009). An estimated 500,000 Iranian lives were lost during the war, and tens of thousands of young veterans were suddenly without a job or other means to make a living.

Despite the damage the war inflicted on the country, a number of events had created new opportunities to transform the auto industry in Iran. From 1980 to 1988, the price of oil dropped from $70 a barrel to $20 a barrel in constant 1988 dollars.[3] Production of passenger vehicles also dropped from 120,000 a year in 1979 to 5,000 in 1989. The banning of imports in the 1980s contributed to a pent-up demand for cars. During the war, participating in a lottery was the only way to obtain a new automobile. (A lottery winner had to place a down payment on the vehicle and wait approximately two years to obtain it.) The demand, however, far exceeded the supply; many of the orders for automobiles could not be fulfilled.

Shifts in the strategy of some key, established automobile manufacturers in the 1980s highly influenced Iran's ability to develop an industry. In the late 1970s, as part of its strategy to increase volume and diversify its product line, Peugeot purchased Talbot from Chrysler's European division. Peugeot failed to update Talbot's products, restricting the company from expanding in European markets. Talbot's survival therefore depended heavily on the Iranian market, but the gradual drop in passenger car production in Iran resulted in a steep reduction in orders for the Peykan knockdown kits. Peugeot subsequently closed the factory in 1988 (Freyssenet, 2009).

Behzad Nabavi, an engineer whose radical ideology was closely aligned with the left and who embraced self-reliance, became the Minister of Heavy Industry in 1985. When Peugeot closed its Talbot factories in Britain in 1988, the manufacturing equipment was put up for sale – thus creating an opportunity for Nabavi to realize his revolutionary ideals of

[2] Adjusted for inflation based on 2008 prices; www.wtrg.com/prices.htm.
[3] www.wtrg.com/prices.htm.

creating a self-reliant industry within an Islamic state. He convinced Mir Hussein Mousavi, prime minister of Iran at the time, to purchase the Talbot factories for $13 million with the proviso that the equipment would be used to build a self-reliant industry by deepening localization of industrial production. Two thousand machines were packed up and shipped to Iran. Iranian managers working in the industry at that time consider the purchase of the Talbot factories as a seminal turning point in promoting local manufacturing: using the factory's equipment meant high, value-added parts could begin to be manufactured in Iran.[4] The Talbot machinery was used to establish eleven large companies.

Within the ministry, concerns existed that Iran would be producing a car with technology that was more than thirty years old. Once the war with Iraq ended in 1988, a second front in the development project began: Behzad Nabavi ordered the managing director of Iran Khodro to strike a deal with a multinational corporation to manufacture a modern car in Iran.[5] Nabavi's policy initiative was to produce the Peykan but phase it out as quickly as possible in favor of using the newly purchased Talbot factories to produce a modern vehicle. Manufacturing a modern car would introduce new technology and enhance the prospects of the industry.

In pursuit of developing a modern vehicle, many of the world's largest vehicle producers were approached – including Volkswagen, Toyota, Nissan, Fiat, Peugeot, and Renault. The choices available to the Iranians were highly constrained by Iran's political relationships with the countries whose multinational corporations were aligned with America's political orientation toward Iran. The managing director of Iran Khodro at that time explained the negotiating process:

> Some companies agreed to work with us, but only to manufacture an old car they would soon discontinue, while others did not agree with manufacturing a car in Iran at all. Of all the companies we approached, only Fiat was interested in manufacturing a new car in Iran, and even they would not agree to work with us directly; we had to work through their Brazilian division. When we were about to sign the agreement with Fiat, we got a call from Peugeot to produce the Peugeot 405 in Iran. We were very happy because it was the newest, highest-quality vehicle in their fleet and it was selling very well in Europe.[6]

---

[4] Interviews with various managers of large business associations and parts suppliers, October 2010.

[5] Known as Iran National before the revolution, Iran Khodro is the country's largest vehicle manufacturer.

[6] Interview with government official of large development organization, October 2010. When released, the Peugeot 405 received rave reviews in the European and British press for its advanced design, fuel economy, and reasonable price. It was designated European

What cinched the deal was the intervention of an Iranian living in France with high-level connections to both the Iranian government and the Peugeot family; he guaranteed that the family would receive a good deal. Peugeot agreed to sell Iran the vehicle initially as a complete knockdown kit at $4,000 each, promising to localize 40 percent of the product within one year of first producing the vehicle and guaranteeing further that 70 percent would be localized within five years.

Restructuring the Political Field: The Rise of Rafsanjani

By the late 1980s, members of parliament began coalescing around the speaker of parliament, Hashemi Rafsanjani. As a former businessman and close associate of Ayatollah Khomeini, he acquired wide support to reconstruct Iran's economy. He was widely perceived as taking a non-ideological approach to solving problems and was seen as someone who tended to avoid extreme solutions (Baktiari, 1996; Moslem, 2002).

When Rafsanjani became president in August 1989, his main objective was to reconstruct and reform Iran's economy after the Iran-Iraq war. The initial restructuring policies had two main components: rebuilding the infrastructure destroyed during the war with Iraq and rebuilding state capacity to implement and manage industrial development. He later supported a new policy initiative to reform foreign policy so Iran could participate in what was perceived as the benefits of the "new" global economy. The left-wing political faction was his primary obstacle in achieving these goals, and for one main reason: even though the left supported his reconstruction policies, they did not support economic liberalization – because their conception of Islamic capitalism favored nationalized industries and nationalized trade. Reforms would also reduce or eliminate their base of support by eliminating subsidies for the urban and rural poor.

To overcome the left's opposition, Rafsanjani implemented two policy initiatives. First, he used his close association with Ayatollah Khomeini as well as his presidential powers to reduce the left's power by appointing his policy supporters to cabinet positions. Second, he transformed Iran's Islamic identity from a left-wing, statist identity to a pro-business identity that would appeal to both the traditional right and the left. Rafsanjani had the support of the traditional right, including the newly chosen Supreme Leader, Ayatollah Khomeini, and most clerics and members of parliament in the traditional right faction. However, simply gaining the support of the Supreme Leader was not enough to bring about change in Iran. The left

Car of the Year in 1988. See "Peugeot 405 Receives Germany's Highest Automotive Honor," *PR Newswire*, November 10, 1987.

still dominated the parliament – the most important organ of government for passing legislation to open up space for industrial modernization. Thus his main objective was to persuade the left-wing members of parliament to support his policies. The remainder of this section will discuss the changes he made in bringing about change.

Restructuring of the Executive Branch

It is believed that Rafsanjani played a large role in convincing Ayatollah Khomeini to restructure executive branch authority with the intention of establishing better management and administration of the country. It was not difficult to convince Khomeini to implement change because by the late 1980s he, too, was concerned that excessive power in the legislative branch had led to factionalism between radicals and conservatives – thus rendering the government incapable of implementing coherent policies. The left dominated the executive, legislative, and judicial branches and pushed through "statist" economic policies such as land reform and subsidies for the poor, whereas the conservatives who supported free market reforms dominated the Guardian Council and vetoed many policies passed by radicals in parliament (Amirahmadi, 1990; Moslem, 2002).

Although Khomeini's ideology was aligned with the leftist faction, he often mediated between the two major factions, siding with one over the other, in such a way that neither could gain the upper hand. Before his death, he set out to resolve factional conflicts by creating further centralization and authority within the executive branch. The new constitution granted greater authority to the Supreme Leader's office to determine the general policies of the Islamic Republic; to resolve the disputes between the three branches of government; and to appoint, dismiss, or accept the resignation of the important members of the branches of the state under the control of the Supreme Leader's office.[7] To reduce conflicts between the parliament and the Guardian Council, the parliament was granted the power to overturn vetoes by the Guardian Council with a two-thirds majority vote.

New powers were also granted to the president's office. Under the old constitution, the presidency was a ceremonial position with little power over the constitution or in making government appointments. The new constitution greatly increased the power of the presidency. The president became the highest official in the country in terms of implementing the constitution and acquired power over financial, economic, and bureaucratic affairs because he was granted the authority to choose cabinet

---

[7] This includes the Guardian Council, the highest authority in the judiciary; the head of national radio and television broadcasting; and the Chief Commander of the Revolutionary Guard Corps, the armed forces, and the police force.

members independently of parliament. The religious authority of the Supreme Leader's office, however, was weakened by constitutional amendment so that the Supreme Leader did not need to be a source of emulation (a Grand Ayatollah or *marja-e taqlid*). This new law opened the possibility for the president to develop his own religious following outside the Supreme Leader's office (Brumberg, 2001).

Institutional Restructuring and Legitimizing of Industrial Development

In the fall of 1989, President Rafsanjani made a number of important speeches to transform Iran's Islamic identity. His interpretation of Iran's economic stagnation was that the war had destroyed the Iranian economy and the situation had been made worse by poor management resulting from Iran's left-wing statist policies. After the revolution, revolutionary-religious orientation and ties to the clerical and political establishment were the main criteria used for choosing managers for government ministries and industrial corporations. Since the left had managed Iran's economy and the war with Iraq, they were blamed for Iran's failing economy. Rafsanjani, therefore, believed it was important to transform the management of government and industries in order to achieve national reconstruction goals. Islamic culture also needed to be reoriented to allow people with the appropriate skills and proper "way of thinking" to manage the economic transformation.

In a series of speeches at this time, he began to reframe the conception of Islamic social justice by claiming that it should be achieved through the building of a self-sufficient society based on industrial production. He claimed Iran was in a state of "dependent capitalism" largely created by left-wing economic subsidies and price controls. In his inaugural speech, he discussed the issue of dependent capitalism within the context of Iran's experience with colonial powers' desire to exploit Iran. He stated that Iran was a country "coveted by the world's greedy vultures, who have always thought of dominating it."[8] He then discussed the need to achieve political independence through industrial production:

> Do you think we can secure independence without serious pro-duction in the country? If we were to continue to buy our wheat, forage, meat, machine tools, and equipment, the machinery itself and our skilled manpower, well – in that case, we would not have any sort of independence, neither political independence nor economic independence. ... Anyone who is so poor and needy certainly cannot raise his head in the world. Can it be said

---

[8] *Hashemi Rafsanjani's Inaugural Speech*, Tehran Domestic Service (in Persian), August 17, 1989. FBIS-NES-89–163, August 24, 1989.

continuously that the poor and hungry people should charge forward with empty stomachs to get killed? Can we protect the people like this? This is not the way.[9]

In this passage, he attempts to address the issue of economic dependency. He criticizes the left for creating a dependent society, but he uses the language of the left – the world is a field of power divided between the oppressed (the poor) and the oppressors (the colonial powers) – to make the case for establishing a new conception of Islamic social justice. The struggle for social justice should result not in a dependent society but rather in one where it is achieved through local industrial production. By supporting local industrial production, he claims to support self-sufficiency – a long-standing policy supported by the left.

Rafsanjani often made references to the conception of work in achieving self-sufficiency. In his view, working hard is directly related to the strength of an Islamic society. He cites the Prophet Mohammad in saying, "a Muslim is happy when his livelihood is sufficient for him and whose strength is ample," but to Rafsanjani it is "completely wrong, and it is an injustice to Islam, to imagine that a Muslim should be a useless, lazy person."[10] Work should not be associated with unbridled greed, which is inherently un-Islamic. On the other hand, without hard work a citizen will be impoverished and will subjugate

> ... him[self] to other material powers, and this is something that always comes about as a result of poverty in individuals, families, and societies that lose their dignity; [it is] something that was strongly condemned by the prophet, lest the Muslims through their laziness leave the field open to the infidels and put the unbelievers in charge of economic affairs. We should eliminate such thinking [that material things do not matter] one-hundred percent from our Islamic society.[11]

Given that Iran and many other Muslim nations are rich in natural resources, it is puzzling that Muslim countries are "weaker from an economic point of view than the infidels." A Muslim is therefore "duty-bound to improve the economy of his society and exploit natural resources for that society."[12] Here he criticizes the left for their position that a society should not be structured around material gain. Yet he again sides with the left, speaking their language, when he sees the world as a field of power divided between the oppressed and the oppressors. Laziness is the cause of poverty, and without hard work Iran's economy

[9] Ibid.
[10] *Hashemi Rafsanjani Gives Friday Prayer Sermon*, Tehran Domestic Service (in Persian), September 29, 1989, FBIS-NES-89–190, October 3, 1989.
[11] Ibid. [12] Ibid.

will be dominated by the "infidels." The message here is that to keep the infidels out of the country, a long-standing position embraced by the left, Islamic culture should embrace hard work.

Rafsanjani's vision of industrial development included establishing ties with Western governments. He believed that in order for the nation to increase industrial production to reduce poverty, Iran would need to obtain the technology from Western countries. This policy, however, would involve a compromise of increasing financial and technical dependence on Western governments. The problem Rafsanjani faced was that the left strongly opposed ties with America and Europe. He attempted to resolve this obstacle by framing the need to establish ties with the West within the context of poverty and current events surrounding the collapse of communism in Eastern Europe:

> At the moment, you can see why it is that the communists of the world have stretched their hands toward the capitalists ... The fact that Poland changes her ideology to attract the attention of the western world is based on economic needs and financial crises. The greatest political powers of today's world have been forced to give up what they followed for years because they cannot run their own lives. Poverty is destroying every aspect of their lives ... The Koran does not wish the Muslims to experience such a day.[13]

By discussing the problem within the context of poverty, a key component of Islamic social justice, Rafsanjani was able to appeal to both the left and the traditional right. He argued, however, that it is better to be friends with the infidels and to be a self-sufficient, developed, and wealthy nation rather than be a poor and isolated one. By 1990, the Iranian government had reestablished relationships with most European countries, including France and Germany, thus creating a more auspicious environment for auto industry development.

Rebuilding State Capacity: The Technocrats and Development Bureaucracies

One of the major policy goals of the Rafsanjani government was to rebuild state capacity. Rafsanjani often emphasized technocratic competency over revolutionary religious credentials. He believed government played a role in providing the resources and creating the environment for entrepreneurship to thrive – but only through a technocratic revolution could a development project realize its full potential.

---

[13] Ibid.

In a *Resalat* interview, Rafsanjani was asked what policy he would follow in choosing directors and ministers. He replied that "[p]ersons should be selected who are revolutionary, expert, and dedicated ... they should combine these qualities with an overall vision. It is not enough to have expertise and be totally bereft of political insight."[14] In utilizing manpower, he responded, "I most certainly do not like to choose someone to assist me, or to reject him, based on reasons pertaining to his gang or political affiliation."[15]

However, it was important for him to legitimize his policies within the context of Islam. One strategy he used was to criticize the left for their support of Hizbollahis (members of the party of God) and their association with mismanagement of the economy. Hizbollahis zealously supported the revolution and behaved as if they had the right to act autonomously in physically attacking opponents of the Islamic Republic (Moslem, 2002). A distinguishing feature of the Hizbollahis was their ascetic lifestyle and scruffy, bearded appearance. Rafsanjani saw the Hizbollahis as harmful to his reconstruction policies and criticized their role as cultural symbols in Iranian society:

> God has created in humans an ornamental and beauty-seeking sense with a disdain for ugliness ... There is a culture in which the lifestyle of priests and Hizbollahis should be unpleasant and ugly. If it becomes a cultural phenomenon that being a Hizbollahi means looking unbearable, this is a sin and Islam has fought this.[16]

Hizbollahis were typically from lower socioeconomic backgrounds, were uneducated, and despised Western culture – all characteristics that Rafsanjani saw as incompatible with reconstruction policies. He instead emphasized the role of highly skilled professionals – but had to legitimize their status so they would be acceptable to both the left and the traditional right. Professionals did not exist at the time of the prophet Mohammed, so Rafsanjani broadly defines professionals as those with skills and who could make contributions to society:

> The prophet's description about these human beings who had the ability to produce was this: God loves a believing individual who has a profession; anyone having a profession, a technical worker, a technician, an engineer, a doctor; any person who having an expertise in providing a service for the society. God loves such

---

[14] Resalat Interviews Hashemi-Rafsanjani, *Resalat* (in Persian), July 26, 1989. FBIS-NES-150, August 7, 1989.

[15] *Hashemi Rafsanjani's Inaugural Speech*, Tehran Domestic Service (in Persian), August 17, 1989. FBIS-NES-89–163, August 24, 1989.

[16] *Ettela'at*, December 5, 1990 (Moslem, 2002).

a person if he is a believer. If a person is both a believer and a professional, he is one of God's favorite servants.[17]

Rafsanjani attempted to elevate the status of industrialists as economic nationalist soldiers burdened with preserving the Koranic commands. In a speech to industrialists, he described them as "forerunners of the revolution," comparing them to crusaders in fighting for economic independence. He stated, "Our great revolution attained victory through reliance on Islam. Now we have to show Islam that we are Muslims who are capable of implementing the Koranic commands." And he hoped that the industrialists would be "good soldiers to the Lord of the Age."[18]

Industrial Nationalists Make a Move toward Self-Reliance

The Left Fights the Left: Industrialists versus Agriculturalists, 1989–1990

When Rafsanjani became president, he used his newly appointed presidential powers to remove those in cabinet positions who either were in the left faction or did not agree with his reconstruction policies. This included Behzad Nabavi and his associates. At that time, Nabavi was a hardline radical, and Rafsanjani saw him as a potential opponent to his reconstruction policies.[19] Rafsanjani appointed twenty-two new cabinet positions, of whom seven had doctorates, nine were engineers, four were educated in the United States, and only four were clerics. Most of those appointed to positions of power were in his pragmatist circle but were competent professionals with many years of experience in the automobile industry or other heavy industries.

The most important cabinet appointee was Nejat Hosseinian, to the position of Minister of Heavy Industry. He had a doctorate in transportation policy from George Washington University. The ministry had strong ties to the automobile industry because it owned the Industrial Development and Renovation Organization (IDRO), which in turn owned the large automobile companies. The second-most important appointee was Reza Nematzadeh, who had earned a master's degree in industrial management at the University of California, Berkeley. Before

---

[17] *Hashemi Rafsanjani Gives Friday Prayer Sermon*, Tehran Domestic Service (in Persian), September 29, 1989. FBIS-NES-89–190, October 3, 1989.

[18] *President Addresses Industrialists*, Tehran Domestic Service (in Persian), March 3, 1990. FBIS-NES-90–043, March 5, 1990.

[19] After leaving his cabinet position, Behzad Nabavi became a member of parliament in the 1990s and 2000s. He resigned from parliament in 2004 and became a member of Iran's reform party.

becoming Minister of Industry in 1989, he was the director of Iran Khodro in the 1980s.

Nejat Hosseinian's goal as Minister of Heavy Industry was to implement Rafsanjani's industrial development reconstruction policies. He was granted the authority to formulate the necessary policies, and one way he did so was to "establish constant contact with managers and experts in the heavy industries sector."[20] Hosseinian established the Automobile Committee composed of thirty executives and experts in the field to create workable policy solutions, to obtain feedback, and to monitor the progress of development. Issues discussed included financing for the industry, technology transfer from Western countries, and laws and regulations that would help the industry develop indigenous local technical capacity. A high-ranking manager in the industry who attended the meetings explained the usefulness of the committee to the industry:

> Bimonthly meetings were held between the ministry and the managers of the largest automobile companies and parts producers. Most of the managers on the committee were young revolutionaries. There was a lot of criticism brought to the ministry. For example, they [the government] were putting a lot of fingers in the companies with rules and regulations, and it was difficult to open a business. The minister eventually got rid of these rules. It was also a place where we could learn about the policies so everyone knew what to do.[21]

The committee was also described as a "community" where camaraderie was established among the young revolutionary industrialists and as a space where industrialists and government officials deepened their contacts. From the minister's perspective, the committee was helpful because members were drawn from both the public and private sectors – so he could be privy to both viewpoints to formulate policy. A case in point was a policy initiative in which an automobile market was created to benefit both the private sector and the government. After the revolution, the left's policies of social justice through subsidies included fixing the price for the Peykan far below the market value to allow people from lower socio-economic classes to purchase a vehicle. At $1,000 per vehicle, the price was far below the real cost for the complete knockdown (which Talbot was selling to the Iranians at $4,500 a kit). As automobile production decreased, the market value for automobiles rose dramatically: by 1988, the real market value for a Peykan was ten times the subsidized price, allowing middlemen instead of the factories to profit from auto sales.

---

[20] *Minister Stresses Industrial Investment*, Tehran Domestic Service (in Persian), March 5, March 11, 1990, FBIS-NES-90–51, March 15, 1990.

[21] Interview, manager at parts supplier company, June 2011.

Nejat Hosseinian eliminated subsidies for automobiles; by doing so, he established a profitable industry in which both the private sector and the government could obtain substantial revenue through automobile manufacturing.

As production increased and government budget resources dramatically decreased, the potential of an indigenous auto industry became more and more attractive. Eventually, the government turned to the automotive industry to solve its own financial crisis and to provide the country with jobs – a much-needed boost after suffering from eight years of war. As Minister of Heavy Industry, Nejat Hosseinian arranged for the government to receive about 20 percent of sales revenue for each car sold.

Despite the growing success of automobile industry development, the signing of the contract with Peugeot was met with fierce resistance by the radicals. They opposed the contract for two main reasons. First, the radical conception of economic development was to support the rural poor; therefore, they believed the focus of development should be on the agricultural sector. Second, ties with multinational corporations were a sellout to the "imperialists" – who presumably would increase Iran's economic dependency on the West.

A movement organized by radical members of parliament and left-wing university elites worked to cancel the contract with Peugeot. The radicals framed their argument around support for the poor and the deprived in rural regions of Iran and around the failure of both the Shah and the economic development projects of the 1980s to develop the agricultural sector. By the late 1980s, only one-ninth of the arable land in Iran was being cultivated – the rest remained fallow. Roundtables consisting of academics and government officials provided a forum for debating policies. Rafsanjani's first five-year plan was debated in one such roundtable; excerpts of the discussion were published in an article in *Keyhan* titled "What Should Be the Priority of the First Five-Year Plan? Agriculture or Industry, Village or City?" Radicals and industrialists engaged in the debate, both sides stating that the plan's goal should be to bring about social justice, a greater distribution of revenues in the country, and an increase in high-paying jobs. The vision of the radicals, however, was to achieve the objectives through bottom-up, village-based agricultural development. A primary objective was that it should maximize employment. After discussing the failures of post-revolution agricultural development in Iran, Dr. Shaditaleb, a radical sociology professor at the University of Tehran, argued for agricultural employment – using the success of agricultural development policies in China as a case study that Iran could emulate:

> Expert research shows we have 3 million hectares of land that can be farmed. Now, if we equip and prepare only 300,000 hectares

of land each year, and if we employ two persons in each hectare, then my calculation shows that we can create 600,000 jobs each year in this way ... What did China do with a large population in villages after the revolution? It used the population for such tasks as soil preparation and irrigation, and for building up the infrastructure with dams and roads. China is now self-sufficient in farming products. They did not even implement complicated methods of heavy machinery used by western countries. My word is clear: What have we done with the 3 million hectares of farming land in Iran? According to farming reports, nearly 60% to 70% of water used in farming is wasted. If agriculture is a central issue in the five-year plan, which we all want it to be, then development must start from villages ... The Peykan has done nothing for us and neither will Peugeot. We want an industry that produces cement pipes for irrigation channels or an industry that produces spades for our farmers.[22]

The industrialists argued for greater ties with Western countries to develop Iran's industrial infrastructure. Their strategy incorporated policies intended to appeal to the radicals by emphasizing that industrial development is not exclusive to automobile production but includes farm industries as well. The ultimate goal was to develop a regional, export-oriented industry marketing to countries aligned with Iran's leftist policies of rejecting dependency on large multinational corporations:

We have high industrial potential, but right now it is dormant. We must activate dormant capabilities by forging smart ties with the world. If the efficiency of our tractors is relatively high, it does not follow that we should ignore our investments in the tractor industry, as well as related industries. There are many under-developed countries that need tractors. Such countries wish to have access to tractors without the presence of multinational corporations. Who is better than we to sell them tractors without political constraints? We should not shut down these industries only because we do not need them right now ... It would be great to launch the Mobarake Steel Corporation, but it is equally important to consider which industries need steel beforehand. We need to invest in those industries.[23]

Resistance to dependency on the West was another cause for opposing the Peugeot project. The conception of capitalism among the left at this time was that technical ties with Western corporations involving imports of

---

[22] "What Should Be the Priority of the First Five-Year Plan? Agriculture or Industry, Village or City?" *Keyhan*, November 14, 1989 (in Farsi).
[23] Ibid.

non-domestically made products was akin to criminal activity. Those who supported these policies were "economic terrorists" because they undermined Iran's economic and political independence. In the case of ties with the French, the initial criticism claimed that the relationship would increase Iran's dependency on a Western country – one that was "an imperialist whose ultimate ambition was to colonize Iran." Interestingly, the British were not considered "imperialists" because the Talbot factories had been purchased by Iran and hence the technology had become indigenized.[24] To the industrialists who supported the project, the radicals were anti-Western fanatics who rejected ties with the West under any circumstances.

The radicals later tempered their position and devised a more conciliatory oppositional strategy. Claiming it would take at least five years to localize the Peugeot 405, they maintained that Iran's currency to purchase the complete knockdown kits during that time would be sent to an imperialist country. They also claimed that any contract with a foreign automobile company should include provisions to localize within two years so as to curtail damage to Iran's independence; if that could not be achieved, the project should be abandoned. Instead, they argued, it would be best to maintain Iran's self-sufficient identity by localizing the Peykan instead of the Peugeot 405: after all, it already had higher local content than any other car in Iran and over the years had become an important Iranian cultural symbol.

Rumors surrounding the Peugeot 405 project suggested that the government would soon abandon it. Although they were pilloried in the Iranian press, the industrialists refused to back down.[25] However, as the conflict continued, the industrialists feared that the leftists would ultimately undermine the national automobile development project. More specifically, Nejat Hosseinian, Minister of Heavy Industry, was concerned that left-wing fanatics would destroy the automobile factories or physically attack factory managers.[26] After the parliament delayed the project for two years, from 1988 to 1990, a compromise was reached. To address the leftists' alliance with the rural poor in supporting the agricultural sector, and instead of investing in cement and piping plants, the Ministry of Heavy Industry would increase development of an agricultural machinery industry. With respect to automobiles, Iran Khodro would not cancel the Peugeot 405 but would shift the emphasis to localizing the Peykan. At the same time, Iran Khodro received permission to enter into a new agreement with Peugeot to replace the Peykan engine with a newer, more fuel-efficient Peugeot 504 engine. In this way, the

[24] In addition, over the years, the Peykan became an important Iranian cultural symbol.
[25] *Ministry Seeking Domestic Vehicle Assembly*, London *Keyhan* (in Persian), April 26, 1990, p. 4. FBIS-NES-90–097, May 18, 1990.
[26] Interview with manager at automobile business association, fall 2010.

ministry achieved a number of goals that appealed to the radicals but also helped advance the cause of the industrialists in modernizing the industry. First, by localizing the Peykan, they were able to claim that the goal was to eventually develop an independent, self-sufficient industry with indigenous local content. Second, in doing so, they would preserve the cultural symbol important to the radicals. Third, although the Peugeot 405 was far more advanced, localization of the new Peugeot 504 engine would partially help overcome the problem of producing an automobile with entirely dated technology.

The compromise, however, did not come without a cost. As a result of the two-year delay in fulfilling the Peugeot 405 contract, Peugeot increased the price of the complete knockdown kit to $8,000. Furthermore, the price of the final vehicle in Iran was raised by an additional $4,000 to ensure profitable returns. The resulting high price of $12,000 for the Peugeot 405 resulted in low economies of scale, which in turn delayed technology transfer via localization by approximately five years.

Industrialists versus Neoliberals and the Rise of Infant Industry Protection, 1990–1992

Rafsanjani began in October 1990 to liberalize the industry by allowing unlimited automobile imports. The official government position was that the leftist policies of banning auto imports and spare parts, policies instituted since the early years of the revolution, had caused unneeded shortages.[27] In 1991, his liberal trade policy eventually became part of a broader reform policy to align economic development in Iran with globalist, free-market economic policies. Framing the justification for the policy shift in the language of the left, he argued that through globalization developing nations could free themselves from exploitation by the dominant world powers to reduce "grave inequalities" in world living standards. He urged other poor nations to adopt similar liberal market policies.[28] These policies included joining the World Trade Organization, funding reconstruction and development projects through foreign direct investment, and borrowing from the World Bank and International Monetary Fund. Reforms to Iran's economy included privatization of nationalized industries, elimination of subsidies to the rural and urban poor, and liberalized trade.

The liberalization of trade had the most immediate impact on the trajectory of the automobile industry. Once the law was approved,

---

[27] *Ministry Lifts Ban on Auto Imports*, London *Keyhan* (in Persian), October 4, 1990. FBIS-NES

[28] Drozdiak, William, *Iran Outlines Shift to a Free Market; Rafsanjani Faults Treatment of Poor Nations*. Washington Post Foreign Service, November 20, 1991.

imports of foreign vehicles increased dramatically – from 537 in 1990 to 7,296 in 1991 and to 50,027 in 1992. The industrial nationalists saw the policy as capitulation to the conservatives, who promoted liberal trade policies. Enriching those who favored imports was also an immediate threat to the long-term vision of the industrial nationalists in building a national, self-sufficient industry based on indigenous technical capacity.

When Nejat Hosseinian became Minister of Heavy Industry, he initially showed mixed support for localization of the automobile industry. A high-level manager at Iran Khodro and member of the automobile committee explained the conflict in policy direction within the ministry at that time: "Nejat Hosseinian was educated in the United States, he didn't know industry well, he was pro-liberalization, and he didn't support localization."[29] The committee was used as a means for the industrialists to express their policy objectives to the minister. Conflicts arose between members of the committee, most of whom had several years' experience in the field, and the minister regarding which policies to adopt. One disagreement concerned the benefits of localizing the industry through infant industry protection:

> Managers in the auto industry were shouting and cursing at him [about the imports]. He initially didn't support localization, and so we lost some opportunities. His position was that to have good local content, it would take seven years; but by that time, the car [produced by the multinational corporation] would be discontinued. So his reasoning was that you needed to have localization within two years, but that was very difficult. He was just a university Ph.D.; he didn't know the pros and cons of industrial development. Members of the committee gradually gave him advice and he began to understand.[30]

Managers in the industry at the time often discussed support for localization as a nationalist struggle. One method used to gain government support was to show the ministers and government officials the progress that had been made. By 1990, localization of parts manufacturing enjoyed significant success, but government officials had to be convinced that it was a project worth pursuing. The managing director of Saze Ghostar, Iran's second-largest supply chain company, explained how he convinced Nejat Hosseinian and other government officials to support localization of the auto industry:

> At the beginning everyone opposed me: they thought that we could not produce parts of good quality, they didn't believe me – not even the suppliers. They said it was too difficult, that auto parts are not easy to make and the effort does not justify it;

---

[29] Interview, manager at automobile business association, June 2011. [30] Ibid.

we should stick to simpler industries. I had a meeting with Nejat Hosseinian and invited him to Saze Ghostar to show him what we had accomplished. He was reluctant to come – they did not believe in what we were doing, his deputies told him not to come; and when he came, he was so impressed. When he left, I had support of the whole ministry; they were astonished that we could produce so many parts.[31]

The role of infant industry protection in the success of the Korean auto industry was also used as a tool to convince those opposed to infant industry protection: "You couldn't expect everyone, including the technocrats, to understand [infant industry protection]. The Korean auto industry was started in the 1960s, at the same time and at the same level as the Iranian auto industry; and we said to them, look at what they have and look at us."[32]

As government officials, particularly members of parliament, were being lobbied to persuade them that localization of the auto industry through infant industry protection was worth the effort, a critical factor arose that determined the fate of the industry. Rafsanjani's liberal trade policies created an economic crisis. Within a year, $20 billion worth of foreign products were imported into Iran. More than 100,000 automobiles accounted for $5 billion of currency that left Iran. This accounted for 25 percent of the currency leaving the country, and the Iranian rial dropped dramatically against the dollar. The ensuing economic crisis opened up new opportunities for expanding the auto industry. High-level executives at the largest auto companies, along with managers at the parts suppliers and key government officials who supported the industry, engaged in collective action to create a coalition to pass infant industry protection:

> As a result of the relationship between the government, the auto companies, and the Ministry of Heavy Industry, we were able to convince a lot of members of parliament to pass the law through lobbying; it worked well to challenge those who were against it, and we won the votes necessary to get it passed.[33]

The new law, the "Automobile Law," instituted a progressive tariff system under which cars imported without local content were subject to a 200 percent tariff, whereas those with local content carried a tariff ranging from 90 percent to zero. The amount of the tariff varied according to the amount of local content: a 90 percent tariff for 30 percent local content, a 60 percent tariff for 60 percent local content, and no tariff for

---

[31] Interview, manager at large development organization, June 2011.
[32] Interview with high-ranking manager at parts supplier company, February 2011.
[33] Interview, high-level automobile executive, February 2011.

100 percent local content. The coalition of industrial nationalists included reformed liberalizer Nejat Hosseinian and two key members of parliament who helped pushed the law through: Ali Akbar Nateq-Nuri, a staunch conservative who supported Rafsanjani and who was an active opposition leader against the left, and Mr. Noroozadeh, head of the Industrial Committee in parliament and member of the leftist faction.

The Automobile Law also included provisions to establish auto manufacturing business associations, including the Iran Automobile Parts Manufacturing Association and the Iran Vehicle Manufactures Association. The idea behind these associations was to create long-lasting ties between the industry and the government to protect the industry. A long-term member of the Iran Automobile Parts Manufacturing Association explained the role of business associations in the industry:

> [Nejat Hosseinian] came to us to create an association for automobiles. He understood how they worked in other countries and saw how they could be helpful to bring the ideas of the people to the government. He saw how imports were hurting the domestic industry and wanted to have growth go toward domestic production and have greater added value in the industry.

Among high-level managers within the industry, the Automobile Law is considered an important factor in creating a "movement." It appealed to a broad coalition in government, and it helped solve an important national economic problem – a currency crisis. Among the industry's leaders, the Automobile Law is considered the most important law for the growth of the domestic auto market by expanding entrepreneurship within the industry and increasing local technical capacity.

Achieving Nationalist Aspirations through Automobile Industrial Development: The Ideological Position and Policies of the Industrial Nationalists

The purpose of this section is to analyze the ideological position and policies of the industrial nationalists who dominated the industry after the passing of infant industry protection in 1992. The nationalists borrowed from Rafsanjani's vision of a post-revolutionary Iran – one that emphasized technocratic management of the economy, a recasting of social justice toward job creation, and ties to Western countries to acquire the knowledge and technology for industrial development. In addition, they believed industrialization should focus on achieving political and economic independence. However, they saw themselves as engaged in an oppositional movement against Rafsanjani's (and the traditional right's) liberalization policies aimed at undermining infant industry protection.

The struggle also extended to the fight over dominance of multinational corporate control over the Iranian automobile market.

The directors and high-level managers were considered "revolutionary nationalists" in that they believed in the goals of the Islamic revolution, had strong religious bona fides, and believed in infant industry protection as the main tool for achieving economic independence. Many participated in the revolution during the 1970s and were jailed for their activities. The majority of them were highly educated technocrats with engineering degrees – approximately 50 percent of them educated in the West and the rest in Iran.

During the Rafsanjani and Khatami eras (1992–2005), the trend was to appoint revolutionary nationalists into positions of power within the industry. Those who rose into top positions at IDRO and the industrial ministries were either high-level managers at the automobile companies or persons who had experience in heavy industry. Reza Veyseh, instrumental in developing the automobile supply chain in Iran, was a high-level manager at Iran Khodro before becoming director of IDRO. He held a bachelor's degree in engineering and a doctorate in management from Sharif University of Technology. Akbar Torkan, with a US degree in civil engineering and who specialized in building prototypes of military vehicles during the Iran-Iraq war, became director of IDRO in the mid-1990s. Ahmad Rafat, with an MBA from the University of Oklahoma, was instrumental in developing the supply chain for Saipa, Iran's second-largest automobile company.

Behzad Nabavi, Minister of Heavy Industry in the 1980s, was one of the early industrial nationalists. Although Nabavi was one of the most prominent non-clerical government officials and was most closely associated with the radicals, he promoted modern industrial development and was unique in his support for establishing ties with Western governments. An associate of Nabavi explained his political orientation and approach to development at that time:

> Behzad Nabavi was a Muslim radical; he used his own hands to fight against the Shah. He was pro-industry because he was educated at the Polytechnic and he believed in modern industries. He was pushing managers to visit different countries to gain the knowledge to develop a modern industry.[34]

Three important characteristics defining industrial nationalists are prominent in this description. First, many high-ranking government officials considered "nationalists" fought against the Shah. Second, education credentials connote competence. Being a highly educated engineer from a well-known university is an important characteristic for managing an

---

[34] Interview, high-ranking manager at automobile business association, June 2011.

industry with relatively sophisticated technology. Third, in pursuing the development of a modern industry, Nabavi established ties with Western countries – a policy that most government officials in Iran's left faction considered a violation of self-reliance policies.

Another major figure considered a revolutionary nationalist – and one of the "fathers" of the Iranian auto industry – is Reza Veyseh, managing director of SAPCO, Iran Khodro's supply chain company. Reza Veyseh is credited first and foremost with implementing an organizational structure instrumental in founding and modernizing approximately 400 automobile parts supplier companies. Like many nationalists with strong religious bona fides, Veyseh often invoked Iranian nationalism above Islam in discussions about the development of the industry. A case in point is an article in an automobile industry trade publication in which he discusses the role of SAPCO as a new phenomenon in promoting total quality management (TQM), in transferring technology, and in improving engineering training. He explains that "SAPCO as an Iranian symbol encompasses three factors – belief in hard work, love of nation, and love of Islam."[35]

Nationalist aspirations are relevant when discussing the struggles of building a local industry. Manuchehr Gharavi, managing director of Iran Khodro for eight years in the 1990s, was a key figure in the development of Iran's indigenous automobile brand and a strong supporter of infant industry protection. In many of his interviews in the trade and popular press, he describes the industry as a "movement" existing in opposition to multinational corporations, whose objectives are to dominate the Iranian automobile market and to undermine Iran's inherent ability to engineer and manufacture modern products locally. In an interview in an international magazine, he states that the greatest reward of the industry's progress is building self-confidence in local manufacturing; he further states that almost all man-made achievements have been applied in auto industries. In a section on "rewarding courage and self-confidence," he expands on his policy views by explaining how the industry has been successful at resisting multinational demands while simultaneously empowering Iran to produce its own modern products:

> The greatest reward of this movement was "self-confidence" for Iranian auto manufacturers. We achieved the self-confidence to say "no" to a foreign company that imposed on us excessive demands … It is a completely national movement, aiming to promote national industry.[36]

[35] *SAPCO: A New Phenomenon for Independence*, the Automobile Industry, December 1997.
[36] "Iranian at Heart, Global in Mind: Interview with Manuchehr Gharavi," *Iran International Magazine*, March 2001, www.iraninternationalmagazine.com/issue% 5F12/text/iranian%20at%20heart.htm.

"Excessive demands" as discussed here are policies by multinationals to import as much of their product as possible into Iran to increase profits and to resist transferring the technology for local, indigenous development. Local manufacturing, however, implicitly requires transformation of a culture from dependency on imports to self-confidence in manufacturing locally.

To the nationalists, Iran's oil curse undermines industrial development. It creates a culture of economic dependence and a country that is open to manipulation by Western powers. Industrialization aimed at creating a self-sufficient industry is a way to lessen the effects of oil; by doing so, it can help in contributing to a "culture of production":

> Since our country is import-oriented and has made a habit of importation, some citizens are not yet accustomed to using Iranian products and supporting local industries. The main problem that our industry is facing is of a cultural nature; it originated several years ago when oil entered the country's economic scene. As a result, we gradually became victims of a cultural onslaught. When foreign-made goods were imported, the young generation lost their self-confidence because they thought they could not produce the same goods ... We should treat industry industrially and with an industrial culture. This is extremely important.[37]

The basic message here is that by resisting foreign demands to control the local market through imports and by making local products, the auto industry is on the vanguard of transforming Iranian culture to one in which local products are accepted. By doing so, the space for industry will expand.

The policies for overcoming the oil curse through automobile industrial development are associated with Islamic social justice and the values of the revolution. When Ali Akbar Nateq-Nuri, head of parliament during the Rafsanjani era (1989–1997), visited the Iran Khodro factory, he explained the automobile industry's role in Iran's economic development. According to Nateq-Nuri, the auto industry is important for jobs – but its main role is the struggle against hegemonic powers that intend to increase Iran's oil dependency:

> The great powers are very influential in manipulating the price of oil. If they want to decrease the price of oil, they can easily do so by increasing supply. So growth and development are the main goal for us in parliament. You cannot find a wise Muslim or sympathetic person who disagrees with us on this matter. But

[37] Ibid.

we say development has to occur while retaining the values of the Revolution, and it is possible. If we attempt to build a nation based on social justice without growth and development, it means that poverty will increase among our citizens. How can we resist the despotic universal powers if we cannot produce enough to provide the essential needs of the populace?[38]

He further explained that parliament's policy goals are to release the economy from oil dependency through investments, to increase automobile production capacity, and to improve quality. And, once the country produces sufficient goods for its internal needs, industrial exports will provide the currency to overcome its oil dependency.

The preceding passages emphasize foreign control and domination over the country and industry; however, internal opposition to the nationalist agenda in Iran has always been very strong. The alliance between merchants and the traditional right, with its policy emphasis on commerce over local manufacturing, has been the main opponent of industry. They claim Iran lacks the capacity to produce automobiles equal in price, quality, and technology to foreign imports. Efforts to develop an automobile industry should therefore be abandoned in favor of importing more advanced, foreign-made automobiles. The nationalists defend their policy by claiming that the merchants and the traditional right have abandoned an important mission of the Islamic state – the self-reliance that breaks dependency on multinational domination over the Iranian economy.

This conflict is typically discussed in terms of the "trade development" and "industrial development" perspectives. An editorial in Iran Khodro's trade magazine, for example, asserts that the trade development perspective supported by the traditional right embraces "traditional capitalism" – giving priority to commerce, economic monopolies, and the export of commodities. It further claims that the trade development perspective does not support industrial development or innovation as important principles in economic development. Moreover, by implementing "backward" management policies, it does not inspire risk-taking. On the other hand, the industrial development perspective is based on an "industrial way of thinking" that incorporates industrial investment, "authenticity" of free competition, and modern management principles. One way the industrial nationalists are able to create legitimacy for their perspective is to reframe support for the auto industry as a modern project that achieves the goal of Islamic social justice:

The authorities of the school of industrial development believe that ... production is the source of wealth, whose distribution is

---

[38] "The head of Parliament among the personnel at Iran Khodro: Commerce and trade sectors must be in the service of production," *Message* of Iran Khodro (in Farsi).

the most important and most evident way to achieve the sacred goal of social justice. In this viewpoint, to avoid the cycle of poverty, capital should be used for industrial production and not for trade relations. This school does not believe raw materials [commodities] have high economic value. In addition, industrialists believe in scientific management, whereas those who support "traditional capitalism" embrace the "old and forgotten methods of management, both in trade and industry." Those who support industrial development need to export their products and therefore need to implement "quality control, standards, innovation, and creativity."[39]

An important point is that social justice must be accomplished with modern sensibilities – innovation combined with an outward, export-oriented policy. Modern management techniques are seen as the basis for criticizing importers and their backward culture – the "bygone" era of how to manage enterprises. The preceding editorial also highlights a distinct role that industrial nationalists play in Iranian society. As engineers, they make things; by doing so, they contribute to the country's national strength. Importers, on the other hand, are concerned solely with making profits – and their actions will guarantee that Iran will remain a rentier state.

Comparing Rafsanjani's "Modern Right" Faction and the Industrial Nationalists

This chapter began by claiming that if either of the two factions extant in Iran in 1988 – the left faction or the traditional right faction – had managed automobile industrial development during this critical period, it would have failed. Rafsanjani attempted to provide an alternative to these two ideological positions when he reoriented the political field toward a more pragmatic, pro-business platform. Instead, when the industrial nationalists won their struggle against the Rafsanjani modern right faction that had pushed for liberalization, they were the group that provided the "alternative" vision. In constructing their policy agenda, the industrial nationalists co-opted key pro-business and technocratic components of the modern right faction but combined them with the leftist policy agenda of developing a self-sufficient, local industry. The industrialists implemented their policy agenda by creating a new alliance with government officials and members of parliament for the purpose of carving out a space for development based on infant industry

---

[39] "Processing view and industrial development," *Message* of Iran Khodro, February 1999, No. 28 (in Farsi and English).

Table 2.2 *Modern Right versus Industrial Nationalist Alliance*

Economic Action	Modern Right or "Pragmatists"	Automobile Industrial Nationalist Alliance
Social justice and Islamic economic orientation	Social justice by creating high-paying, highly skilled jobs through industrial development.	Same as modern right.
Trade and infant industry protection	Modern economy established through free markets, free trade, and economic liberalization.	Support ban on imports or infant industry protection. Infant industry protection should be "progressive" to force multinational corporations to transfer technology to local companies.
Ties to society	Ties mostly to conservatives (traditional right) and technocrats who support liberalization policies.	Diffuse ties with social groups: elite universities, left-wing technocrats in positions of power, members of parliament, and clerics who support industrialization.
Policy toward Western governments and their multinational corporations	Ties to Western countries, allowing foreign direct investment and liberal trade.	Ties to foreign governments and multinational corporations necessary to obtain technology and expertise to build an industry – as long as industrial policy eventually leads to independent "national" industry.
Corporate ownership	Support for privatization.	Support for privatization, but state should own large industrial corporations.

protection. To understand how their policies were successful in achieving industrial development goals, it is important to understand the differences between their ideological orientation and those of the Rafsanjani faction (see Table 2.2).

The Rafsanjani faction is often referred to as the pragmatist or "modern" right faction. In their view, Islamic social justice should be achieved through job creation via industrialization. This includes an open policy toward the West to attract foreign direct investment and joint ventures with multinational corporations. Although they support industrialization, they also embrace free markets, liberal trade policies, and privatization of smaller industrial corporations. Large industrial corporations and the development organizations, however, should be managed by technocrats – more specifically, engineers having the knowledge and skills to manage and coordinate industrial activities. The modern right obtained most of its support from the traditional right and from technocrats who supported liberalization policies – such as neoliberal economists.

The industrial nationalists, similar to the modern right, believe that Islamic social justice is best achieved through industrialization. But they differ strongly from the modern right on how it can be best achieved: the industrial nationalists favor infant industry protection or a ban on imports. Ties to Western countries should involve not unlimited imports but rather progressive infant industry protection laws to force multinational corporations to transfer the technology for development. Like the modern right, they maintain that privatization is the best way to inspire entrepreneurship; however, they do not support full privatization of industries. In their view, large industrial corporations should be state-owned, whereas entrepreneurs should own smaller parts supplier companies. The industrial nationalists' ties to society are diffused among government agencies, universities, members of parliament, and left-wing technocrats in positions of power who support localization of the industry.

3

An Era of Coherence: State-Led Development and the Deepening of Automobile Industry Ties to Society

Introduction

An era of coherence in the Iranian automobile industry began in 1992 when elite autonomous alliances helped defeat the political factions opposed to industrialization. The state apparatus and the industry were now aligned to create coherent industrial policy. Development organizations with sufficient institutional power to coordinate development activities supported the agenda of the industrial nationalists. Infant industry protection was a contributing factor that led to rapid production volumes and space for entrepreneurs to develop a local parts supply chain. In addition, the development of high local manufacturing content was achieved through ties to multinational corporations that transferred the technology and knowledge to local Iranian companies.

In analyzing the era of coherence, this chapter has three objectives. First, it will inform current scholarship of what "autonomy" looks like in a country where a pocket of efficiency is important for the success of a development project. Most development organizations in intermediate states, particularly those in the Middle East, are not meritocratic organizations (Moore, 2001, 2004). These development organizations, however, can be successful when state actors carve out a space within the larger state apparatus to protect the organization from predatory behavior (Geddes, 1990; Hout, 2007; Hertog, 2010). This concept is consistent with the claim that successful industrial development depends less on the Weberian characteristics of the bureaucracy and more on its "institutional power" to discipline agencies within the state apparatus to develop coherent industrial policies (Chibber, 2002). Other scholars have argued that development organizations can also achieve successful industrial development without meritocracy if they can provide a social space where state actors, motivated by a nationalist agenda, can effectively facilitate and organize the project (Breznitz, 2007). This chapter will make a similar claim in that it will show that autonomy is associated with the ability of pro-industry technocrats to be united by a nationalist agenda.

This refinement of the conceptualization of autonomy informs the scholarship on state capacity in two ways. First, the creation and maintenance of autonomy is a more dynamic process: autonomy leads to rapid industrial development that results in greater industry embeddedness in society. The embeddedness helps the industrialists to effectively coordinate industrial activity. Second, the preservation of the ideological orientation in place of bureaucratic coherence solves, at least partially, the "fragility" problem related to the pocket of efficiency being "swept away" by social forces or political factions opposed to development (Evans, 1998).

The second objective of this chapter is to lay the groundwork for the theoretical discussion behind the underpinning of Iran's automotive mini-developmental state. Important for this theoretical framing is the feedback between autonomy and embeddedness that maintained the state and industry alliance through ties to society. In doing so, I will argue that that over time the industrialists needed to have sufficient power to protect autonomy. This power emanated from ties to key actors in the state apparatus and to social groups in society that were willing to protect the industry's legitimacy. In addition, the analysis of social groups in this chapter will later build on the concept of embeddedness – ties to social groups or factions willing to support the industry in exchange for benefits to their constituents.

The third objective is to analyze the extent to which the industrialists built the organizational and technical capacity of the industry. I will show that the building of this capacity was important for the transfer of higher value-added technology from engineering consulting firms later in the decade. These firms in turn helped deepen state capacity by transferring their organizational and technical capacities to the industry.

Fortunately for the industrialists, the formation of state capacity occurred at a time period when the conditions required for rapid growth and localization of the industry began to develop. These conditions included the ability to work around US sanctions to establish relationships with multinationals to transfer technology for the industry, the educational capacity to localize production, and the development potential of an automobile market.

US sanctions against Iran were a key factor in shaping its ability to obtain the technology to develop the industry. By isolating Iran through economic sanctions and political pressure, the United States succeeded in preventing Iran from joining global institutions such as the World Bank, the International Monetary Fund, and the World Trade Organization (Brzezinski, Scowcroft, & Murphy, 1997; Fayazmanesh, 2010). However, the sanctions were unilateral, and many European and Asian countries refused to follow their guidelines (Amuzegar, 1997a). These policies allowed large European and Asian multinational corporations, as well as small engineering consulting firms located in these regions, to establish long-term technical relationships with Iranian automobile companies.

Local engineering talent is particularly important for establishing indigenous technical capacity. The Shah established a number of modern universities and technical schools, but after the revolution many of the faculty fled and funding to universities stagnated due to the drop in oil revenues starting in the mid-1980s. In the 1990s, President Rafsanjani and his successor, President Khatami, increased funding for education, resulting in a dramatic rise in the number of university graduates, research institutions, and engineering schools. In 1979, total student enrollment at universities in Iran was 154,000 but by 2005 had increased to 2,117,489 (Hamdhaidari, Agahi, & Papzan, 2008). Of these, 578,526 were in engineering programs. Many universities also increased funding to mechanical, electrical, and industrial engineering departments with established automobile engineering programs or with ties to automobile companies where students worked on engineering projects. Consequently, scientific output in Iran since 1990 has grown eleven times faster than the world average, and Iran is currently the fastest-growing country in the Middle East in terms of scientific output (MacKenzie, 2010).[1]

A population explosion in the 1980s and an increase in the middle class with strong purchasing power increased the market potential for automobiles. The population explosion from 40 million in 1980 to 72 million in 2011 in Iran was largely a result of the Islamic government's abandonment of family planning in the 1980s. In the decade after the revolution alone, the population increased by 50 percent. This increase in population was coupled with an increase in per capita GDP. The minimum per capita GDP required to support the purchase of an automobile is known to be approximately $6,000 (Ernst & Young, 2010). By the late 1990s, Iran reached the minimum threshold: the per capita income increased from $1,037 in 1993 to $7,006 in 2011.[2]

This chapter begins with a discussion about the role of nodal organizations responsible for development of the auto industry. The next section in the chapter covers the era of coherence and analyzes the ways in which the industrialists coordinated activities to build the industry. During this time period, production and entrepreneurship increased dramatically, and organizational techniques were transferred from abroad to help build

---

[1] Rates are based on publications in academic, peer-reviewed science and engineering journals. Data compiled by Science-Metrix Canada and published in a 2010 report titled "30 Years in Science: Secular Movements in Knowledge and Creation," http://rosmu.ru/activity/attach/opinions/111/30years-paper.pdf.

[2] http://databank.worldbank.org.

a modern industry in Iran. Consequently, the automobile industry became more deeply embedded in society by becoming the largest source of employment in Iran.

The Organization of the State and Its Role in Automobile Development

From the early 1990s to the present, the Ministry of Industry (previously the Ministry of Heavy Industry), IDRO, Iran Khodro, and Saipa were responsible for development of the automobile industry (see industry hierarchy in Figure 3.1). The highest-level organization, the Ministry of Industry, receives its financing from the parliament. Its role is to establish political support for industrial policies; the ministry works with the industrial committee in parliament to ensure proper funding for projects, favorable lending to entrepreneurs, and implementation of policies to

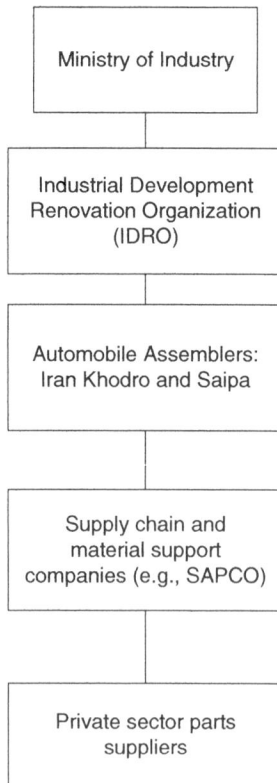

Figure 3.1 Industry Hierarchy

ensure the success of the industry. In addition, the Ministry of Industry can independently decide which projects it will fund without the need to seek approval from the parliament.

The Ministry of Industry works with IDRO, an industrial development holding company, to facilitate and organize automobile development. IDRO has remained largely a heavy-industries holding company with 117 subsidiaries, with the auto industry as the most profitable among the industries in its portfolio. It engages in policy development and implementation and facilitates interactions with multinational corporations for transferring technology and modern management techniques to its companies. IDRO assigns the CEOs to the industries it owns and often places new employees at companies to restructure them if new managerial direction or strategy is needed. Recently, IDRO has engaged in publishing quality evaluations of all vehicles sold in Iran. In a major change in the mid-1990s, the organization invested 25 percent of its profits into building research and design centers and expanding training in modern management techniques such as TQM, lean work, and 360-degree evaluations. Additionally, IDRO's role in the auto industry has been to arrange contracts with foreign companies for localization and to create long-term planning for the industry.

For their part, Iran Khodro and Saipa are responsible for the heavy lifting of industrial development: building the organizational capacity for development, establishing R&D facilities and building factories, and working directly with multinational corporations to transfer technology for the creation of local technical capacity. The private sector is largely responsible for producing the automobile parts assembled in the large Iran Khodro and Saipa factories.

Although the organizational chart of automobile industrial development follows a well-structured hierarchy, the role of the development organizations has varied over time. The previous chapter shows how industrialization of the auto industry began in the late 1980s when Behzad Nabavi, then Minister of Industry, became directly involved in automobile development by arranging for the purchase of the Talbot factories for Iran Khodro. At the same time, IDRO was directly involved in localization of the Renault 5 for Saipa. During these early years, the Ministry of Industry together with IDRO functioned as commander of industrialization via a top-down process in which the minister and IDRO managers called most of the shots related to coordination of the industry. During the Rafsanjani presidency, as discussed in the previous chapter, industrial managers at Iran Khodro and Saipa became more active in formulating policy by means of a middle-up process of voicing their ideas and vision to the Ministry of Industry and IDRO. Throughout the 1990s, this middle-up strategy remained largely in place. Although these managers were official state employees, they functioned as quasi-state employees because they were granted the autonomy to develop and implement policies. A high-ranking manager of Iran's parts supplier business association who was directly involved in creating automobile industrial policy explained how auto policies were created in the 1990s:

> The automobile policy went according to who was in charge of the industries at the time. For example, Manuchehr Gharavi [former managing director of Iran Khodro] made the policies by himself; he decided what cars to design and manufacture. There was no policy in place to tell him what to do.[3]

These policies, however, were coordinated among the various automobile organizations and associations under the supervision of the Ministry of Industry and IDRO. A high-level manager in the Ministry of Industry in the 1990s recalls how the ministry facilitated automobile industry development during this time period:

> We had a planning and policy-making meeting twice a month. We invited the heads of the auto parts association and the large auto companies, experts in the industry, and the policy-making departments. We also invited one auto parts company that was doing well in order to recognize its quality improvement. We had everyone involved, so we were able to execute what we wanted.[4]

Attendees included the managing director of IDRO, the Minister of Industry, and the important managing directors of Iranian banks. These meetings helped managers coordinate the type of car each company would produce, production number targets, and the number of vehicle models. According to one manager at a parts supplier company, the main objective of the meetings was to "bring all of the important managing directors of the most important organizations in Iran to share knowledge among the managers working in the industry so everyone knew what to do." From 1992 to 2005, the parliament and the industrial managers were largely in agreement with the proposals by the industrial managers, so there was little resistance.

From 1992 onward, the Minister of Industry and IDRO functioned jointly as facilitator and organizer for three main reasons. First (and most important), the relationship between the state and the industry became institutionalized within the state and industrial field. By helping resolve the currency crisis of 1991, the industrial nationalists were viewed as important contributors to the economic stability of the country and

---

[3] Interview, high-ranking manager at parts supplier company and business association, June 2011.

[4] Interview, high-ranking manager of large development organization, October 2010.

were granted the autonomy to continue with their work. Second, the reconfiguration of industrial production made coordination of the industry and transfer of technology among large multinational assemblers, parts suppliers, and engineering consulting firms a more complicated affair. Managers at Iran Khodro and Saipa – the vast majority of whom were engineers – were better positioned to coordinate these activities. Third, the industry was highly profitable during the 1990s, and its profits contributed to funding other industrial projects. The state, therefore, did not want to interfere with cash flow.

The bureaucratic structure of IDRO is much like that found in Western countries: it has a CEO, a vice chairman, and a board of directors. Its most important departments include finance and economic planning, marketing, human resources management, industrial, entrepreneurship, systems and information technology development, and high-tech industries. Each of these departments has sub-departments engaged in the development of industries such as automobiles, oil, heavy industries, and high technology. Its core personnel consist of engineers and others with experience in the field, all of whom must pass a written exam to enter the organization. In 2005, 17 percent of them held a doctorate, 39 percent a master's degree, 41 percent a bachelor's degree, and 3 percent an associate's degree or less. IDRO's size increased over the years, growing from a staff of thirty-five in 1988 to more than 300 by the mid-1990s; it numbered more than a thousand by the early 2000s. It is currently located in an eight-story building on Vali Asr Avenue – a high-status location in Tehran.

It is important to recognize that IDRO and the Ministry of Industry do not resemble ideal or even typical Weberian bureaucracies. The government chooses its top managers, who are responsible for hiring deputies (sub-division managers) to fill mid-level positions within the bureaucracy. These positions change with the election of a new president. The political influence on the industry raises an important issue with regard to competency. In choosing deputies, the top managers engage in what is termed "bus management" – meaning the top managers "bus" in close associates for key positions within the industrial bureaucracies. Thus the Ministry of Industry and IDRO are in reality only semi-autonomous, semi-meritocratic organizations, given that the government selects the top managers and these positions are generally occupied by engineers experienced in the industry. One way IDRO enhances competency is by hiring employees with several years of experience in the field instead of hiring new university graduates.

The Failure of Privatization and Control over the Industry

Although the previously described organizational structure led to effective development of the industry, the conservative push for the privatization of large state-owned enterprises in the 1990s threatened to undermine it. The failure of implementing privatization, however, meant that the alignment between the state apparatus and the industry to create coherent industrial policy remained largely intact. This section will briefly cover the privatization policy in the 1990s, why it failed, and how it influenced the automobile industry.

After the presidential elections of 1989, Rafsanjani became the first post-revolution leader to push for privatization of state-owned enterprises. Rafsanjani's technocratic approach emphasized that a modern and competitive market economy would create a more prosperous economy. His neoliberal vision for the economy incorporated foreign direct investment requiring the state to privatize its industries. The leftists, who still had significant power in parliament, fiercely attacked the plan as capitulation to Western capitalism that would replace self-sufficiency with dependent development. During this time period, high-level automobile industrialists were aligned with the leftists and opposed privatization. In 1992, Rafsanjani and his allies retaliated against the left in parliament by aligning themselves with the conservatives in the Guardian Council to purge leftists from the political field by disqualifying them from running in the parliamentary elections.

Shortly after the purge, the economic crisis of 1992 forced Rafsanjani to abandon his liberalization policies. Privatization, however, continued to inch along. In the mid-1990s, the government identified 391 companies out of 790 that could be privatized according to Article 44 of the constitution (Harris, 2013). However, instead of being put up for auction, many state-owned enterprises underwent "negotiated sales" to buyers with strong connections to Rafsanjani and the state apparatus. This policy, criticized by both left and right, was regarded as fraught with corruption; as a result, in 1994 the parliament prohibited the sale of companies through negotiated sales. Instead, transaction houses were created to sell the organizations to large foundations (*bonyads*) whose constituencies included war veterans, families of martyrs, and members of the *basij* (among others) with revolutionary sentiments. At the end of the Rafsanjani era, about half of the selected companies were sold off; the other half were told to become financially self-sufficient. Hard budget constraints, however, were not strictly enforced. Large government-owned organizations, such as those in the automobile sector, were not sold to Islamic organizations. Instead, they remained under the control of the Ministry of Industry.

When the reformist Khatami became president in 1997, a highly conservative Guardian Council vetoed reforms associated with radical change. Khatami thus avoided adopting privatization as a major aspect of his reform package. Instead, his government granted more licenses for establishing private industries. As a result, the private sector flourished and began competing with sectors once occupied by state monopolies. With respect to the automobile industry, most industrialists maintained the leftist stance of opposing privatization of large, state-owned automobile enterprises: even as the private automobile parts sector grew rapidly during the Khatami era, Iran Khodro was at its peak in developing a successful industry – and privatization would disrupt their vision of creating a self-sufficient, national industry.

The remainder of this chapter discusses the role of development organizations in Iran's automobile industrial development.

An Era of Coherence: State-Led Development and the Deepening of Industry Embeddedness, 1992–2000

After Talbot's Hillman Hunter (in Iran, the Peykan) was discontinued in 1988, industrial development focused on developing the Saipa and Iran Khodro parts supply chains. Although Iran Khodro would become the main company to push forward development of a modern parts supply chain, Saipa was a key organization in initiating development of the first independently established supply chain. During the 1990s, when the Ministry of Industry and IDRO were more engaged in commanding state-led development, they streamlined the ability of entrepreneurs to found auto companies:

> At that time, if someone wanted to start an auto company they had to go to lots of bureaucratic departments to obtain permission, and this took a lot of time. There were also lots of ambiguities as to how a company should make the parts, so we created a separate company in IDRO to establish parts manufacturers.[5]

This company, named Saze Ghostar, was founded in 1990 to manage the Saipa automobile supply chain during localization of the Renault 5. The company was placed under the management of Ahmad Rafat, an employee of IDRO. Rafat was highly aligned with the nationalists and inspired employees with the slogan "I want to work under the flag of Iran; what about you?" Employees who worked with him were required to shake his hand and commit themselves to the national cause of building a local auto industry. According to one such employee, the policy "was parallel and equal to the trajectory of the revolution – the 'masters' of the revolution in those days wanted to produce national products."[6]

---

[5] Interview with ex-director of large auto company, February 2011.
[6] Ibid. The "masters" of the revolution were the high-level clerics and intellectuals who struggled and fought alongside Ayatollah Khomeini to defeat the Shah. Khomeini produced a number of slogans denouncing economic dependency by promoting the localization of products.

Since a large automobile parts supply chain had never been created in Iran, one of the main concerns was how it should be organized. Like most auto companies producing automobile parts during the early 1990s, Iranian manufacturers were inspired by the Japanese production system as a more advanced model for industry organization. When Ahmad Rafat visited Japan in late 1990 to investigate how to manufacture an engine component for the Nissan Patrol,[7] he was impressed with their production system:

> We were assigned to build a large casting factory in Iran for the Nissan Patrol. We visited Japan and met with Nissan employees to discuss what we needed for the project. Building the factory was not at all successful, but I learned about the way of manufacturing in Japan called outsourcing. When I returned to Iran, I thought about building a similar production system in Iran. Instead of investing 150 million dollars in a new factory, I thought to myself, "Why don't we just use the existing capacity of the factories in Iran to produce what we need?"[8]

He located a list of all of the factories in Iran and what they produced and coaxed them into making automobile parts. One of the initial goals was to recruit the entrepreneurs based on four criteria: owning an existing factory, experience in manufacturing parts, a willingness to produce high-quality parts, and a commitment to the industry. If an entrepreneur didn't have the first three, experience in the field or an engineer who could vouch for him would do. For those who were chosen, 30 percent of the cost of production was loaned to the companies as up-front capital. If the company did not have the capability to produce a part, the company was promoted to obtain investment and buy the machines. Since there was a huge demand for automobiles, most of the financing in the auto industry at this time came directly from buyers, who were required to pre-purchase the cars up to one or two years in advance.

Reverse engineering was used to initially obtain the technology to produce the parts domestically. The discontinuation of the Renault 5 provided one of the strongest incentives for localization, since many of its parts could not be imported from France. Reverse engineering involves removing a part (or parts) from a vehicle and disassembling it, creating a drawing from its dimensions, and then producing it by using available machinery. Reverse engineering was carried out systematically, as a manager in one development organization explained. "We created four divisions within the organization to carry out reverse engineering: number

---

[7] The Nissan Patrol, a pickup truck first produced in Iran in the 1970s, continued to be produced through the early 1990s.

[8] Interview, executive at parts manufacturer and a former government employee, February 2011.

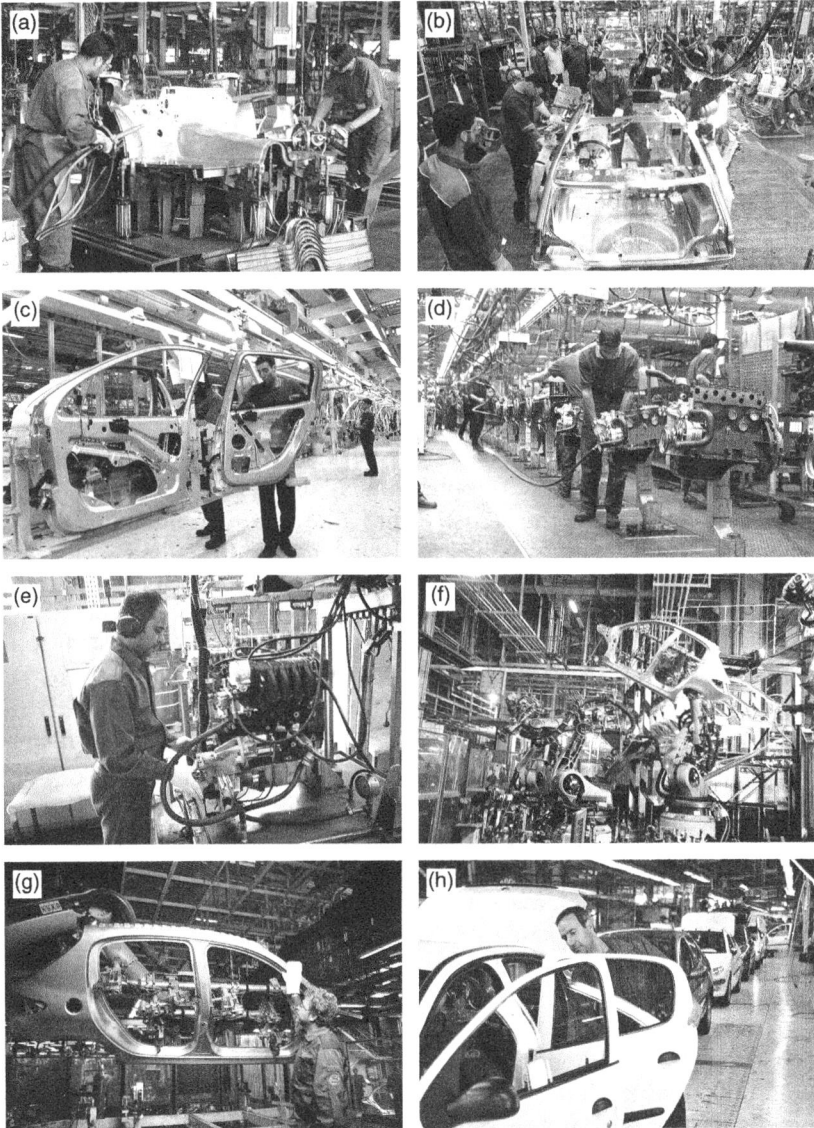

Figure 3.2 (a) Body Making Line for Peugeot 206. Welding Bottom Piece and Firewall (b) The Final Stage for Welding Body Skeleton (c) Installing Doors for Peugeot 206 (d) The Final Line of Engine Assembly, Preparing for Installation of Peugeot Cylinder Head (e) Engine Testing (f) Robotics Assembly: Vehicle Frame Is Lifted (g) Robotics Assembly: Prepared Vehicle Frame Placed on Hangers after Assembly Phase (h) Finished Vehicles Coming Off the Line

one was sheet-metal forming, number two was rubber and plastics, number three was die-casting and forging, and fourth was quality standards."[9] The benefits of this process were that it was cheap and Iranian companies no longer needed to pay license royalties to foreign companies.

Although Saze Ghostar was Iran's first independent automobile supply chain and would have a lasting and positive impact on building entrepreneurship within the industry, the Renault 5 suffered from quality problems when management attempted to rapidly localize all parts in-house, particularly the complex ones. It could therefore not reach sufficient production volumes to support a profitable parts supplier network.

Iran Khodro, however, became a highly profitable company. It was in the vanguard of modern corporate development, technology transfer, and high-volume production of higher-quality vehicles. The company's development took off after the 1992 passage of the Automobile Law and the compromise agreement to localize the Peykan. As noted in the previous chapter, the purchase of Talbot manufacturing equipment had been important in localizing the industry but had not provided manufacturing capabilities for all parts supplied to the vehicle. Because the Peykan had been discontinued in the United Kingdom, Iranian companies could not depend on foreign manufacturers to produce needed parts. To remedy this problem, the "Peykan without Talbot" project was initiated at Iran Khodro, using reverse engineering to build the majority of the parts. Reza Veyseh, a high-level manager at Iran Khodro, was assigned to manage this project. He sourced from Iranian companies the parts that could be produced in Iran, and unlike Saze Ghostar, instead of rapidly manufacturing all parts locally, it obtained more complicated parts from the United Kingdom, Italy, Japan, and Korea.[10] Once the project was complete, Iran Khodro was able to source 1,200 parts from local Iranian suppliers and the remaining 150 parts from foreign parts suppliers.

The new car, the Peykan 1600, had an initial production run of forty vehicles a day, and the target was to ramp this up to 300 a day. During this time, a major problem arose with supplying good-quality parts on time. To remedy the problem, Veyseh envisioned and implemented an independent supply chain modeled after Saze Ghostar and called SAPCO.[11] According to a high-level manager who worked with him, the government initially did not want to lose control of its parts supply network:

> He had a conflict with Iran Khodro and the government; they did not want a separate supply-chain company that was independent

---

[9] Ibid.

[10] The complicated parts included crankshafts, transmission gears, axles, bearings, cam shafts, connecting rods, and so on – typically requiring more sophisticated machining and casting.

[11] In this context, *independent* means "not controlled by the government."

of the internal organization of Iran Khodro. Fortunately, he was the vice president of Iran Khodro and a member of its board, so he had the power to create the company.[12]

Once he got the go-ahead, he engaged in aggressive recruiting and poached the best people in the industry to work for him by offering them top-level jobs with significant salary increases.

Veyseh implemented a modernization strategy oriented toward establishing new companies in the supply chain and in producing parts with higher-quality standards. He induced Iranian companies to become part of the supply chain network by placing newspaper ads and holding a conference to encourage the private sector to begin producing parts for the auto industry. Those willing to found companies to make parts were given financial support and offered guaranteed purchase of their parts for five years. This policy increased the Iran Khodro tier 1 parts supply network from fifty in 1990 to 600 by the early 2000s. Another method was to develop ownership and knowledge-transfer relationships with a select number of parts suppliers, as one manager of a large components company explains: "Iran Khodro took over 30 percent of the shares of our company, and the remaining 70 percent remained in private hands. This gave us a chance to have a partner in the world; Iran Khodro assigned representatives to the board of our company for weekly meetings to transfer ideas, philosophy, and strategy."[13]

The majority of entrepreneurs who founded companies represented a mix of post-revolutionary technocrats with engineering backgrounds and skilled technicians who owned small manufacturing enterprises, metal foundries, or stamping shops. By the mid-1990s, the vast majority (about 95 percent) of the entrepreneurs were technocrats and graduates of Iran's elite engineering universities. Many of them had very close relationships with management at Iran Khodro or Saipa. A high-level manager at a parts supplier company, with thirty years' experience in the field, explained the process of founding parts companies:

> It was all based on relationships. The companies [Iran Khodro or Saipa] would announce a financial support plan to establish a parts component company, and an employee would quit to start that company. The founders of the company would then approach a foreign company to license their parts; most would respond positively because Iran was a good market for them.

Those entrepreneurs with backgrounds in commerce (the *bazaaris*) were, on the whole, excluded from the industry.

---

[12] Interview with high-level manager at Iran Khodro, February 2011.
[13] Interview, manager at large parts supplier company, February 2011.

According to Iran Khodro's parts manufacturers, Veyseh's strategy was to increase the capacity to produce higher-quality parts. He became familiar with many of the necessary techniques by traveling to Japan to benchmark its parts supplier system:

> Many of the parts companies at that time [the early 1990s] were not capable of producing high-quality parts. Veyseh wanted to increase their knowledge and so began teaching these companies how to produce the parts and [how to apply] the technology in a systematic way. He forced us to implement ISO 9000 standards, and he encouraged the adoption of TQM methods.[14]

Transferring the knowledge needed to increase quality required changing the paradigm between customer and supplier. This was achieved primarily by establishing a parts supplier grading system based on an ABCD scale: those companies not supplying either A or B level–quality parts were removed from the group. According to a parts supplier manager, the success of SAPCO is related to its autonomy:

> Although the government owns SAPCO, it is not directly under the control of the government; it is under the control of Iran Khodro. The company has played a very positive role in the industry because it has good relations with factories, parts manufacturers, and the auto parts associations. Most important, they have good relationships with foreign companies that provide the knowledge that is transferred to the Iranian parts suppliers.[15]

As the industry developed further, more of the coordination activities relating to the parts supplier network, factory maintenance, and tooling were transferred to the large automobile companies. Along with SAPCO, two other Iran Khodro subsidiary companies were established to provide coordination of manufacturing activities. These include TAMKO, an engineering service company that builds factories and buildings for Iran Khodro in Iran and abroad, and ISEIKO, which provides factory maintenance and material support services.

Establishment of modern after-market sales and service companies was also an integral part of building a modern automobile industry. Even into the mid-1990s, a standardized after-sales service support system did not exist for either Iran Khodro or Saipa. People who had purchased vehicles relied on local garages often staffed with untrained personnel that provided low-quality service. To resolve this problem, Iran Khodro founded the after-service company ISACO and Saipa founded Saipa Yadak. With the assistance of the Ministry of Science, the companies established

---

[14] Interview, manager of parts supplier company, October 2010.
[15] Interview, manager at large parts supplier company, October 2010.

training programs for more than 2,500 mechanics and agents who service automobiles throughout Iran; furthermore, faculty departments at vocational and technical schools incorporated advanced scientific curricula. Today, most mechanics must have at least an associate's degree in order to obtain a license to repair automobiles. Training of mechanics also included "repairmen's cultural" issues such as how to be polite to customers and respect their desire for good service. The after-sales companies also worked with the Department of Environment to educate owners in the care of their automobiles to reduce pollution.

As the industry developed, its success increased employment opportunities for veterans of the Iran-Iraq war. Iran Khodro had reached its lowest point in automobile production in 1989, when 50 percent of its staff – including factory workers – were laid off; it directly employed only 6,000 factory workers and engineers. However, by 2004 the number of employees had risen to 50,000, making the industry an important source of employment for blue-collar workers. Many of the soldiers who had fought during the war belonged to a volunteer paramilitary unit, the Basij; most of these were from working-class religious backgrounds strongly committed to the revolution. Men closely aligned with this ideal type were often referred to as *hezbollais* (members of the party of God). In discussing Iran's "revolutionary Renaissance" that was occurring in the mid-1990s, President Rafsanjani explained that the role of industrial development must include participation and economic improvement for veterans of the Iran-Iraq war:

> One fundamental outcome of the revolution has been the liberation of great multitudes of people who had been imprisoned at the very bottom of the socioeconomic scale. These people are now the leadership and driving force of this process of revolutionary Renaissance. Eight years of Holy Defense [during the Iran-Iraq war] have shown the ardor and courage of a noble and peace-loving people who sacrificed themselves to suppress the aggressive enemy. The Iranian nation owes every inch of its land to the blood of its martyrs.[16]

Ties between the veterans and the industry included personal visits to the factories by military leaders, who met with its managers. Mohsen Rezai, commander of the Iran Revolutionary Guard Corps that controlled the Basij Army, visited the Iran Khodro factory in 1996 to push for further employment opportunities for *hezbollais*. He reminded management of the veterans' role in defending the country in the Iran-Iraq war and pressed them to employ these men in the factory. An article written

---

[16] Introduction in Abdolhossain Harati's *Iran's Industrial Panorama,* Tandis Press, 1998.

about Rezai's reception by Manuchehr Gharavi, managing director of Iran Khodro, explained the purpose of his visit:

> Mr. Gharavi was very glad that Mr. Rezai was visiting the company. Mr. Rezai said, "During the war, Iran Khodro was the most important company for soldiers. Right now we are in an industrial war, and soldiers and labor must work together to win on another front. We [the Basij] are good soldiers, and we want to contribute to Iran Khodro's success." One of Mr. Rezai's deputies, Mr. Savari, said, "The production revolution will influence all aspects of political and economic life in Iran. If the *hezbollais* work in industry and participate in the economic front, inflation will disappear and production will become ten times greater."[17]

During the Iran-Iraq war, the automobile industry became an "important company for soldiers" when it was converted to producing munitions. By employing war veterans, Rezai proclaimed that Iran Khodro would continue with its nationalist mission. During the visit, he suggested that Manuchehr Gharavi build a statue at the entrance of the factory to commemorate Iran's most famous martyr, thirteen-year-old Hossein Fahmideh, so that "Everyone knows who our leader is: Hossein Fahmideh."[18] Once the statue had been created and placed at the factory entrance, two aphorisms were inscribed on its base: "We are proud we are eating working-class food" and "Thank God our children are reaching their goals." The deepening of ties between the religious working class and the industry would prove beneficial after 2005, when the industry sought protection from social groups who opposed national automobile production.

The industrial nationalists achieved their goal of creating a "production revolution" partly by reorganizing the industry to make it more profitable. Akbar Torkan, director of IDRO in the mid-1990s and former Minister of Defense, was a key figure in this endeavor. To increase production and reach economies of scale, he merged the dozen or more automobile companies into two large conglomerates: the Iran Khodro and Saipa groups. Each group had large divisions for passenger vehicle manufacturing, engine production, research and development, and commercial vehicle manufacturing. Market specialization and ties with multinational corporations determined the role of each conglomerate: Saipa was assigned to produce cheaper compact cars; Iran Khodro got the nod for mid-priced and luxury sedans. Those companies with ties to East Asia were merged into Saipa and those with European ties into Iran Khodro.

---

[17] "In Honor of Basiji Labor," by Mohsen Rezai (commander of the Basij army during this time period); *Message* of Iran Khodro, 1996.
[18] *Message* of Iran Khodro, 1996, Vol. 3.

Table 3.1 *Types of Parts Produced Locally and Value-Added Content, 1988 and 2011*

Value-Added Content	Number of Companies, 1988	Number of Companies, 2011	Types of Parts Produced
High	2	72	Engines, pistons, ball bearings, crankshafts, axles, engine cylinders, etc.
Medium	5	61	Spark plugs, shock absorbers, alternators, auto glass, springs, etc.
Low	12	667	Batteries, radiators, mufflers, tires/tubes, etc.

The growth of the industry raises the question of whether development policies have created value-added jobs. The number of parts suppliers increased from thirty-four in 1988 to almost 800 in 2011.[19] Furthermore, 4,115 automobile manufacturing supplier companies existed by 2004. Among these companies, 128 were categorized as having 100 or more employees, eighty-six companies had fifty to ninety-nine employees, and 3,530 companies had fewer than ten employees.[20] Table 3.1 compares value-added categories in 1988 with those in 2011. Notably, the number of companies in the high value-added category has increased significantly. The industry currently has the capability to produce all engine components except the electronic control units (fuel injectors and computer controls).

[19] Data from the Iran Automobile Manufacturers' Association.
[20] Iran Statistical Yearbook, 2003–2004.

4

Using Global Corporate Networks as a Path to National Industrial Development

Introduction

The previous chapters discussed how industrial nationalist became dominant players in building a local industry. This chapter covers how they were able to overcome global isolation and US sanctions to achieve the goal of building local, indigenous technical capacity through ties to engineering consulting firms. In pointing out the implications of this case for existing theories of industrial development, the chapter will build on recent network-centered industrial theories that argue that the reconfiguration of industrial production has created new opportunities for industrial development (O'Riain, 2004; Block, 2008; Whittaker et al., 2010; Block & Keller, 2011; Breznitz & Murphree, 2011; Keller & Block, 2012). By building on current theories, it will analyze engineering consulting firms as important global network actors in transferring technology for automobile industrial development. The concept of global technology "networks" is important because local ties to engineering consulting firms enable countries in the global south to develop automobile industries with greater local indigenous technical capacity and to design and produce products independently from lead automobile assemblers.

A contribution to this line of scholarship that has gained attention in recent years is the developmental network state. According to this perspective, rapid innovation and industrial fragmentation prohibit countries from relying on large, national firms in transferring technology for industrial development. Developing countries now need to diversify their acquisition of technology through joint ventures or foreign direct investment or by establishing R&D laboratories that enable high-level knowledge and technology acquisition (O'Riain, 2004; Breznitz, 2007; Block, 2008; Keller & Block, 2012; Negoita & Block, 2012). The state should be conceptualized as a facilitator and organizer in connecting a global network of technology to local networks of learning among engineers, businesspeople, and government officials in order to generate innovation (Negoita & Block, 2012). The state should also motivate the private sector to make long-term commitments to developing local technical capacity. The idea here is that countries can develop industries when ties from the global to the local create a technical synergy whereby local entrepreneurs create new innovations that "bubble up from below." This strategy differs from the older developmental state model, where the state acts as the "commander" of industrial development to conquer already established markets.

Compressed development scholars make similar claims about new opportunities arising from the global restructuring of production. According to these scholars, the reconfiguration of industrial production and rapid innovation are "compressing" the time and space for development to such an extent that developing countries can target different stages of development simultaneously (Whittaker et al., 2010). Once basic assembly and parts manufacturing is established, developing countries can upgrade their technology when multinational automobile assemblers establish ties to local suppliers to license their technology in order to meet product quality, process efficiency, environmental, and labor standards. Developing countries can also move up the global value chain by acquiring higher value-added proprietary technology through outward foreign direct investment, such as by purchasing a multinational assembler in the industry. According to this perspective, the state should be "adaptive" in that it should proactively create an innovation system conducive to global engagement and industrial upgrading.

The common thread underlying these theories is that the global reconfiguration of industrial production has created new opportunities for developing countries to acquire and upgrade technology when they strategically link their industries to a global and more diversified network of technology. These new strategies have been used by newly developing automobile industries, most notable in China, India, and Malaysia, to create national brands and to deepen local, indigenous technical capacity. Here, the state played a significant role in facilitating ties between multinational automobile assemblers and global parts suppliers through inward foreign direct investment and joint ventures for the transfer of technology to local automobile companies (D'Costa, 1995; Sit & Liu, 2000; Harwit, 2001; Abbott, 2003; Thun, 2004, 2006). Infant industry protection and mandatory local content quotas were primary tools used to begin the transfer of technology to assemble and manufacture basic components.[1] To develop higher value-added technology, these countries

---

[1] A case in point: in the 1990s, when Chinese industry was growing rapidly, protection was accomplished through tariffs on imported vehicles. These tariffs amounted to as much as 220 percent, depending on the type of vehicle. A progressive import substitution law reduced the tariffs to 50 percent if the foreign firms agreed to reach 80 percent local

expanded their ties to global technology through the development of local research and development labs (Noble, 2013). They also used outward foreign direct investment, such as establishing overseas offices near the heart of Western automobile design industries and through the acquisition of foreign automobile companies. In the case of China, the acquisition of foreign auto companies allowed local automobile companies to purchase the intellectual property rights over patented technology to avoid being subject to the World Trade Organization's intellectual property rights laws.

More recently, some companies are developing their industries by relying heavily on sourcing inputs form the automobile global supply chain. A case in point is Chery of China, which used this strategy to quickly become a major exporter of automobiles. It did so by establishing a network of ties to source parts, sub-systems, process engineering, and design technology from engineering consulting firms and global parts suppliers (Whittaker et al., 2010).

Although network-centered theories provide a powerful frame for understanding current industrial development strategies, empirical studies have primarily focused on countries that are members of global institutions and hence are more integrated in the global economy. The development of technical capacity in isolated countries, such as Iran, is particularly challenging because they do not have the opportunity to obtain higher value-added technology through more conventional means. Isolation can be particularly troublesome during the final stage of industrial upgrading. An upper limit on technology is often reached when multinational assemblers protect their market share by resisting the transfer of higher value-added technology.[2] For this reason, multinational automobile assemblers relegate the developing country to the manufacture of parts at the low and middle end of the global value chain (Humphrey, 2003; Rugraff, 2010). The acquisition of higher value-added technology through inward and outward foreign direct investment and joint ventures are common ways developing countries reduce the impact of these limitations. For instance, in 2000 the combined foreign direct investment on average to China, Malaysia, and Turkey was twenty-seven times the foreign direct investment into Iran.[3]

---

content by the eighth year of implementation. In the 1990s, Malaysia implemented similar tariff policies, while India banned imported vehicles.

[2] High, value-added technology is defined as the engine and its components (such as fuel injection systems and electronic control units). Mechanical moving parts (including such parts as pistons, crankshafts, ball bearings, and engine cylinder heads) require sophisticated manufacturing to reach tight tolerances.

[3] In 2000, the amount of FDI in Iran amounted to US$1.35 per capita compared to $12 in Turkey, $31 in China, and $68 in Malaysia. (From *Strategy Document to Enhance the Contribution of an Efficient and Competitive Small and Medium-Sized Enterprise Sector in Iran*, United Nations Industrial Development Organization. February 2003, p. xxiv.)

Given the geopolitical constraints by the United States that succeeded in preventing Iran from joining global institutions such as the World Trade Organization (Brzezinski et al., 1997; Fayazmanesh, 2010) and Iran's own internal political constraints that limited foreign direct investment, Iran had to develop a more insular policy to acquire high technology. On the one hand, Iran's isolation from global institutions allowed the country to rely on reverse engineering without repercussions from global institutions. As discussed in the previous chapter, these development policies led to an exponential increase in local content, production, and entrepreneurship. On the other hand, by the late 1990s Iran's political and economic isolation prevented local companies from relying on more conventional ties to sources of global technology for developing higher value-added technology. During this time period, Iran's parliament heavily restricted foreign direct investment. Furthermore, the United States placed pressure on its allies to prevent the establishment of meaningful financial ties with the Iranians through inward or outward foreign direct investment. The Iranian state thus relied more heavily on engineering consultancies to obtain higher value-added technology to achieve industrial development goals.

Apart from restrictions on higher value-added technology, multinational automobile assemblers also limit the local manufacture and marketing of their vehicle brands in developing countries. These restrictions include royalty payments to license the multinational assembler's vehicles and its parts and on establishing independent relationships with the multinational assembler's global supply chain to design more advanced vehicles. Most agreements between developing countries and multinational automobile assemblers also restrict the sale of locally manufactured completely assembled vehicles to local markets only. While multinational assemblers are important in obtaining the vehicle assembly and licensing technology, these limitations restrict a country's ability to develop indigenous vehicle brands and to export them on foreign markets.

By analyzing the case of the Iranian automobile industry, this book builds on current network-centered theories by showing that new opportunities are currently available for nations to overcome these limitations. The key point of this chapter is to show that the global reconfiguration of industrial production has opened up a space for engineering consulting firms to play a critical role as key network actors to assist in building greater local, indigenous technical capacity for automobile industrial development. While engineering consultants are most useful for a country that is isolated, an analysis of their role in Iran will shed light on current possibilities available to all developing countries engaged in automobile industrial development. In doing so, I will show that engineering consulting firms achieve two goals. First, they transfer higher value-added technology and knowledge as well as their own intellectual property rights to local firms. In this way, developing countries can move up the automobile global value chain by acquiring rapidly innovating technology without the need to depend on lead automobile assemblers. An important point is that engineering consulting firms can be valuable intermediary actors in the diffusion of global technologies because their core business is in technology transfer, and unlike multinational automobile assemblers, they are not themselves manufacturers.

Second, consulting firms use their own network of ties to global parts suppliers to help developing countries create local industries with independent, national brands. This is accomplished when they link local parts suppliers to a network of global parts suppliers to license and manufacture parts locally. While developing countries will likely still remain dependent on licensing higher value-added, highly patented parts from the global parts suppliers, these relationships allow them to develop national brands by eliminating lead automobile assembler royalty payments and parts manufacturing restrictions. In this way, they allow developing countries to gain greater control over local vehicle design and manufacturing processes. Furthermore, when they develop national brands, they eliminate restrictions to export vehicles in foreign markets.

Consistent with recent findings by developmental network state scholars, in Iran the state functioned as a facilitator and organizer to support industrial entrepreneurs to utilize engineering consulting firms to build indigenous technical capacity. More specifically, the technology transferred by consulting firms was facilitated and managed by two state organs. First, the Ministry of Industry and the Industrial Development and Renovation Organization arranged financing for the project, including favorable loans to entrepreneurs to establish parts companies. The second key state organ was Iran Khodro: it was granted the autonomy to establish and manage relationships with consulting firms and to work directly with them to transfer the technology. This included setting targets, drafting technology transfer agreements, and monitoring the quality of the technology transferred. The facilitation by these state agencies helped develop a more robust innovation system in the automobile sector that compressed developed scholars claim is key to a successful development project.

Scholars have discussed the theoretical importance of engineering consulting firms and their role in technology transfer and innovation systems (Lall, 1992; Kim, 2004) as well as their role as intermediaries (Bessant & Rush, 1995; Hargadon & Sutton, 1997). This research builds on that work in two ways. First, it provides empirical evidence to show how engineering consultancies can transform an industry in a developing country by deepening its technical capacity. Second, it shows how consultancies are positioned in a global network of technology transfer and describes the strategies that can be used to obtain the technology and knowledge from that network.

This chapter will first explain the role of engineering consulting firms in automobile industrial development. Next, using qualitative process-tracing analysis, it will show how engineering consulting firms were employed by the state in Iran to transfer technology to the industry. Quantitative social network analysis will be used to describe graphically the network position of engineering consulting and their global technology transfer ties to the Iranian auto industry. The analysis will show the specific technology transfer relationships between the engineering consulting firms, the lead assemblers, and the global parts suppliers to local industry. It will then discuss how the use of engineering consulting firms in Iran informs network centered development and current industrial development strategy.

The Role of Engineering Consultants in Building Local Technical Capacity and Their Position in the Global Network of Technology Transfer

Engineering consulting firms provide services to their clients that can vary from the design of an entire vehicle or engine to the design of specific components. The service can be focused on obtaining a design, training the engineers, and transferring the technology and knowledge to outsourcing the capacity to the consulting firm. For example, if a company would like to obtain the capacity to design an engine independent of the lead assembler or to upgrade its current line of engines with the latest advanced technology, it can hire an engineering consulting firm to achieve this task. The firm can then work with the client company to incorporate the knowledge and technology to help build indigenous technical competence and capacity within the client's organization.

Consulting firms occupy a specialty niche in either engine or body design and styling. To attract clients, they position themselves in the market by offering an array of engineering services and expertise. Table 4.1 lists the activities performed by engineering consultants. The first column lists the needs of the developing country (the customer) in the development of indigenous technical capacity; the second column lists which services are performed by the consulting firm.

As the primary customer need, companies in developing countries often must design and produce products with higher value-added technology. For example, some companies have hired FEV of Germany and Ricardo of the United Kingdom to transfer hybrid electric technology or to upgrade their engines with higher-performing, lower-emission gas direct injection.[4]

---

[4] See www.fev.com or www.ricardo.com.

Table 4.1 *Engineering Consulting Firm Services*

Customer Needs	Engineering Consultancy Service
High technology products	Transfer technology to design products with value-added technology or provide a design that meets customer needs.
Ownership over intellectual property rights	Transfer proprietary designs and technology that can be domestically designed and exported to global markets.
Independent technology licensing network	Establish ties to multinational parts suppliers outside multinational assembler network of suppliers to license technology.
Access to knowledge database	Provide access to a knowledge database that can be used for benchmarking customer designs.
Increase in engineering team technical capacity	Provide access to consulting engineers with expertise in specific technology, increasing project team engineering capacity and speeding up design process.
Access to testing equipment	Provide access to consultancy's high-tech equipment to test and improve designs.

Another customer need is ownership of intellectual property rights for the desired technology in order to avoid multinational assembler royalty payments and to be able to export to foreign markets without restrictions. Engineering consultants create proprietary technology designed in-house that can be sold to customers. Many firms also bundle new designs with their own proprietary software, allowing clients to use computer simulation to design products independently.

Engineering consulting firms also provide engineering training. Their consultants work alongside engineers in developing countries to transfer tacit knowledge in designing entire vehicles or just engines or specific components. The objective of this training is to enable countries to design their own products independently of the consulting firm.

A case in point to illustrate how a developing country can obtain the technology and training from an engineering consulting firm is the indigenization of engine design. This is accomplished in three primary stages. The first is the design layout of the engine, which includes its major components such as the intake ports, fuel injection system, pistons, engine blocks, and cylinder head. When the firms work with their customers to design the engine, they transfer the knowledge and technology so that developing countries can design the engine independently from the consulting firm. In addition, if the consulting firm has developed its own patented combustion technology, it can integrate it into the engine design and work with global parts suppliers to manufacture the parts for the new technology. Furthermore, customers can use the advice of engineering consulting firms to increase the technical capacity of a project team and to speed up the design process. Once the engine is designed, it becomes a patentable product that is owned by the client. The client can therefore change or redesign the engine at will or rehire an engineering consultancy to do so.

The second stage is the manufacturing process. Important engine parts include fuel injection systems, pistons, and the electronic control units. If the developing country cannot produce the parts locally, the engineering consulting firms can function as key intermediary actors in establishing independent ties to a network of global parts suppliers. Global parts suppliers are willing to transfer technology to local parts suppliers except for patented technology, which is highly protected. The transfer of higher value-added parts is therefore mostly limited to licensing. Engineering consultants will often recommend global suppliers they have worked with in the past and can trust as competent technology partners in working with their customers. These relationships help reduce the risk of incompetence or opportunism that could contribute to project failure (Schrank & Whitford, 2011).

The third stage is testing. For this stage, the consulting firms offer access to a knowledge database developed over years of experience from the synergy between lead assemblers and the consulting firm. This knowledge base can be used to benchmark the customer designs. Furthermore, should the customer lack the facilities or know-how to further develop or test the product once a prototype is created, the consulting company's equipment can be rented or used collaboratively.

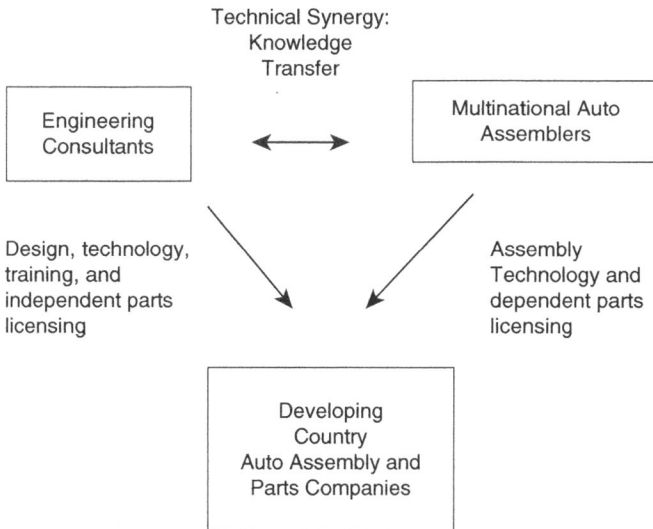

Figure 4.1 Engineering Consultancies and the Global Network of Technology Transfer

Figure 4.1 shows how the engineering consulting firms are embedded within a global network of technology transfer ties. Multinational automobile firms transfer assembly technology and establish licensing ties between their network of parts suppliers to parts suppliers in developing countries. However, these licensing ties are *dependent* since their production is limited to the vehicle manufactured in the developing country. When a developing country hires a consulting firm they tap into the highly advanced *technical development synergy* produced by the existing relationships between lead automobile firms and the engineering consultancies. Ties from engineering consultants to developing countries include knowledge, training, technology transfer, and independent ties to global parts suppliers.

Building Local, Indigenous Technical Capacity: The Role of Engineering Consultants in Iran

Soon after the passing of the infant industry protection laws, nationalists dominated the policy agenda, and by the mid-1990s they had pushed for two objectives: to develop a national Iranian brand and to reduce technical dependency on the West. This two-pronged policy was embodied in the development of a sedan called the Samand. For this project, Iran Khodro received permission from Iran's Ministry of Industry to hire British consulting firm CGI to provide support in managing the project. CGI claims the main reason for hiring the firm was to reduce Iran's dependence on Peugeot. "The basic problem that they wanted to address was that they were subservient to PSA (Peugeot/Citroën) of France for automotive technology, and they had little control over their own destiny and economic development."[5] The British consulting firm was particularly useful because its primary areas of expertise were intellectual property transfer and building an "indigenous in-market supply base" in developing countries.[6]

Once the project was given the go-ahead, key actors in the state apparatus, namely IDRO president Mr. Khamooshi, Minister of Industry Reza Nematzadeh, and the director of the Central Bank, were instrumental in facilitating the project. However, the project between Iran Khodro and CGI was entirely funded by Iran Khodro cash flow. Manouchehr Gharavi, President of Iran Khodro, and his team managed the project. Responsibilities included meeting annual goals of the quality of the work provided by CGI, setting delivery targets, arranging licensing

---

[5] CGI website at http://stevemurphy.co.uk/portfolio/iran/.
[6] www.cgi-consulting.com/. This firm's markets reside in the Middle East, India, China, Iran, and Central Asia.

agreements between global parts suppliers and Iran Khodro's supplier network, and the establishment of a research and design lab to absorb the technology.

The Samand project had three objectives: to produce a car that would increase local content, to produce a mid-sized vehicle to replace the dated Peykan, and to produce a car that could be sold on global markets.[7] To achieve the local content objective, the consulting firm recommended that Iran Khodro take advantage of the manufacturing structure that already existed (i.e., machines, tooling, and organizational structure) by redesigning the Peugeot 405, a vehicle that was currently in production in Iran. According to one of the top managers who worked on the project, "The trick is to get a product that is in production – for example, the Peugeot 405 – and what you do is design a 'top hat,' which requires using the same platform but redesigning and upgrading the interior; in that way, the design process is very rapid. It's a great way of entering the market while increasing your technical ability."[8]

Before the design process could begin, financing of the project and localization of the manufacturing had to be arranged. To facilitate financing, the Central Bank of Iran worked directly with the consultants to create stable financing for the project. When Iran Khodro wanted to purchase equipment and material for a project, it had to wait for weeks to convert the currency. The Central Bank of Iran, with help from the consultants, set up a financial system whereby France's Elf and Total purchased $2 billion in oil futures and used that money to pay Peugeot directly for proprietary parts for the vehicle. This meant that Iran Khodro did not need hard currency to fund the Samand project. The consultants also helped the bank place the Samand project on the Tehran Stock Exchange, which brought in $480 million in capital for the project.[9]

To localize manufacturing, the consultants worked with Iran Khodro management to employ a two-step strategy. The first step was to help Iran Khodro purchase the production facilities for the Peugeot 405 from a Taiwanese company. This allowed Iran Khodro to reach 50 percent local content in eighteen months. The consultants also brought in parts supplier tooling and established joint ventures with some foreign companies to speed up the process. The next step was to reduce Iran's technical dependence on Peugeot's technical licenses by getting it to agree that any component of the vehicle that Iran invested in could be used by Iran in future Iran Khodro products with no royalty payments.

---

[7] The contract signed with Peugeot allowed the Iranians to manufacture within Iran, but the vehicles produced there could not be exported to foreign countries.

[8] Interview with Mike Ross, October 2010. More specifically, the car was built on the Peugeot "platform" – everything in the vehicle that is not visible to the user, such as the engine, transmission, axles, and so on.

[9] http://stevemurphy.co.uk/portfolio/iran/.

Once the financial and manufacturing issues were resolved, the consultants began training the Iranian engineers. The consulting firm coordinated various design activities among several global parts producers in Europe and East Asia. In this role, the consultants functioned as brokers to ensure that the engineers received the necessary skills from a portfolio of companies they could partner with on the project. This was accomplished by nominating an Iranian to be project team manager for each component of the vehicle; for example, there was one team for the engine, one team for body design, and so on. Teams were sent to Japan, Italy, and the United Kingdom to be trained in their respective engineering trades. Project managers interacted with the consultants to ensure that the project was properly integrated and that each team received the engineering knowledge before returning to Iran. A high-level state manager working for the Ministry of Industry in Iran recalls how the technology transfer was facilitated to ensure Iran obtained the capacity to design the vehicle:

> We sent 25 Iranian engineers to England to be trained and to make a basic design, and then we asked the company to train our engineers in Iran on how to design the body and suspension. Six engineers were sent from Britain, and they stayed in Iran for one month ... we made an office in Iran and employed 200 young Iranian engineers, and we got them all together to design this car. They made clay models and thousands of sketches; we spent a lot of time designing the body so it was appealing to the customers. Iran Khodro now has a good design center. During this project we learned all the different aspects of car design, manufacturing, machining, and training.[10]

The design center was expanded into a full research and design center employing 1,200 engineers and was used as a point of technology transfer between Iranian parts suppliers and Iran Khodro. As explained by a manager at a private parts manufacturer that supplied parts to the Samand, "Our company designed seven parts for the Samand; there was a direct link between the supplier OEMs, the R&D center, and our company's R&D center; there were several thousand hours of discussions until the car was born."[11]

An important component in developing a legitimate industry is building the capabilities to design vehicles of good quality. The key is obtaining technology. The consulting firms helped bridge this legitimacy gap by building the research and design center and implementing computer engineering tools to test the vehicle for design defects. An Iranian engineer who worked on the project recalls, "We did computer aided design

---

[10] Interview with manager at government development organization, 2010.
[11] Interview with manager at parts supplier, February 2011.

modeling and simulation on the vehicle, and we were horrified to see that it [the Samand] would fall apart on impact ... we were able to use the tools to redesign it."[12] The engineering consulting firms also implemented the use of computer tools in Iran to improve the quality of the reverse engineering processes. For instance, computer tools for advanced mechanical stress and computational fluid dynamic analysis improved designs that were being reverse engineered by the Iranian parts companies. When a final prototype was developed, managers at Iran Khodro required final testing of the performance, quality, and safety of the vehicle at facilities in Britain.

Indigenizing engine design was the second step to develop national brands based on greater local technical capacity. To facilitate this project, IDRO with financing from the Ministry of Industry created a subsidiary of Iran Khodro called the Iran Power Train Company (IPCO) to work directly with FEV of Germany. FEV helped IPCO develop three types of engines: gas, dual fuel, and turbocharged engines primarily used for the Samand.[13] A meeting was held between FEV, Iran Khodro, and SAPCO – Iran Khodro's automobile parts supply Chain Company – on April 22, 2004, in Tehran to coordinate the transfer of the technology. The role of FEV, as explained in the meeting notes, was described as follows: "FEV realized that technology transfer is a key element of the program. Therefore, FEV agreed to transfer the know-how on the job without limitation, including all complete models."[14] The transfer included engineering modeling, lubrication and bearing analysis, engine intake systems, and management of designing the project. This included all design documents and 3D-CAD models, timing of product release, and cost of parts and materials. FEV, Iran Khodro, and SAPCO jointly worked on testing the engines, the bill of materials listing what was needed to produce the parts, and the request for quotation (RFQ) to invite suppliers into the bidding process. Prominent among the global parts suppliers that licensed technology to Iranian parts suppliers were Bosch, INA, and Mahle, all German companies.

Designing the engine autonomously from a multinational assembler was a key factor in transferring the knowledge and skills. A manager who worked on the project explained the process:

> They established mutual design teams and they helped Iran Khodro to find suppliers for each part. The contract involved training

---

[12] Interview with Iranian project engineer, February 2011.

[13] $80 million was required for the first phase of investment for the national engine, and $400 million for the design of the Samand.

[14] EF7 program review meeting at IPCO on LOI Milestone, April 22, 2004; http://www.isaco.ir.

Iranian engineers; they rented a house in Germany for eight months
to train the engineers, and there was a lot of high-level knowledge
and technology transfer.[15]

Working on mutual teams was very important, since most of the transfer
consisted of tacit knowledge and it was important for the Iranian engineers to learn specific engineering techniques. An engineer who worked on
the computer simulation for the project recalls, "The thing that was really
useful was, they taught us what to emphasize in understanding what parts
of the simulation were important – no one else could teach you those
things, and you can't learn them in the journal articles."[16]

To ensure the engineers were well trained to engage in autonomous
engine design, the training was implemented in two phases. The first step
consisted of thorough immersion in engine design, training on how to test
and calibrate engines, and using computer simulation software for new
engine designs. The second step, required by the management of Iran
Khodro, was a test of the quality of the services provided by the consulting
firm. It involved a test of the knowledge and skills of Iranian engineers to
evaluate whether they could design a new engine independently of FEV.
This step was accomplished by sending the design of an entirely different
engine to FEV for evaluation; the German company provided feedback
and recommendations for improvement. The engine benchmarking information obtained from previous FEV projects was particularly useful in
evaluating how the performance characteristics of the Iranian engine
compared to engines produced by large, well-known multinational automobile assemblers. The relationship with FEV helped Iran to establish
a complete infrastructure for engine design that included design conceptualization, engineering analysis, emissions reduction, and fuel economy opti-
mization. The Iran Powertrain Company and its affiliates currently employ
3,470 engineers, technicians, and production workers. Ten percent of the
personnel are dedicated to research and development, and among this
group 80 percent have graduate degrees in engineering.[17]

The contract with FEV, however, was not without complications.
Friction in the relationship between Iran Khodro and a multinational
assembler developed when the Iranians attempted to initially obtain modern engine technology. An Iranian who worked on the project explained:

> We were selling the [multinational assembler's] engines in Iran
> and they were old; they were from the 1980s and had low
> fuel economy and high emissions. We approached [the multina-
> tional assembler] to upgrade the engines, but they kept on

[15] Interview with manager at parts supplier company, July 2011.
[16] Interview with project engineer, January 2012.
[17] Iran Khodro Powertrain Company, company profile.

delaying ... when they finally agreed, they said we could use it on some vehicles but not others. They wanted to be a single source of technology so they could continue to sell their old engines in Iran, and they were selling a lot of them. We didn't want that.[18]

Although the multinational assembler had a highly advanced engineering research and development center, managers were concerned that, even if they agreed to transfer the technology, complications would likely arise: unlike FEV, they were not in the business of selling knowledge.

The old engines the multinational assembler sold in Iran had Euro 1, or worse, emission standards, whereas the new design provided by FEV met Euro 4 standards. This leap in technology resulted in significant technology upgrades to the Iranian parts suppliers. Meeting the new standards required more sophisticated tooling and materials in order to reach tighter tolerances in parts manufacturing, to produce more sophisticated electronic systems, to carry out software upgrades, and to provide better quality control technology. Since FEV is not a specialist in all aspects of component design, it functioned as an intermediary between the global parts suppliers and the Iranian parts supply chain in transferring the necessary technology for local manufacturing.

A case in point is the relationship between Bosch and the engine research center in Iran in transferring the know-how and technology to calibrate engines to Iran's diverse weather environment. This calibration function is vital in preventing engine failure. The technology transfer resulted in high-level training for Iranian engineers and a reduced overall investment in the development of the engine.

The founding of research and design companies by most of the large assemblers in Iran began soon after the Samand project was initiated. At first, these companies provided engineering services to the parent company. The companies, however, were set up as entrepreneurial ventures and – although most were owned or partly owned by the government – were required to be profitable. They did so by expanding their business. Consulting firms provided capabilities to these small firms, as explained by an Iranian project engineer:

> Most of the technology was obtained from European consulting firms – British, German, and Italian companies. Experts [at our company] learned a lot from these companies when they worked on various projects. Once we obtained the knowledge, we decided to expand our business with other companies in Iran.[19]

Establishing ties with engineering consulting firms resulted in Iran's producing three national vehicle brands and two national engines with

---

[18] Interview with project engineer, January 2012.
[19] Interview with company manager, October 2010.

advanced technology. These include the Samand and the Runna, produced by Iran Khodro, and the Tiba, produced by Saipa. The Runna and the Tiba are equipped with ABS brakes, airbags, and electronic steering. The two national engines include a gasoline and a diesel engine produced by Iran Khodro and Iran Khodro Diesel, respectively. The EF7 gasoline engine is a sixteen-valve, four-cylinder dual-fuel, turbocharged engine that currently meets Euro 4 emission standards. The development of national brands, particularly the Samand, has allowed Iran to engage in export promotion of its vehicles. The Samand is now manufactured as knockdown kits in countries such as Syria, Venezuela, Belarus, Azerbaijan, Egypt, and Senegal. In all, overseas factories produce approximately 50,000 vehicles a year. Iran currently exports approximately $500 million in vehicles to Middle Eastern, Central Asian, and African countries.[20]

Regression Analysis Predicting High Value-Added Technology Transfer

An important benefit to hiring the engineering consulting firms was to build an independent, local parts supply chain. In all, from 1991 to 2008, Iranian parts companies engaged in 156 technology agreements with global parts suppliers to transfer and license such technology as ceramic catalysts, pistons, fuel systems, windshield wipers, and so forth.

An ordered logistic regression analysis was conducted on the technology transfer ties between multinational parts suppliers and Iranian parts companies. The purpose of the analysis was to show which ties are important to transfer the technology to a developing country in an era of fragmented global production. According to the network centered development perspective, it is incumbent that the state facilitates ties between industrialists in developing countries and multinational parts suppliers to transfer higher value-added technology. For instance, when a company is developing the technical capacity to design an engine that can be exported on global markets, it requires the ability to design an engine that meets strict global emission standards. Ties to multinational parts suppliers are key in obtaining the technology to meet these standards.

This analysis helps illustrate which type of technology transfer agreement produced higher value-added technology, from which region of the world higher value-added technology came, and what the returns on the transfer of value-added technology were over time. The type of technology

---

[20] These are 2011 export numbers prior to the current round of sanctions. Data from World Trade Organization Statistical Data Base at http://stat.wto.org/.

transferred was coded *high, medium,* or *low,* according to its value-added content.[21] These codes were constructed into an ordered logit dependent variable. Because the objective was to determine "high" value-added content transferred, the ordered logit was 1 for low, 2 for medium, and 3 for high value-added transfer. The independent variables in the analysis are a categorical variable indicating country, a categorical variable indicating type of technology transfer agreement, and the time period of the transfer. The analysis was run with country of transfer as a categorical variable and included Germany, France, Spain, South Korea, Japan, and Taiwan.

The type of technology transfer agreement included *license, technical cooperation, technical assistance,* or *joint venture.* Since technical cooperation and technical assistance are very similar (multinational suppliers provide direct assistance during transfer, such as sending engineers to the site), they were aggregated into a single variable. The year of the technology transfer was aggregated into three periods, early (1991–2000), middle (2001–2004), and late (2005–2008). The early period spans a larger time frame because few technology transfer agreements were made in the early to mid-1990s.

The results of the analysis are illustrated in Table 4.2 and show strong associations of the independent variables predicting high value-added technology transfer.[22] The first column is the variable coefficient, the second is the standard error, and the third is the odds ratio. Variables that were not statistically significant were dropped from the model. Turning to the year, the prediction shows that in the late period there is a 2.29 odds of high technology transfer compared to the middle and low period combined. These results show that Iranian parts suppliers transferred low and middle value-added technology earlier in the transfer time span; when they built greater competency in absorbing the technology in later years, they established ties with multinationals to transfer high value-added technology.

In the country of technology transfer, France was the reference value. The results show that high value-added technology is 3.71 times more likely from Germany compared to France and 0.7 times less likely from South Korea compared to France. I ran a separate regression analysis aggregating the countries into Europe and East Asia, and the results

---

[21] The parts coded as "high" value-added are electrical or mechanical moving parts that require the most sophisticated manufacturing. These include such parts as pistons, crankshafts, ball bearings, and engine cylinder heads. Those coded as "medium" value-added require less sophisticated manufacturing such as the use of presses and moderate amounts of machining; they include parts with mixed materials such as auto glass, door panels, spark plugs, and alternators. Those parts coded as "low" include parts with the least sophisticated technology, such as fuse boxes, mirrors, cables, seat belts, springs, and electric motors.

[22] Calculation conducted in R using the generalized linear model.

Table 4.2 *Ordered Logistic Regression Predicting High Value-Added Technology Transfer from Multinational Parts Suppliers to Iranian Parts Suppliers*

Independent Variable	B	SEβ	exp(β)
Year Period Late	0.83*	0.48	2.29
Germany	1.31**	0.43	3.71
South Korea	−1.17*	0.57	0.30
Transfer Agreement: License	0.75*	0.42	2.13
Transfer Agreement: Cooperation and Assistance	2.24**	0.77	9.47

* $p < .05$.
** $p < .01$.

revealed that high technology transfer is 3.7 times more likely from Europe than East Asia. These results show that the Iranian parts companies benefited more from their ties to European, most importantly from Germany, rather than East Asian, parts suppliers. One important reason why the results are so skewed in favor of the European region is that the majority of high-tech engineering consulting firms engaging in technology transfer are located in Europe. For instance, two high-powered engine consulting firms (FEV and AVL) are located in Germany and Austria, respectively. Here, they establish close ties between parts suppliers in their own region with whom they have close contacts (i.e., Bosch, Freudenberg) and Iranian parts suppliers. None of the engineering consultancies are located in East Asia.

The analysis of the type of technology transfer agreement is also insightful. The reference variable in this analysis is joint venture agreements. The odds of transferring high value-added technology, compared to medium and low combined, by means of cooperation and assistance agreements is 9.47 times more likely compared to joint ventures. The odds of transferring high technology through licensing is 2.13 times higher compared to joint ventures. The reason for this large variance is that companies engaged in joint ventures typically produce parts with lower value-added technology to break into the lower end of the global parts supply market. In addition, these technology agreements are called "cooperation" and "assistance" because they involve the transfer of higher value-added technology that requires personnel from the multinational corporation to live in the developing country in order to manage the transfer of the technology.

Time Series Graph of Technology Transfer

Figure 4.2 shows a time series graph of the number of cumulative technology transfer ties established from 1997 through 2008 and the value-added technical content of those ties. The rate of ties increased exponentially from 2000 through 2006 and occurred at the same time as the development of national vehicles and engines. Since American companies were excluded from establishing ties with Iranian companies, the vast majority of the ties were with global parts suppliers located in Europe and East Asia. In addition, the proportion of high (compared to medium and low) technology transferred increased from 8 percent in 2000 to 22 percent in 2008. This increase was due largely to FEV acting as a broker to establish independent ties to mostly German and French parts companies in order to license technology for the national engine project. Of the ties coded as "high" in their value-added content, 44 percent are with German companies, 33 percent with French, and 8 percent with English companies; the remaining 14 percent are with other countries including Italy, Spain, South Korea, and Brazil. In all, the proportion of companies producing

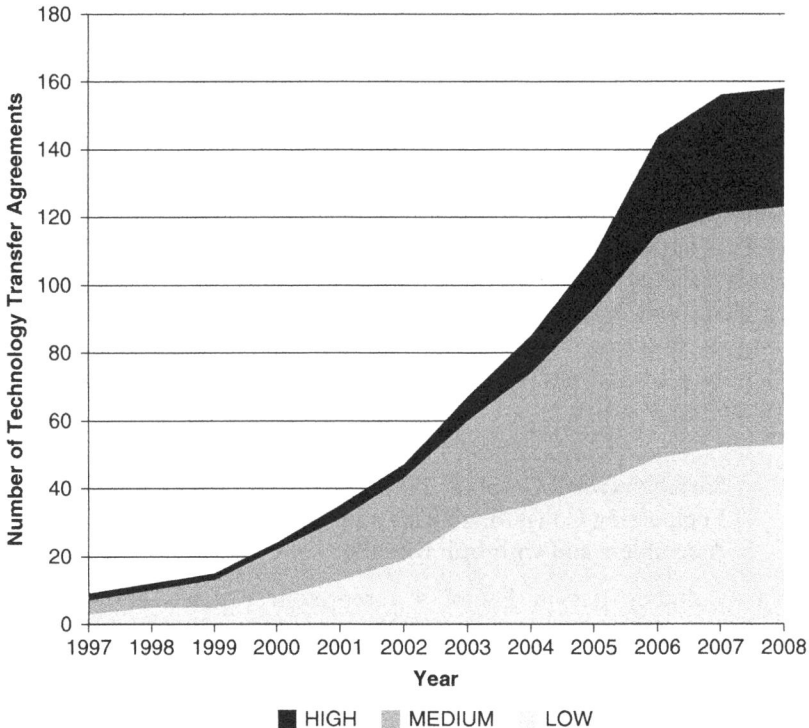

Figure 4.2 Time Series Technology Transfer Agreements between Iranian and Global Parts Suppliers

higher value-added parts in Iran increased more than threefold, from 2.7 percent in 1979 to 9 percent in 2010.[23]

The development of an industry in Iran based on greater indigenous local technical capacity is largely the result of establishing ties with engineering consulting firms. The firms also reduced technical dependence on Peugeot by linking the Iranian automobile companies to a network of global parts suppliers outside of Peugeot's supply chain. The state played a key role as facilitator and organizer at various stages of the project. At the beginning it helped provide the financial resources. During the projects, it facilitated the synergy between the consulting firms and Iranian engineers, transferred technology to local parts suppliers, and built the R&D centers to absorb the technology. Toward the end of the projects, when it tested the products it evaluated the quality of services. The relationships established with the consultancies to build technical capacity build on the idea of network-centered development theory by illustrating the diversity of the global networks that the state can play a role in constructing.

Networks of Technology Transfer

This section provides empirical evidence to illustrate the network position of engineering consulting firms within the global relationships of technology transfer. Even though Saipa has also used engineering consulting firms in its development strategy, the discussion will focus only on Iran Khodro in order to make a strong argument to illustrate the technology transfer networks. Three network graphs will be analyzed. The first will show the technical synergy ties among engineering consulting firms, multinational assemblers, and Iran Khodro. The second graph will show the local technology licensing ties in manufacturing vehicles in Iran. The third will combine the two previous graphs to show the entire global network of technology transfer.

Social Network Graph 1: Technology Synergy between Engineering Consulting Firms and Multinational Automobile Assemblers and with Iran Khodro

The consultancy ties in Figure 4.3 represent the ties between the engineering consulting firms and the multinational assemblers and between the consulting firms and Iran Khodro.[24] The important engine

---

[23] Data before the revolution are from Salami, 2004. Data after the revolution are from the Golden Key Directory of Automobile Producers in Iran, 2010.

[24] Ties obtained from annual reports, press releases, and company websites.

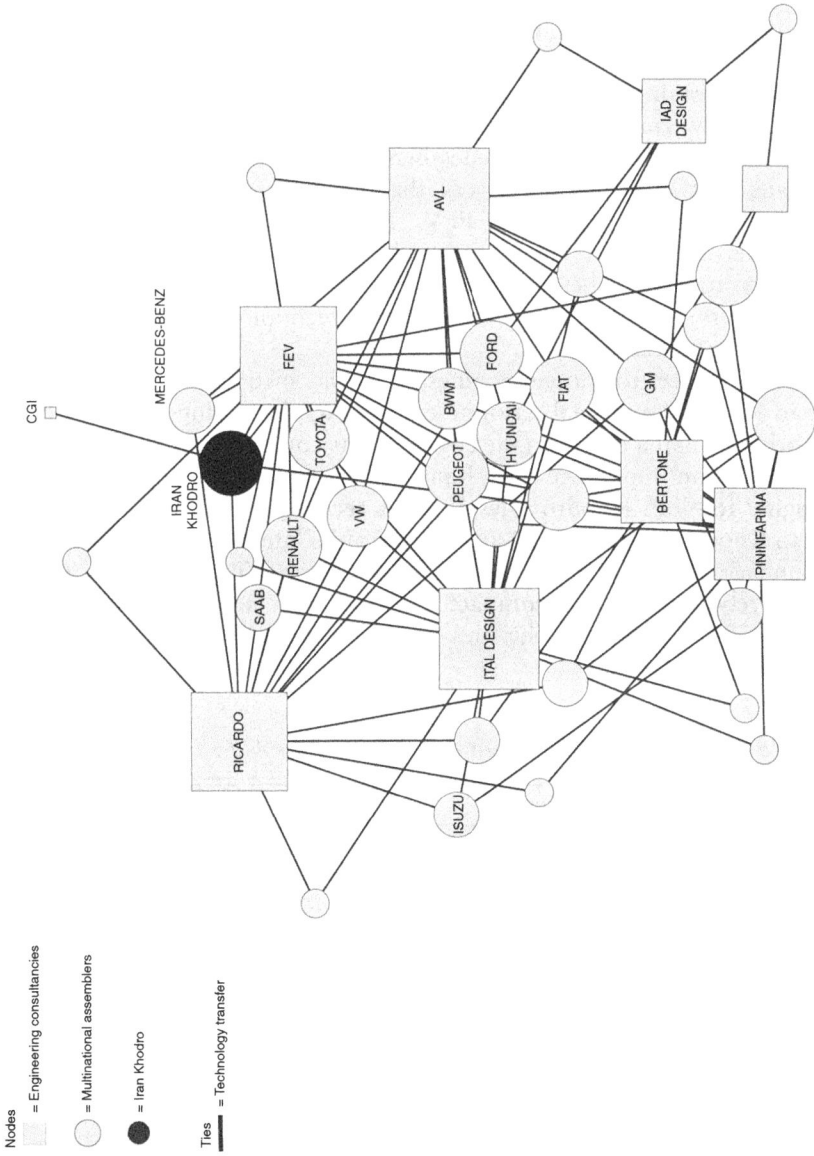

Nodes

☐ = Engineering consultancies

◯ = Multinational assemblers

⬤ = Iran Khodro

Ties

▬ = Technology transfer

Figure 4.3 Engineering Consultancy Ties to Multinational Assemblers and Iran Khodro

consultancy firms include FEV (Germany), AVL (Austria), and Ricardo Engineering (United Kingdom). The other consultants are the body and styling firms, with Italian companies (such as Pininfarina, Bertone, and Italdesign) the most prominent in the field. Many of the world's major automobile companies have been clients of these firms at some point. A sample of engineering consulting firms' clients in developed countries includes Peugeot, Citroën, Renault, Mercedes-Benz, Volkswagen, Porsche, Audi, BMW, Saab, Fiat, Volvo, Toyota, Nissan, Subaru, Suzuki, Nissan, Honda, Isuzu, Ford, GM, Chrysler, Hyundai, Daewoo, and Kia.

The most interesting aspect of the graph is that Iran Khodro is structurally equivalent to many large multinational assemblers including Renault, Toyota, Mercedes-Benz, Volkswagen, and Saab. This means that it acquired services through ties to similar engineering consulting firms, including FEV, AVL, Ricardo, Pininfarina, and Bertone. The major exception is that CGI that was hired by Iran Khodro to design the Samand sedan and has no ties to multinational assemblers because CGI focuses only on technology transfer to developing countries.

With respect to Iranian engines, FEV was instrumental in designing Iran Khodro's national gasoline engine, supplementing the consulting work with Saipa to design the engine for its compact car called the Tiba. AVL was an important consultancy in designing Iran's national diesel engine for Iran Khodro Diesel. Most recently, Pininfarina is helping Iran Khodro with the body and styling of its latest compact vehicle, the Runna, and Bertone is assisting with Saipa's Tiba. Both are small, relatively inexpensive compact cars popular among Iran's middle class. Table 4.3 lists the ties between consulting firms and Iran Khodro and Saipa.

Table 4.3 *Engineering Consultancy Ties to Iran Auto*

Consultants	Type of Company	Ties to Iranian Companies
CGI	British consultancy specializing in body design	Iran Khodro
	Italian company specializing in body design and styling	Iran Khodro
Bertone	Italian company specializing in body design and styling	Saipa
FEV	German engineering consultancy specializing in gas engines	Iran Khodro and Saipa
AVL	Austrian engineering consultancy specializing in diesel engines	Iran Khodro
Ricardo	British engineering consultancy specializing in engines and control systems	Iran Khodro

Social Network Graph 2: Local Production: Iranian Auto Assembler and Parts Company Ties to Multinational Assemblers and Global Parts Suppliers

The graph of local manufacturing ties, seen in Figure 4.4, shows two large nodes: Peugeot on the left (light-colored sphere) and Iran Khodro on the right (dark-colored sphere). There are two types of ties in the graph. The first are tier 1 *parts supplier* (these are global parts suppliers such as Bosch, Mahle, and others) *ties* that go directly either to Peugeot or to local parts manufacturers that supply directly to Iran Khodro. The horizontal ties are the *licensing* ties from the global parts suppliers to the local Iranian parts suppliers. The technology is licensed either *independently* if they supply to one of Iran Khodro's national vehicles or the national engine or *dependently* if it is for the production of the Peugeot 405, for one of the varieties of the 405 (such as the Peugeot Roa and the Peugeot Pars), or for the Peugeot 206.

The list of global parts suppliers with relationships to Iran Khodro parts suppliers includes a number of large, well-known corporations, including TRW France, Bosch, Behr, ZF, Valeo, and Faurecia. The development of Iran's national engine expanded high-tech license agreements with a variety of European manufacturers, including Mahle, INA, Bosch, Freudenberg, Reinz, and Johnson Matthey to manufacture pistons, engine valves, exhaust manifolds, heat shields, and catalytic converters.

Social Network Graph 3: The Global Network of Technology Transfer

Figure 4.5 combines the technical synergy graph (social network graph 1) and the local manufacturing graph (social network graph 2) to show the entire network of technology transfer on a global scale. The graph illustrates how the global reconfiguration of industrial production has created a diverse network of ties to develop an automobile industry. The top portion of the graph illustrates the *technology synergy* among the engineering consulting firms and the multinational automobile assemblers. Peugeot and Iran Khodro are now shifted down because they exist in the Iran local manufacturing space. As can be seen from the graph, the engineering consulting firms doing business with Iran Khodro and Peugeot function as gatekeepers in transferring higher value-added technology from the technical synergy among developed countries to the local Iranian developing space.

Peugeot and its subsidiary, Citroën, have proven to be one of the most important companies in diffusing technology from engineering consulting firms to Iranian companies. Most notably, the Peugeot 405 platform, designed by Pininfarina, was used in producing Iran's national vehicle

114

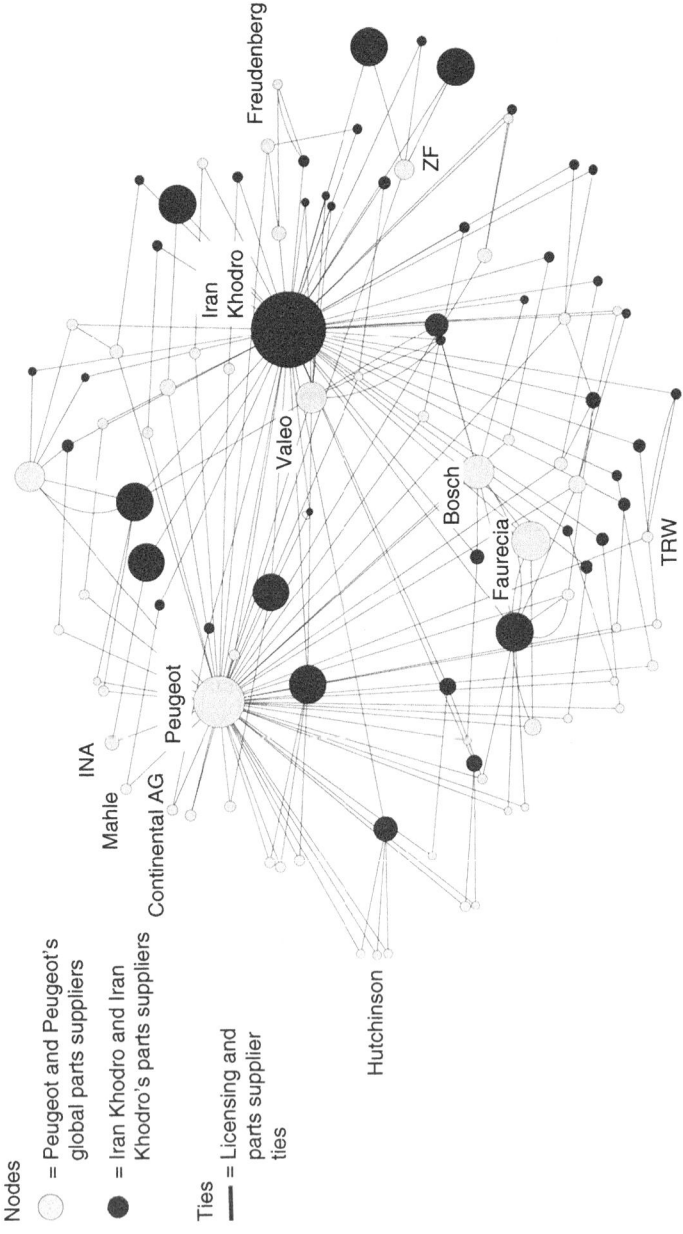

Figure 4.4 Local Manufacturing Ties

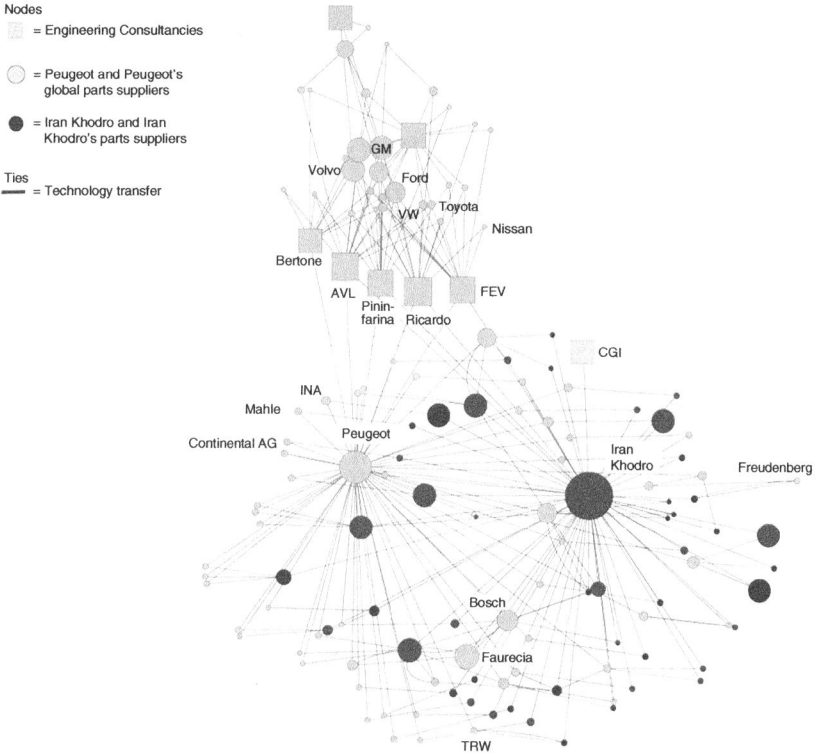

Figure 4.5 The Global Network of Technology Transfer

(the Samand), a project managed by CGI. For body design, notable projects include Pininfarina's design of the Peugeot 405 and 406 and Bertone's design of the Citroën Xantia and ZX.[25] The Peugeot 405 and Citroën Xantia are currently manufactured in Iran.

---

[25] Besides designing Peugeot vehicles since the mid-1980s, Pininfarina includes among its clients Honda, Ferrari, Alfa Romeo, Rolls-Royce, Maserati, Jaguar, Fiat, Lancia, Mitsubishi, Citroën, Hyundai, Daewoo, and Volvo. In addition to work for Citroën, a sample of Bertone's client list since the mid-1980s includes Lamborghini, Chevrolet, Daewoo, Opel, Fiat, BMW, Alfa Romeo, and Jaguar.

5

From Industrial Protection to the Rise of the Stakeholder Model of Corporate Ownership

Introduction

Despite the industry's progress, by 2005 liberalization policies promoted by social groups and political factions in the state apparatus threatened to undermine local manufacturing. The liberalization policies incorporated two initiatives: the dismantling of infant industry protection and the privatization of the industry. The industrial nationalists viewed the abandonment of infant industry protection as a significant threat to their national project of building an industry based on local technical capacities. It opened up a conflict among conservatives, who wanted to completely liberalize the industry in order to support their constituency of importers, and the industrial nationalists, who wanted to support their constituency with the technocratic elite. In addition, the automobile parts manufacturers, who were represented by the Iran Automobile Parts Manufacturers Association, were particularly interested in maintaining protection because, according to their perspective, without it they could not survive against foreign competition.

The privatization of the automobile industry was part of a broader initiative to privatize all industries in Iran. Since the early 1990s, ownership of industrial organizations has been a contentious issue. Those in the state apparatus who favor privatization argue that state ownership of Iran's largest industrial organizations has led to widespread mismanagement and economic malaise. In addition, in Iran privatization is promoted as a way to create modern and competitive industries because it would force firms to economize costs and increase performance. As discussed in Chapter 3, privatization of state-owned enterprises under the presidencies of Rafsanjani and Khatami did not gain traction. With Ahmadinejad's election to the presidency in 2005, however, the political dynamic around privatization changed. He positioned himself as a populist with the platform that he would finally improve Iran's economy by ridding it of corruption and inefficient state-owned enterprises. The industrial nationalists, however, saw privatization as a threat because government ownership of the industry insulated it from social groups who did not share the policy interest of building a national industry.

In this chapter I will argue that the industrial nationalists engaged in strategic action to protect the industry from those opposed to local manufacturing. They did so by deepening their political ties within the state apparatus and by expanding their alliance with politicians and social groups in Iranian society who were willing to support the industry. I will then extend the argument by showing that the industrial nationalists further protected the industry from groups, such as the Iran Revolutionary Guard Corps, by gaining ownership control of Iran's largest automobile assemblers. Furthermore, the government's attempt at privatization was responsible for creating a stakeholder model of a large number of passive investors that opened up space for the industrial nationalists to further insulate the industry from actors opposed to national industrial development. The stakeholder model builds on previous findings about Iran's pseudo-privatization, where state institutions and quasi-state organizations such as pension funds, banks, and cooperatives gained ownership control over Iran's largest enterprises (Harris, 2013).

By making these arguments, I will make two contributions to the industrial development literature. The first is I will refine theoretical arguments about the concepts of embeddedness in intermediate states. Classic embeddedness is characterized by feedback between development organizations and industrial managers – feedback that allows state actors to monitor projects and correct bad policy decisions (Evans, 1995; Kohli, 2004; Chibber, 2006). In this chapter, however, I will argue that in intermediate states where factionalism is an important independent variable that determines development outcomes, the concept of embeddedness needs to be clarified to define how it operates. The scope should include ties to social groups or factions willing to support the industry in exchange for benefits to their constituents. States cannot rely solely on embeddedness between the development organization and the industry but instead must rely on industrialists to engage in strategic action to build alliances and coalitions to protect the integrity of industrial policy.

The second contribution is to the scholarly literature on privatization. This literature can be divided into the path dependency and conceptions of control scholarship. Since the early 1990s, much of the privatization scholarship has focused on the theoretical concept of path dependence to explain the transition from a planned to a market economy. Stark (1991) argued that countries in Eastern Europe initially adopted four typologies for privatizing state owned enterprises: sales of shares of the enterprise to multinational corporations in East Germany; distribution of shares to citizens in the Czech Republic; mass privatization and liquidation of companies in Poland; and sales of shares to institutional investors, such as pension funds, in Hungary. In devising these strategies, path dependency (Mahoney, 2000; Pierson, 2004) played a large role in the formation of privatization strategy. While state actors and social groups demanded a say in the process of change, their choices were constrained by the existing set of institutional resources. Thus in Eastern Europe, the rebuilding of organizations and institutions did not occur on top of the ruins of communism but *with* the ruins as they redeployed available resources in response to their immediate practical dilemmas (Stark, 1996, p. 995). For instance, in Hungary reformed communists faced weak and fragmented opposition; the country's enterprise managers, who had become the most powerful social group in the 1980s, became the most powerful social actors in society. During the transition period, these enterprise actors were able to negotiate with the opposition party to transfer the shares of enterprises to institutional investors.

Research shows that in China, when the government created a market economy, it produced a mixture of public and private enterprises. The government did not privatize large, state-owned enterprises. Instead, during the transition, a new dynamic sector of public enterprises owned by counties, townships, and villages emerged (Walder, 1995). A significant private sector of newer, entrepreneurially oriented enterprises emerged that currently exist side by side and compete with public enterprises (Fligstein, 1996; Guthrie, 2001).

The idea of conceptions of control was first introduced by Fligstein (1993), who studied the restructuring of American industrial enterprises. He argues that, with the passage of laws allowing corporations to form profit-centered holding companies, American corporations shifted from a manufacturing to a financial conception of control. This organizational form became more widespread following the economic crisis of the 1970s. Studies of restructuring in Japan show that, when corporations engaged in widespread cross-shareholding, industries became insulated from outside forces that threatened a manufacturing conception of control (Gerlach, 1997). Cross-shareholding insulates an industry because the purchase of shares from within the group reduces or eliminates the ability for outsiders to take over the firm. For instance, when America and Western Europe pressured Japan to drop its trade barriers in the early 1960s to allow foreign firms to purchase shares of Japanese companies, cross-shareholding among Japanese companies increased substantially.

The findings in this chapter build on current privatization and industrial development research by showing that privatization in the automobile sector in Iran led to two major restructuring events that insulated the industry from actors opposed to national, local manufacturing. First, consistent with Harris' findings, privatization led to the rise of diverse structure of ownership. In this study, I use the concept of "stakeholders" to more accurately describe the ownership structure because they are largely passive investors who hold the shares without making profits by buying and selling on a market. As a group, the stakeholders by their presence prevented investors from outside the industrial group from taking over the firms. Second, during privatization, the industrial nationalists (who were deeply embedded within the political and industrial fields) engaged in strategic action to maintain the nationalist conception of control over the industry by using the already existing and legally recognized "cooperative corporation" to purchase major shares in Iran's largest automobile assemblers. The industrialists took this action at a time when the state, faced with the dilemma of losing control over the industry, began a more serious push for privatization.

In this way, Iran borrowed from Eastern Europe in that the industrial nationalists redeployed available resources to prevent loss of control over the industry. More specifically, as in Hungary, privatization resulted in ownership's shift to a diverse number of institutional investors. However, in Iran the stakeholder model had a more instrumental function: it insulated the industry from outside interests intent on changing the internal dynamics of corporate control in their favor. In this way, the formation of the stakeholder model is similar to that of Japan – except that the stakeholders in Iran were a mix of state and quasi-state actors, whereas in Japan they were private investors associated with the industrial group.

This chapter begins with a discussion about the conservative opposition to infant industry protection and the strategy used by industrial nationalists to build coalitions to protect it. A discussion about the privatization policy under President Ahmedenijad and the industrial nationalist opposition to it follows. The remainder of the chapter will cover the action taken by the industrial nationalists to gain ownership control over the industry. Lastly, a social-network analysis will show the position of the activist cooperative organization within the industrial field and the structure of power between government organizations and Islamic leadership. It will also provide empirical evidence to show how post-revolutionary privatization policies led to diffuse ownership among several institutional investors.

Attacks on Infant Industry Protection and Political Coalitions to Protect It, 2005–2011

After President Ahmedenihad's election in 2005, the conservative faction in parliament and groups within the state apparatus who controlled trade imports began to push for the liberalization of the industry and the abandonment of infant industry protection. The push toward liberalization opened up a conflict among conservatives, who wanted to completely liberalize the industry in order to support their constituency of importers, and the industrial nationalists, who wanted to support their constituency with the technocratic elite and automobile entrepreneurs – most of whom were parts manufacturers. The Iran Automobile Parts Manufacturers Association and the after-sales service companies and agencies were particularly interested in maintaining protection because, according to their perspective, without it they could not survive against foreign competition.

To promote trade liberalization, the conservative faction began to criticize the automobile managers as an insular "Mafioso" group who sought benefits primarily for themselves and their constituents. And they saw an opening to gain ground and promote their constituency via the issue of automobile quality. Quality became a more serious issue in 2006, when about two dozen people perished due to vehicle fires caused by faulty fuel lines in the Peugeot 405. Conservatives rallied support by promoting policies that would resolve the quality problem through a more competitive automobile market, one without infant industry protection and open to foreign imports.

The industrial nationalists fostered support for infant industry protection by establishing stronger ties to the Islamic leadership, particularly the ties between the large automobile companies, together with the Iran Automobile Parts Manufacturers' Association, and the Supreme Leader's office. An Iranian business consultant explained how these relationships strengthened the nationalist position over the years:

> It is mostly related to the lobby of the automakers and parts manufacturers. There are lots of small and medium spare parts companies in Iran that have relationships to politicians and government bodies. In the past 20 years, these relationships have become very strong. One example is the relationship between Iran Khodro and the Islamic leadership. Mr. Babai, the public relations and sales director of Iran Khodro, has a very close relationship with the Supreme Leader.[1]

Although the main components of the Automobile Law have remained on the books since its passing, in 2005 the parliament allowed foreign imports into the country. A tariff of 90 percent to 120 percent was applied to these vehicles, depending on the price. In 2010, however, the parliament attempted to pass a proposal to reduce the import tariff by 15 percent because of concerns that Iranian auto companies were producing low-quality cars. The Iranian Automobile Manufacturers' Association

---

[1] Interview with business consultant, June 2011.

opposed the law, lobbying the parliament heavily with the claim that the new law would destroy jobs. It relied on its connections to defeat it:

> A 90% tariff is not a problem for us, but a 15% drop is too risky. Our major concern is competition with foreign autos; the association did a lot of lobbying in the parliament and lots of negotiations went on. The industrial commission in the parliament supported us, but we also showed members of the parliament the Iran Khodro factories so they could see for themselves the jobs that would have been lost.[2]

In its lobbying efforts, the association (together with Mr. Babai of Iran Khodro) contacted the Supreme Leader's office to help defeat the law in exchange for greater effort to resolve quality problems: "The Supreme Leader has all of the data about the Iranian economy and knows that Iran Khodro is very important for jobs; it is the most important industry in Iran outside of oil."[3] Shortly after this lobbying effort, the Supreme Leader emphasized in a speech the need for the industry to "double down on improving quality." He then went on to discuss his position and the solution to the problem:

> A nation with a glorious past, talented youth, and high aspirations demands a flourishing industry in the Muslim world. Having abundant and inexpensive products is good, but more important is the growth of local industry. The gates should not be opened to imports according to mostly baseless reasons ... The philosophy and logic often raised is that increasing imports will enhance the quality of local products, but there are better options to reach this goal, one of which is enforcing policies and regulations for enhancing the quality of local products. The conjunction [the synergy] between industry and universities is very important, and a strong relationship should be established between these two sectors so that industrial progress can be achieved.[4]

After this speech and the association's lobbying efforts, the parliament eventually abandoned the planned tariff reduction. The Supreme Leader came down on the side of the automobile producers, primarily to protect industry jobs.

Maintaining strong infant industry protection laws allowed the industrial nationalists to insulate the industry from social forces opposed to local manufacturing. In the late 1990s, as the automobile industry became

---

[2] Interview with manager at auto parts business association, February 2011. [3] Ibid.
[4] *Iran Khodro Press*, April 4, 2010; also in the *World of Finance*, April 17, 2010, and the *Iran Economist*, April 10, 2010 (in Farsi).

more profitable, the Iran Revolutionary Guard Corps entered the Iranian automobile market by purchasing Bahman Motors. Infant industry protection laws, however, prevented the company from obtaining a significant share of the market. The business plan was to make money by selling the Mazda 3, a low-priced sedan selling for approximately $16,000 in the US market. The company has not been able to gain greater than 30 percent local content for this vehicle, which has relegated it to the high tariff category: it sells in Iran for about $45,000. In 2009, only 7,221 Mazda 3 vehicles were sold, representing 0.61 percent of the sedan market. It is rumored that the Revolutionary Guard is attempting to withdraw from the automobile industry and has put Bahman Motors up for sale.[5]

The industrial nationalists also sought protection of the industry through alliances with members of the parliament. Consequently, the automobile industry began to increase employment opportunities in less developed regions of Iran in exchange for industry support. In 2006, the government provided incentives for large auto companies to build factories in districts outside Tehran. These incentives existed in the form of larger loans and a five- to ten-year tax haven, along with other benefits – depending on the size of the factory. The Iran Auto Parts Manufacturers' Association has become a key player in forming these alliances with the goal of supporting domestic production. A high-ranking manager in the industry and board member of the association explained:

> We go to the parliament to tell them what matters and what is good for the country and good for progress. Fortunately, members of the parliament come from all over Iran; we have close relationships with some members, and they listen to us. The policies that we want implemented at times involve a trade-off to open factories in other regions in Iran.

As a result of these alliances, Iran Khodro has in the past few years engaged in a decentralization policy, opening ten factories outside Tehran in such places as Semnan, Khorasan, Mazandaran, Tabriz, and the northwestern district of Azerbaijan. These factories were built with the capacity to produce 100,000 to 200,000 vehicles a year in joint projects involving the company, local provinces, and private capital. In one project in Semnan, the province provided $50 million to build the factory; Iran Khodro provided the required technical knowledge, equipped the production lines, and trained the factory workers.[6] Some large parts supplying companies are following Iran Khodro's lead: the second-largest parts supplier in Iran, Sazeh Ghostar (managed by Saipa), has committed to

---

[5] Interview with automobile executive, February 2011.
[6] *Iran Khodro Group Magazine*, March 2011, No. 76, p. 6.

expanding its factories in the "deprived" areas of Iran.[7] By supporting the nationalist agenda, members of the parliament are able to deliver jobs to the districts. Although some of the factories have the potential to become profitable, many auto executives see them as government handout projects rather than profitable investments.

Strategic Action to Protect Ownership over the Industry

Shortly after Ahmadinejad was elected as president in 2005, he was able to gain support from both the Supreme Leader and the parliament to implement privatization more aggressively. He framed privatization efforts within the context of populist Islamic social justice by embracing a "justice shares" program, whereby each Iranian family would receive shares of divested state-owned enterprises. This was a "just" policy because the poorest members of society would receive the greatest shares; at the same time, it would diversify stock ownership to create greater incentive for privatization. Provincial committees oversaw the establishment of cooperatives to manage investment of the shares. During the process of distribution, the shares were transferred to welfare entities such as the Imam Khomeini Relief Fund, low-income villagers and nomads, public-sector retirees, young addicts in treatment, construction workers without labor contracts, and so on (Harris, 2013). The structure of industrial enterprise ownership therefore transformed from entirely state-owned enterprises into one in which various institutional investors in the form of government and state organizations owned a "stake" in the industry.

By 2009, 60 percent of Iran Khodro and Saipa was owned by government-affiliated institutional investors such as the Social Security Investment Company (SHASTA) and other companies with strong ties to the automobile industry. These investment companies have two main functions: to invest in the Iranian economy and to produce profits for the organization. However, as "passive" investors that typically do not sell company shares to make quick profits, they also provide stability. A high-ranking manager in the development organizations explained SHASTA's role in the Iranian economy:

> SHASTA is a big company in Iran, and they have a very important role in the economy. They have a lot of money to invest, and they put their money into all fields in Iran that are profitable, such as the automobile industry, oil, gas, and agriculture. Sometimes the government gets money from SHASTA; when it wants to

---

[7] www.sazehgostar.com/Home_en.htm, under "Communication with Society."

compensate them, the government will give them a factory or a company. SHASTA has to hold on to these properties; they can't sell them.

By 2011, Ahmadinejad was pushing privatization more aggressively. This pressure threatened the automobile industry because it opened up the field to actors that favored imports over local manufacturing and that could gain ownership control of key organizations within the industry. These groups included those associated with the conservative factions in Iran, groups within the Iran Revolutionary Guard Corps (IRGC) or the *basij* cooperative, or private-sector individuals with neoliberal sentiments toward industrialization. The state-affiliated organizations are considered the greatest threat because of their cash reserves, which they can use to purchase shares of industrial organizations. They are considered semi-governmental organizations because they not only receive money from the government but also can invest that money like private sector investors. Their modus operandi is essentially as follows: they receive a budget from the government, and excess budgetary funds can be used to invest in businesses of their choosing. They invest in startups if, after investigating the business plan, they think they can make money on the venture. Many of these companies, however, are interested only in quick profits and thus invest only in such businesses as importing or construction. The criticism levied against the organizations is that there is little or no accountability and profits are made among a small group of high-level managers using state money to enrich themselves. Given a chance to control the largest auto companies, such as Iran Khodro or Saipa, local industry would suffer in favor of the large amounts of money to be made on importing cars.[8]

In 2011, IDRO owned a 40 percent share in both Iran Khodro and Saipa, but the new privatization laws required it to reduce its share to 18 percent for each company. (Owning greater than 15 percent of the shares in any company in Iran guarantees a position on the board to shape corporate policy.) To the industrial nationalists, the sale of 22 percent of the company's shares threatened to open up space for social groups opposed to local manufacturing to influence industrial policy. To eliminate the threat to Iran Khodro, the industrialists engaged in strategic collective action by creating a "network committee" to found a cooperative with the Iran Automobile Parts Manufacturers' Association, the workers' syndicate of Iran Khodro, the Automobile Industry Pension Fund, Iran Khodro Diesel, and SAPCO. A similar cooperative was formed among Saipa-affiliated companies and workers' groups to purchase Saipa's shares. The network committee of Iran Khodro claims it is a "grassroots" organization with the intention of preserving local

---

[8] Based on interviews with employees of semi-government organizations, January 2010 and February 2011.

manufacturing in Iran.[9] When asked "why" the action was taken, a manager of a prominent auto parts company who was also a member of the networked committee responded:

> Privatization has raised a new challenge in the industry; in my opinion, it is good for the private sector if the shares of Iran Khodro are out of government hands. There was a major concern among Iran Khodro and the workers' syndicate that if someone else controls the company, it will not be good for them or for us. We share the same values – and if we buy the shares, we can continue the same way as before. We have seen how companies have been changed by outside people, and they have often ruined the company. We can run the company much better: that is what we believe.[10]

When asked about the role of semi-governmental organizations, he responded that "they are profit-oriented: they make money by buying and selling shares in companies; we are production-oriented."[11] Many of the organizations that have bought shares in Iran Khodro or Saipa are considered the "second-hand government" in that they are smaller agencies or companies founded by the government to purchase shares in the industry. This action guaranteed that the dominant shares of Iran's largest automobile companies would remain in the hands of the government and of the industrial nationalists who supported domestic production.

This action, however, raises the question: if the government is sincere about pushing privatization to improve Iran's economy, why would it tolerate the formation of a government-centered stakeholder model? One reason given is that the country lacks private-sector investors interested in purchasing companies from a government not committed to securing profitable investments. In the 1990s, Behzad Nabavi, a former Minister of Industry and president of IDRO, discussed these problems in an interview:

> We are seeking true privatization, but we currently do not have a powerful private sector. This means that we have no other choice but to apportion industries to such organizations as the Social Security Organization or the Iran Pension Agency, and these are by no means private. If we are seeking the true sense of the term [privatization], we should admit that we don't have powerful private organizations in Iran to run Machine Sabzi Arak, Iran Khodro, Saipa, or the Sadra Machine units.[12]

---

[9] www.tavonikhas.ir/ [10] Interview with parts supplier manager, February 2011.
[11] Ibid. [12] *The Role of IDRO and Industrial Development in Iran*, 2000 (in Farsi).

The previous section in this chapter showed how ties between the industry and the Supreme Leader were important in preserving economic stability. Another reason why these ties are strong is that high-ranking government officials need to control the automobile industry to achieve geopolitical goals. As the industry grew throughout the years, it became an important political tool to strengthen Iran's ties to foreign countries friendly to Iran. Since 2005, Iran Khodro and Saipa factories have been established in Venezuela, Syria, Belarus, Azerbaijan, and the Sudan – countries that typically harbor anti-American sentiments. Most corporate and government managers interviewed regarded these as "political" projects in which the government's goal was to improve economic relationships by opening factories in parts of the world neglected by Western European and American companies. But such political goals are one reason the industry has not privatized: "The factories abroad have never been profitable; we have not seen a dime from the Venezuelan operations. This is one of the reasons that the industry is not private, because the factories abroad will not make money and a private company will never invest in such a project."[13] The companies are not profitable largely because the number of vehicles produced in foreign factories remain relatively low – approximately 50,000 vehicles a year.

Social-Network Analysis of Corporate Ownership

The aim of social-network analysis of corporate ownership is to provide empirical evidence for the deepening of nationalist ties within the automobile industry and to show how it is insulated from actors opposed to domestic production. Data for the analysis was obtained from a large, reputable consulting firm in Iran that had conducted shareholder-mapping research of Iran Khodro and Iran Khodro Diesel for a foreign automobile client. Data consisted of major and minor shareholders of all firms connected to Iran Khodro or Iran Khodro Diesel. All organizations in the network have at least one major shareholder, approximately 40 percent of the firms have minor shareholders, and 60 percent have major shareholders only.

The social-network analysis will achieve three specific objectives. First, a *major shareholder* analysis will show the positional importance of the activist cooperative organization within the industrial field. Second, the major shareholder analysis will compare the distribution of power between the industrial field, government financial organizations, and Islamic leadership organizations. Third, a *minor shareholder* analysis will show how post-revolutionary privatization policies have diffused

---

[13] Interview with parts supplier manager, February 2011.

ownership among several institutional investors, including the Islamic leadership.

Major Shareholder Analysis

The Activist Network of Power and Control over the Industry. Major shareholder analysis is important in measuring power within the network: any firm that is a major shareholder of another firm can have a seat on that firm's board to control company policy. The higher the number of firms in which it owns major shares, the greater is its power over policy direction within the network. Figure 5.1 shows the graph of the major shareholders in the ownership network. The graph shows three main clusters: the Iran Khodro industrial cluster to the left, the government financial cluster in the middle, and the Islamic leadership cluster on the lower right. The Iran Khodro industrial cluster shows the structure of the activist network committee ownership and major shareholders within Iran Khodro's industrial cluster (left side of figure). Arrows show direction of a board member: if firm A is a major shareholder in firm B, the arrow points from A to B. There are two types of nodes: government organization (spheres) and the activist network cooperative (triangle).

Within the industrial cluster, Iran Khodro, IDRO, and the activist network cooperative Tavani Khas Iran Khodro are the actors with the most power. Iran Khodro is a major shareholder of eight companies including SAPCO (100 percent), ISACO (100 percent), Rena Investment (15 percent), Samand Investment (43 percent), Iran Khodro Investment (80 percent), Iran Khodro Diesel (23 percent), and various material support companies. In the cases where ownership is 100 percent, it directly controls that company's board; in the cases where it is a major shareholder, it has at least one member of the company on the board. All these companies are important for Iran Khodro's manufacturing operations.

IDRO is a major shareholder of two companies, Iran Khodro (21 percent) and Rena Investment (39 percent), and sends at least one board member to those companies. The Ministry of Industry wholly owns it.

The graph's most important aspect is that the activist network cooperative has a board member on Iran Khodro because it owns 18 percent of its shares. This ownership arrangement allows the activist network cooperative not only to influence policy around assembly operations but – most importantly – to influence the parts supply chain through SAPCO and after-sales service and parts supply through ISACO. The parts supply chain is particularly important to the committee. The Iran Automobile Parts Manufacturing Association was a key organizer behind the founding of the activist cooperative because its members have much to lose if actors unfriendly to local manufacturing gain ownership control over the industry.

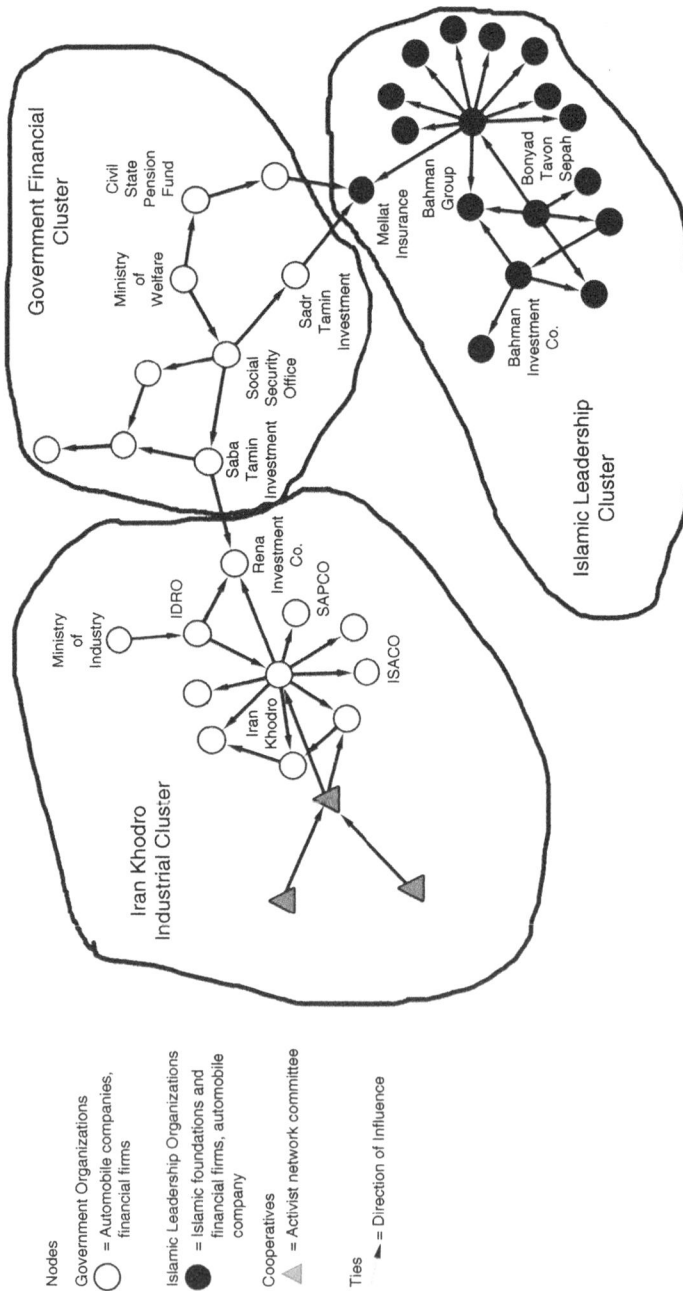

Nodes

Government Organizations
○ = Automobile companies,
  financial firms

Islamic Leadership Organizations
● = Islamic foundations and
  financial firms, automobile
  company

Cooperatives
▲ = Activist network committee

Ties
◄— = Direction of Influence

Figure 5.1 Major Shareholder Structure of Iran Khodro and the Islamic Leadership, 2009

The Structure and Distribution of Ownership between the Iran Khodro Industrial Group, Government Financial Organizations, and the Islamic Leadership. The Islamic Leadership cluster (lower right) and the government financial cluster (upper right) portion of the graph show two additional structural characteristics of the ownership network. First, the Islamic leadership cluster and the Iran Khodro industrial cluster are separated by five degrees of freedom via the government financial cluster, indicating very little influence of the Islamic leadership on government-controlled industry. The government financial cluster therefore functions as institutional "gatekeeper" because it has members of its board in both networks. With $4 billion invested in various firms within the automobile industry and other industrial organizations in Iran, the Social Security Office (SHASTA) is the most important organization in the government financial cluster connecting the Iran Khodro industrial and the Islamic leadership clusters. With respect to the government cluster, the Social Security Office is a major shareholder of Saba Tamin Investment, a major shareholder of Rena Investment. Because IDRO and Iran Khodro are major shareholders of Rena Investment, it is therefore a focal point where IDRO, Iran Khodro, and the Social Security Office meet. As part of the Islamic leadership cluster, the Social Security Office sends a board member to Sadr Tamin Investment, which in turn sends a board member to Mellat Insurance. The Bahman Group and the Civil State Pension Fund also each have a board member on Mellat Insurance. Mellat Insurance is therefore a meeting point between the Islamic leadership and the government.

The second structural characteristic is the Islamic leadership has a distinct organizational cluster engaged in automobile development. Within the Islamic leadership cluster, the Bahman Group, the Bonyad Tavon Sepah, and the Bahman Investment Company are the organizations with the most major shareholders. The official purpose of the *bonyads* is to provide "aid to the needy and deprived classes of the Islamic Nation."[14] One way to do so is by establishing a reliable infrastructure for collecting cash and non-cash revenue through Islamic *zakat* and *khoms*.[15] In recent years, *bonyads* have increased revenue through investments in automobile manufacturing – most notably, through the Bahman Group and their automobile company called Bahman Motors, best known for its ties to Japanese automobile companies. It produces the Nissan Patrol, a pickup truck, and the Mazda 3 passenger car.

---

[14] www.emdad.ir/index_en.asp.
[15] *Zakat* is the donation of a fixed portion of one's income to charity, and *khoms* is the giving of one-fifth of one's income to charity.

The Bahman Group is a major shareholder in ten companies, most of which are affiliated with the IRGC. These include various financial firms and construction companies in which it also owns 100 percent of the shares. The Bonyad Tavon Sepah is a major shareholder of five companies including the Bahman Group (45 percent), a trade company (Trade Arya 45 percent), and a commercial industrial firm (Asr Bahman 66 percent); it is also a dominant shareholder of two investment companies. Most important to its ownership arrangement, it is a member of the board of the Bahman Group. Bahman Investment Company is a major shareholder of Trade Arya (20 percent), Asr Bahman (34 percent), and Salim Investment (100 percent). Its major shareholder is Tavoni Etebari Samenolaeme, which is wholly owned by the Bonyad Tavon Sepah.

Minor Shareholders

The Institutional Stakeholder Model of Passive Investors. Direct interaction between the government and Islamic ownership networks occurs among minor shareholders. Figure 5.2 represents minor shareholders only. Government organizations are circles, and the Islamic organizations are squares. Minor shareholder ties exist only among industrial organizations and financial firms. The ties in this network represent *direction of influence* from one organization to another. For instance, if firm A owns shares in firm B, the tie is directed from A to B.

The graph illustrates three important aspects of minor shareholder ties. First, most of the organizations have several minor shareholder ties to organizations that have no other ties in the network (zero-degree

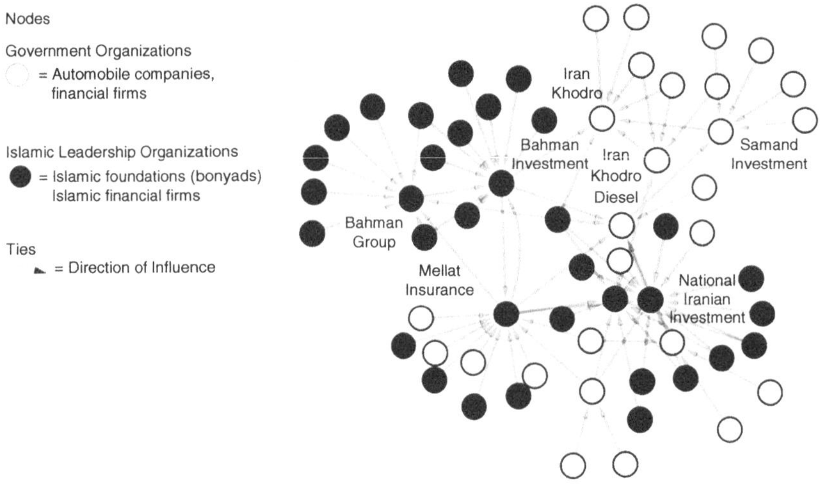

Figure 5.2 Graph of Minor Shareholders, 2009

Table 5.1 *Minor Shareholder Centrality*

Company	Affiliation	Centrality
Mellat Insurance	Islamic	0.47
Bahman Investment	Islamic	0.30
National Iranian Investment	Islamic	0.25
Iran Khodro Diesel	Government	0.23
Bahman Group	Islamic	0.17
Iran Khodro	Government	0.15
Melli Investment	Islamic	0.15
Samand Investment	Government	0.13
Tadbir Invest Co.	Islamic	0.09
Sepah Investment	Government	0.07

centrality). These organizations function as stable shareholders because they are passive: they do not sell their shares, and (since they are minor shareholders) they do not have a seat on the board. Second, while government and Islamic organizations have a diverse number of cross-shareholder ties, two distinct ownership blocs exist because most of the firms own shares within their own network (upper right is government owned Iran Khodro and upper left is Islamic owned Bahman group that owns Bahman Motors). This arrangement reinforces their position as passive investors because they have similar interests in maintaining the ownership structure. Third, as seen in Figure 5.2 and in Table 5.1, organizations associated with the Islamic leadership are the most central actors in the network. Of the top five most central actors, four are affiliated with the Islamic leadership, whereas only one is associated with the government.

Although Islamic organizations are the most central actors in the minor shareholder network, the government organizations – most importantly, Iran Khodro and Iran Khodro Diesel – remain insulated from the Islamic leadership. Iran Khodro has eight minor shareholders, five of which are government organizations: Social Security Investment Company (8 percent), Rena Investment Company (8 percent), Samand Investment Company (7 percent), Civil State Pension Fund (5 percent), and Civil State Pension Investment Company (3 percent). Two of the minor shareholders belong to the Islamic ownership network: Tadbir Investment Company (1 percent), wholly owned by the Imam Khomeini Relief Foundation, and Bahman Investment Company (0.1 percent), owned by IRGC.

Iran Khodro Diesel has six minor shareholders; the Islamic leadership is the most prominent minor shareholder but holds only 4 percent of the shares through Tadbir, Bahman, and National Iran Investment Company. The major shareholder of the National Iran Investment Company is IRGC.

Among the companies in the Islamic leadership ownership network, a few investment firms have government companies as minor shareholders. This arrangement exists only among financial firms such as Melli Investment and Mellat Insurance. None of the minor shareholders in the Bahman Group (the organization that produces automobiles) is associated with the government.

Comparing Government and Islamic Structure of Ownership

This section will compare the structure of ownership in the government and in Islamic leadership, including major and minor shareholder ties. Table 5.2 shows this comparison. The numbers of government major and minor shareholder ties are relatively equal: thirty-two and thirty-seven, respectively. Looking at the Islamic leadership's ownership structure, however, twenty-two of the ties are major shareholder ties and sixty-three are minor shareholder ties. Interestingly, each government firm has on average 1.8 major shareholders and 4.1 minor shareholders, whereas the Islamic leadership has 1.2 major and 10.5 minor shareholders per firm. This shows that power among the government organizations is more diffused to organizations outside the firm, and even though the Islamic leadership has less power sharing at the top, the shares are distributed over a greater number of minor shareholders within the network.

Table 5.2 *Comparing Structure of Ownership between Government and Islamic Leadership in the Network*

	Government	Islamic Leadership
Number of major shareholders	32	22
Avg. number major shareholders per firm	1.8	1.2
Number of minor shareholders	37	63
Avg. number minor shareholders per firm	4.1	10.5

6

Factors Determining Iran Auto's Survival: Industry Fragility, the Quality Issue, and the Conflict over Globalization

Introduction

The previous chapters showed how specific state structures and field stabilization opened up space for industrial nationalists to become dominant players in the automobile industry. The industrialists implemented nationalist policies focused on infant industry protection, acquisition of technology from multinational corporations and engineering consulting firms, and strategic action to protect the industry. This chapter evaluates the overall success of these policies and the debates around the future of the industry. The basic finding is that, although the Iranian automobile industry has generated high employment, the industry is currently facing a number of challenges related to vehicle quality, profitability, political instability, and sanctions.

This chapter informs two theoretical perspectives of the book. First, it explores the "fragility" component of the pocket of efficiency argument (Evans, 1998). Second, it shows how institutions shape outcomes in automobile industrial development. With regard to the former, the industry's success in Iran depended largely on the network position of the industrial nationalists and their unity in developing coherent policies to help resolve national economic problems. A complicating factor, however, in resolving industry problems is that coherence became weaker after the industrial faction splintered between two industrial nationalist groups with different conceptions of the ways in which to construct a profitable, modern automobile industry. These conceptions were tied into which globalization model the industry should best adopt on the future path of development. Biggart and Guillen (1999) argue there are currently three models of automobile development: (1) a logic that favors large automobile assemblers and the sale of products on the global market, (2) small firms that sell parts on a global supply chain, or (3) linkage to the global economy through foreign ownership. In Iran, one industrial group pushed for the second model of developing a robust small-parts suppliers network to sell parts on the global supply chain; the other pushed for the first model – focusing on large firms developing local vehicles and sales of the vehicles on a global market. The ensuing conflict weakened state capacity, but as discussed in Chapter 3, the industrial nationalists were united in defeating neoliberals who sought to privatize the industry and dismantle its protection. These cross-cutting patterns of conflict and unity created pockets of coherence and incoherence: the industry continued to produce vehicles at high volume, but local content suffered and the industrialists wasted resources on a project that produced mixed to negative outcomes.

Another factor that weakened state capacity was the contradictory policies implemented after the election of President Ahmadinejad in 2005. His policies of eliminating favorable loans to the industry and implementing automobile price controls squeezed industry profits, forcing about 20 percent of the parts companies to go out of business or to source cheap parts from China. Consequently, local content suffered. Even though the structure of close ties between the state apparatus and the industry remained largely intact, many of the industrial nationalists who had built the industry in the 1990s were forced out of their positions or had to move out of the automobile industry into lower-status jobs within the state apparatus. The overall result of these policies was to reduce feedback between the industrial and political fields. Some of the factors influencing industry outcomes, however, were forces outside the control of the industry or the industrial development organizations. These included the US-led global sanctions against Iran and the rise of the Chinese global parts supply chain as an inexpensive source for automobile parts.

The second theoretical perspective this chapter informs is how institutions shape outcomes in automobile industrial development. Biggart and Guillen (1999) argue that automobile development depends on linking a country's historical pattern of social organization with opportunities made available by global markets. During the process of development, key actors in countries either can create space for industries to develop or can undermine development by enacting laws that inhibit the growth of national industries. The previous chapters discussed how key actors created space for the industry to develop; this chapter builds on this research by analyzing three important factors for shaping industry outcomes. First, the conflict among the industrialists constrained Iran's ability to develop an industry based on the sale of automobile parts on a global market. Second, the rise of China as a cheap source of global parts opened up opportunities for parts suppliers to resolve profitability problems by sourcing parts from Chinese firms. Third, geopolitical forces constrained Iran's ability to integrate the industry into the global economy. For instance, Iran cannot rely on foreign ownership and joint ventures to improve quality or to increase industry profits by selling its product on the global market. All these factors helped to shape and reinforce a model of development focused around large state enterprises and sales of completely built-up vehicles on a global market.

This chapter begins by discussing automobile quality in Iran. It is followed by discussions of the conflict over the joint venture with Renault-Nissan, vehicle pricing, and sourcing from Chinese automobile parts firms. It ends with a comparative analysis between Iran's auto industry and those of other countries to assess the progress of the Iranian automobile industry.

The Quality Problem

A major concern for global automobile producers is closing the quality gap. Countries are often pressured to provide citizens with good-quality vehicles to satisfy customer needs. Overall automobile quality is shaped by "perceived quality," which is defined by "the customer's subjective judgment (overall feeling) about the general excellence of the product or service with respect to its intended purpose, relative to its alternatives" (Cole & Flynn, 2009, p. 67). The general excellence of a vehicle delivered to a customer is influenced largely by three important variables: design, materials, and manufacturing technology. A vehicle needs to be well designed to function properly over long periods of normal driving conditions. Components produced with low-quality materials or with poor manufacturing technology will increase the probability of component failure, which in turn will lead to low-quality products.

The history of worldwide postwar automobile development reveals that only Japan and South Korea advanced to produce vehicles that meet global quality standards. Automobile companies in China, India, and Malaysia have made improvements, but – according to J.D. Power and Associates – they still lag far behind Japanese, American, and European vehicle manufacturers.[1] J.D. Power's quality rankings are determined by an overall initial quality score based on reports per 100 vehicles (PP100), with a lower rate of problem incidence indicating higher quality. In China, on average, the domestic brands score 158 PPO, whereas international brands have an average score of 104 PPO.[2] Mercedes-Benz and Lexus are ranked highest, followed by Beijing Hyundai and Shanghai General Motors. Quality results are very similar in India and Malaysia, but Japanese automobiles have the highest quality rankings.

---

[1] J.D. Power China Initial Quality Study, http://autos.jdpower.com/content/press-release/uiiKtTY/2013-china-initial-quality-study.htm.

[2] Ibid.

Table 6.1 *Iran Automobile Vehicle Quality Ratings*[3]

Vehicle	Country of Origin	Local Content	Production	Price ($US)	Quality Grade
Mazda 3	Japan	0.30	7,224	$45,000	A+
Renault Xantia	France	0.42	14,537	$20,000	A
Renault L 90	France	0.50	25,117	$15,000	A
Peugeot 206	France	0.50	114,983	$16,000	A
Kia Rio	Korea	0.19	16,991	$15,000	A
Iran Khodro Samand	Iran	0.70	105,356	$12,000	B
Peugeot 405	France	0.70	174,601	$12,000	B
Saipa Saba (Kia Pride)	Korea	0.70	544,170	$8,000	C

J.D. Power does not evaluate the Iranian automobile market, but IDRO has produced similar quality ratings. Table 6.1 shows the 2009 rankings of vehicles with greater-than-5,000-per-year production volume, with ranks according to letter grades of A, B, C, or D. Variables include local content, annual production numbers, and vehicle price in US dollars. The table shows that the vehicles with the highest local content (>70 percent; these include the Samand, the Peugeot 405, and the Kia Pride) have grades of B to C. Vehicles with lower local content (<40 percent) are graded A+ to A.[4] Furthermore, the lower the vehicle price, the lower the quality. In sum, the table shows that the Iranian market is bimodal: it is composed of high-volume, low-priced vehicles with substantially lower quality and a lower production volume of higher-priced vehicles with higher quality.

Although the Iranian automobile industry is similar to those of China, India, and Malaysia because they have not reached global quality standards, Iran differs from the other countries in that, in recent years, Iranian automobile quality has not improved at the same rate as in other countries. For this reason, quality has become a national problem threatening the integrity of industrial policy because it undermines the industry's legitimacy. Quality became such an important national issue that in 2001, the Minister of Industry and Mines publicly apologized for the low quality of Iranian-made vehicles.[5] In addition, as discussed in previous chapters, the quality problem strengthens the argument for those who oppose development of a local industry in favor of imports.

China, India, and Malaysia have continued to close the quality gap, particularly in recent years, through joint ventures with multinational

---

[3] Three years of monthly quality reports (2008–2010) show little change in quality.
[4] These are 2009 quality rankings. Data downloaded from IDRO website at www.idro.org.
[5] *Prices and Quality: High and Low, Iran International Magazine*, Automobile Special Issue, Issue 13, 2001.

corporations. Joint ventures are particularly beneficial to local automobile firms, because multinational corporations typically have an interest in exporting the products and therefore are committed to transferring the organizational techniques and the technology in order to reach quality and process efficiency goals. India and Malaysia have relied heavily on Japanese automobile assemblers for their joint venture projects, whereas China has relied on a mix of automobile assemblers from the United States, Germany, and Japan.

Iran, however, does not have the same opportunities to close the quality gap through joint ventures. Iran's isolation from the global economy, particularly the United States, has constrained its ability to establish relationships with multinational corporations. For instance, one reason behind quality problems is that some of the higher-production vehicles licensed by Iranian companies were designed and produced by multinationals for the middle and the low end of the global automobile market. The low-end vehicles licensed by Iran had inferior quality because they were built with cheaper materials and were designed with more rudimentary technology. A multinational corporation's desire to strike a deal for new vehicle production in Iran was influenced first by its internal policies of locating factories in Iran and second by the size of its American market share. A high-ranking engineer who held positions in Iran's development organizations explained what Iran has faced since the revolution in establishing ties with multinational corporations:

> When the managing directors of the Iranian companies negotiate with the foreign companies, the deal they can get depends on the policies of the foreign companies and whether they agree with the localization laws in Iran. Most foreign companies just want to sell their cars; they do not want to localize, particularly if they think the political conditions are poor. The common thinking in Iran is that we prefer Japanese or German cars because they are high-quality – but these companies don't want to produce cars here. The French are interested because they are free from the challenge of the United States, and the Koreans are interested because their policy is to outsource cheap cars in developing countries.[6]

These constraints existed when Iranians shopped around for a multinational corporation to produce a car in the late 1980s. Toyota refused to sign a contract with Iranians for fear of antagonizing Washington. During the Iran-Iraq war, Toyota sold thousands of pickup trucks to Iranians; as a consequence, it was pressured by the United States to align its policies with US sanctions against Iran. However, with respect to the case of Kia, Ford entered into a strategic alliance with Mazda and Kia to design and

---

[6] Interview, manager at large development organization, January 2011.

market the Ford Festiva for the American and Asian markets (Nohria & Garcia-Pont, 1991). In Korea, this model was sold as the Kia Pride; in the early 1990s, Kia purchased the rights from Ford to license the technology abroad. Kia was therefore able to sell the rights to manufacture the Pride in Iran. A vehicle designed in the 1980s for the low-end market niche, the Kia Pride therefore has inherent quality problems.

The reverse engineering process instituted in the early 1990s to localize French and Korean vehicles was an important variable that undermined quality. With reverse engineering, engineers dismantle a part produced by the multinational corporation in order to measure the component's dimensions, recreate the part's drawing based on the measured dimensions, and then manufacture the part based on the drawings. Reverse engineering is attractive to developing countries because they can indigenize component manufacturing without the need to pay royalties to the multinational corporation that produces the part. The disadvantage is that the drawings produced from this process can never match the drawings from the original parts; therefore, the parts are produced with varying tolerances – increasing the likelihood of component failure. Once the process was instituted within the organizations in Iran, it became difficult to upgrade the technology to produce higher-quality parts. According to a high-level manager with forty years of experience in the Iranian industry, reverse engineering in Iran has greatly damaged industry quality: "When you do reverse engineering you are copying without knowing the exact composition of the material and the part's tolerances; you become a copier, and you don't know how to design or develop the parts – you become a copying machine."[7] Furthermore, the problems worsened when many of the components were produced with old machines that had not been upgraded.

Based on interviews with managers in the industry, one of the reasons Iran has not been able to close the quality gap is that the men who own many of the parts companies have a "traditional" management sensibility as opposed to a "modern" one. Traditional managers seek rents through close relationships with government officials. These companies reject modern management techniques for improving quality and are primarily concerned with short-term profits. Managers of these firms are "traditional" because they conceive of ties to society through patrimonial relationships, they judge their subordinates based on "emotion" instead of modern "objective" criteria, and they treat their workers as if they were members of a family. A business consultant with many years of experience in advising Iranian firms and foreign firms in Iran explained the organizational impact of the traditional versus the modern approach:

---

[7] Interview with manager at business association, June 2011.

> A company is modern if it has a human resources department
> [and] a corporate governance structure and uses modern technol-
> ogy. If the managers graduate from universities that are in foreign
> countries, they will have "modern minds" and will employ "mod-
> ern concepts." A traditional company, for example, doesn't use
> modern information technology to manage the company; all of
> the important information of the company is in a single, hand-
> written notebook. Even if the company grows and grows, there is
> no tendency to change or implement modern technology or
> techniques.[8]

Even though most of the managers at the companies are engineers, they are
not familiar with modern management techniques and are not provided
with proper incentives to learn and implement them. Not all companies,
however, follow the traditional management style. Although most local
parts companies survive on close relationships with the government, a small
number of high-performing companies are considered "progressive"
because they embrace modern management techniques. These companies
are currently exporting their products abroad and therefore produce parts
with higher quality than do most local suppliers. A case in point is Ezam,
which supplies pistons to Peugeot.[9] In this way, the Iranian auto industry is
bimodal: its success relies on protectionism and patrimony, but it also
contains pockets of modern high technology and techniques.

Of the two largest automobile assemblers, Saipa is considered to be
more traditional in its management style. This is due largely to the close
relationships between management and its parts suppliers. The Kia Pride,
the highest-selling vehicle in Iran, is a cash cow for the company because it
purchased the rights to manufacture the vehicle and does not have to pay
royalty payments to Kia. The Pride is the lowest-priced vehicle in Iran, but
it is also the vehicle with the lowest quality. When Saipa began to localize
the vehicle in Iran in the mid-1990s, the entrepreneurs who founded parts
companies had very close relationships with its management:

> Many of the entrepreneurs who started parts companies were
> managers at Saipa. When a manager wanted to start a company,
> he approached his colleagues with his idea and they had a meeting
> among themselves to decide whether he should be allowed to
> establish a company. All of the managers have good relationships
> with each other and many of them who started companies were
> connected to each other through family relations. Although the
> parts companies established were private companies and

---

[8] Interview with business consultant, June 2011.
[9] The export volume, however, is low. Iranian parts suppliers export approximately
$70 million in parts each year.

independent of Saipa, the manager could keep his position at Saipa while he managed his company.[10]

About 70 percent of the managers of the company have dual roles, as a manager of Saipa and as an owner of a parts company. The tight social relationships de-emphasize the need to produce parts with high quality: the ability to get a parts contract is not based on the ability to produce quality parts but rather on familial or patrimonial ties to management.

Iran Khodro's vehicles rank higher than Saipa's vehicles for three reasons. First, in the early years, its parts component entrepreneurs founded companies that were independent of relations with management. Second, they forced the parts companies to meet quality standards or be expelled from the group. Third, they transferred higher technology through engineering consulting firms with the objective of closing the quality gap. Nevertheless, Iran Khodro vehicles are not without quality problems. The main problem is that, even though there is stiff competition among the tier 2 and tier 3 parts suppliers to supply lower value-added parts, there is little or no competition among the tier 1 parts suppliers. In addition, parts suppliers are forced to localize parts rapidly to meet local content rules. In 2006, a version of the Peugeot 405 had fire problems when fuel lines were not tested properly. According to an engineer at Iran Khodro, one reason for the fires was that, in the process of reaching local content quotas, the company had "permission to use the parts for the vehicle without inspection on a trial basis with the agreement that the parts would pass inspection at a later date."[11] Unfortunately, no one enforced the inspection at the later date.

The major factor given for the inability to close the quality gap is the lack of competition. As discussed in the previous chapter, despite the push toward privatization the major ownership actors are government and state organizations. According to interviews with Iranian quality consultants, the companies most interested in instituting quality control are private companies. State-owned enterprises lack the incentive and therefore have a merchant mentality because they "can't see beyond the tip of their nose" in focusing on profits over quality. A quality movement began in the mid-1990s under Khatami's presidency and continued through the 2000s, culminating with many automobile companies receiving ISO 9000 certification. Quality certification, however, was not meaningful because companies were not forced to implement systematic, long-term quality improvements. Furthermore, the rationalization and reorganization of the automobile industry in the late 1990s into two large conglomerates exacerbated the quality problems. After reorganization, the two large automobile companies occupied a market niche – Saipa produced cheap Korean automobiles and Iran Khodro the more expensive European vehicles – and did

---

[10] Interview with manager at large automobile company, October 2010.
[11] Interview, engineer, October 2010.

not compete with each other for market share in their respective niches. For these reasons, automobile managers have been accused by various government agencies and Iranian politicians of being a *mafioso* gang that is "milking the cow" because they are not being held accountable for churning out low-quality products. Although the government is currently forcing Saipa and Iran Khodro to upgrade vehicle technology by mandating higher safety and environmental standards for their vehicles, the government is not pushing for dramatic reorganization of the industry.

The flight of qualified engineers with the capability to implement modern management techniques and technology for quality improvement is another reason given for the poor quality of Iranian vehicles. According to the International Monetary Fund, Iran has one of the highest "brain drain" rates per capita of any country in the world (Khajehpour, 2014). Every year, about 150,000 highly educated people leave the country to pursue higher education but never return. The number leaving Iran increased dramatically after the 2009 election conflict. Many of the managers interviewed reported skilled engineers quitting their jobs and leaving the country after the election. The flight of engineers has particularly hurt the research and design labs established by the engineering consultants. Many of the engineers trained by the consultants found jobs at automobile companies abroad. The brain drain creates vacancies for jobs that cannot be filled domestically and leaves in its wake an internal network of local engineers with limited expertise in quality control. Many companies must compete for personnel from this labor pool because spending money on training younger, inexperienced engineers becomes a sunk cost:

> We always hire engineers from the best technical universities in Iran. But if we train them, in one or two years they leave Iran and go to Canada, Europe, or America. It is a big problem because we put a lot of money into training them. So now we hire only those with experience because we know they have made a decision to stay in Iran and won't leave.[12]

Many of the engineers leaving the country are middle-range engineers who are more likely to do the hands-on processing work important for improving quality.

Conflicts over Globalization Policy and Improving Vehicle Quality

The vast majority of managers and engineers in the Iranian automobile industry consider joint ventures with multinational corporations as the

---

[12] Interview with manager at parts supply company, October 2010.

most effective way of improving quality. Joint ventures force local auto-mobile parts suppliers to incorporate the technology and modern manage-ment techniques to meet global quality standards, thus creating a more competitive automobile market that delivers higher-quality goods at bet-ter prices. Joint ventures also help resolve the brain drain by creating a more dynamic international industrial field for engineers to work in. An important added benefit is the increase in profitability of the industry by creating a global export market for local parts suppliers and vehicle manufacturers.

The industrial nationalists pushing for joint ventures were led by Reza Veyseh, who wanted to create an industry focused on small and medium parts suppliers who would sell parts on the global automobile market. In the early 2000s, his group benchmarked automobile industries in other countries (such as Turkey, China, India, and Malaysia) and concluded that a more profitable industry, producing higher-quality parts, could be built around automobile parts exports through joint ventures. The liberalization of the Turkish automobile industry was used as an example of what Iran could achieve with greater global integration. When Turkey privatized its industry in the 1980s, many large multina-tional corporations purchased Turkish automobile companies; by the early 2000s, the industry was exporting $20 billion in automobile parts each year. These global integrationists opposed rolling back infant indus-try protection but also believed greater foreign control in the industry would lead to an increase in quality and profits.

However, the national developmentalist group, headed by Iran Khodro's managing director Manuchehr Gharavi, wanted to continue with the nationalist policy of building an industry centered around locally assembled vehicles created with indigenous capacities and independent of multinational corporations. It criticized the Turkish liberal model as a "sellout" to countries with imperialist ambitions and believed this would create an industry too dependent on multinational corporations.

When Reza Veyseh became managing director of IDRO in 2001, he gained the upper ground in this debate. With the successful development of SAPCO, Veyseh became a rising star in the industrial field and used his established connections within the state to begin pushing his agenda through the state apparatus. He wanted to achieve three major objectives with a multinational joint venture.

His first objective was to obtain the organizational techniques and technology to improve quality. According to members of parliament and other critics of the industry, Iran's inability to produce automobiles equal in quality to those of European and Asian manufacturers meant that the Iranian automobile industry was a failure. The Korean automobile indus-try was held as a counterexample against the Iranian automobile industry: it was founded at the same time and had achieved much greater success at producing higher-quality vehicles at higher volumes. To resolve the quality issues, high-ranking conservative members of parliament requested a reduction in tariffs to allow more imports and thus create a more competitive market. Reza Veyseh, on the other hand, opposed tariff reductions. Instead, he championed joint ventures as an alternative to imports by claiming that "it is better to import the carmaker than their cars."[13]

Veyseh's second objective advocated increased revenue to local parts suppliers through exports to foreign countries and through increased local production. He intended to produce a modern vehicle with high local sales potential and to increase exports to the lower end of the global automobile market. The export regions of interest included Africa, Central Asia, and the Middle East. To this end, vehicles needed to be sold for no more than $8,000. Because Iran owned the production rights of the Samand and the Peykan, these were Iran's only vehicles that could legitimately be sold locally and for export to foreign markets; however, neither could attain local and export profitability goals. The Peykan did in fact sell for $8,000, but it was an old vehicle with no export market value. In addition, due to its role in aggravating Tehran's growing pollution problems, manufacture of the Peykan was discontinued by an act of the Iranian parliament. As for the Samand, its local and global sales were hampered because it could not be sold profitably for less than $12,000.

As a third objective, Veyseh also wanted a multinational corporation that would promote the manufacture of both an Iran Khodro vehicle and a Saipa vehicle using the same platform. Building multiple vehicles on the same platform would allow the companies to design a unique vehicle to reach a specific market niche but without the added high cost of designing a new engine and power train.

In 2003, Veyseh approached various multinational automobile companies (including Fiat, Daimler-Chrysler, Renault-Nissan, and Peugeot-Citroën) to sign joint venture projects with Iran. Renault-Nissan showed the most interest by agreeing to produce its low-cost Logan L90 with all the conditions that Veyseh demanded. The most important provision of this joint venture was Renault-Nissan's willingness to allow Iran to export the automobile to foreign countries, contingent upon its owning dominant shares in the joint venture. The vehicle's low cost (selling price would be approximately $5,000) would optimize Iran's capability to reach high production volumes both at home and abroad. A joint venture with Renault-Nissan was signed in 2005, and both parties agreed to invest $500 million in the project. This was a radical agreement for Iran in two ways: it was the first agreement since the revolution to allow a foreign company majority ownership (51 percent Renault-Nissan) of an

[13] Ibid.

industrial enterprise and the first to include joint ownership by Iranian companies – Iran Khodro and Saipa each owned 24.5 percent of the joint venture.

Veyseh, known to be a highly competent and organized manager, wanted to ascertain the potential benefits of the project before signing on. To do so, he established a twenty-two-member committee composed of managing directors and high-ranking managers from IDRO, Iran Khodro, Saipa, and a consulting company managed by an Iranian engineer who had previously worked at General Motors. The representative from IDRO explained how the committee managed the relationships with Renault in localizing the parts:

> There were negotiations on all aspects of the contract, including economics, trade, technology transfer, and local content. For example, to understand whether we could localize the parts, we needed to know whether we could produce the parts with more advanced technology. At the time, we had 600 parts producers in Iran, so my job was to locate the capacity to make the new parts among these companies.

The committee was structured to deal with problems that arose from localization difficulties:

> There was a hierarchy in the committees to resolve the problems. When the parts supplier companies negotiated with the foreign companies, IDRO was at the top of the hierarchy. If there were any problems – for instance, if the parts company did not agree with Renault's demand – it was brought to the committee and we would try to resolve them. If we could not, it went to the president of IDRO and he negotiated directly with the French.

Disagreements with the French included conflict over royalty payments as well as the type, quantity, and quality of the technology transferred. About 20,000 hours of work on the project took place before the contract was signed.

As soon as the agreement was signed, Hamid Reza Katouzian, chairman of the industrial committee in parliament (he had close ties to Gharavi), began mobilizing against it. He attacked the project as a sellout to a "colonialist power" with ambitions to dominate Iran's automobile market. In addition, he attacked Veyseh for signing an agreement that would undermine Iran's project of creating indigenous technical capacity through the development of national brands. Members of parliament who were aligned with Katouzian and Gharavi in opposing the project claimed they were not against the presence of multinational corporations in Iran but considered themselves "economic activists" who were using "legal capacities as the people's representatives" to get a better deal from

Renault-Nissan in order to "protect the people's rights as well as Iran's interests."[14] Katouzian began attacking the project by criticizing the majority ownership provision, which, according to his perspective, would shift the balance of power within the industry from Iran to the French – who, he believed, intended to dominate Iran's automobile market. According to this perspective, the economic activists were obliged to protect the industry from an insular *mafia* of technocrats led by Reza Veyseh and Minister of Industry Jamshid Jahangir – who were in cahoots with the French in creating a "rent-seeking industry" that undermined technical advancement.[15] These technocrats needed to be taken to task for "wronging their country" by pushing through a project without consulting members of parliament. Katouzian spoke about the greater value of the Samand's contribution to Iran's national vehicle capabilities, adding that if it is not the mission of Iranian automobile manufacturers to build indigenous design capabilities, then the industry should shut its doors.[16]

Katouzian pushed his agenda by demanding that Iran should amend the Logan L90 contract in order to force Renault-Nissan to transfer the organizational and technical capabilities in exchange for access to the Iranian market. He proposed that all L90 vehicles produced by Renault-Nissan for the global market should source 20 percent of their parts from local Iranian parts manufacturers. Reza Veyseh and his group opposed the amendment, claiming that the current agreement was the best deal Iran had ever obtained from a multinational corporation. Parliament suspended the project for two years while the two groups sorted out their disagreements. In the end, Renault-Nissan refused to incorporate the local content amendment. In response, Katouzian and his supporters forced the company to sell its dominant shares in the joint venture. In response to this action, Renault-Nissan did not pull out of the joint venture entirely but did remove the provision that would allow Iran to export the vehicles abroad.

The conflict between the global integration and the national developmental industrialists damaged, but did not destroy, the industry. However, it nixed any chance of integrating the industry into the global economy through joint ventures. According to a high-level executive at one of Iran's largest parts manufacturers, "based on the Renault-Nissan experience, there is not a chance another multinational will enter into an agreement in such a toxic political environment." In addition, the decline of the Iranian rial against the euro doubled the price of the automobile and led to low sales volumes. The vehicle did not sell more than 50,000 units

---

[14] Interview with Hamid Reza Katouzian in "From Assembly to Manufacturing," *Iran International Magazine*, March 2006, No. 39.

[15] "L90 Project in Limbo," *Iran International Magazine*, May 2006, No. 40.

[16] "MPs Slam Opponents of Car Design Plans," *Iran International Magazine*, January 2006, No. 38.

a year. The industry, however, did transfer organizational techniques from Renault-Nissan in the form of the Nissan production system, a variant of the Toyota production system.

Cost Control and the Challenge from the Chinese Parts Supply Chain

When Ahmadinejad became president in 2005, he implemented a contradictory policy of cutting state financial support for the industry while controlling the price of automobiles. Cutting back on favorable loans from state banks resulted in a shift of borrowing to private banks. Of course, borrowing from private banks requires a much higher rate of return compared to borrowing from government-owned banks. Iran's deteriorating economic condition, caused by high inflation, prompted the president's economic advisors to suppress the price of automobiles for the eight years he was president.

The aggregate of these factors, along with the failure of the Renault-Nissan joint venture, dramatically reduced profitability for automobile parts suppliers.[17] Ahmadinejad's decision to curtail favorable government loans to the companies while maintaining the price of completely built-up vehicles proved to be especially dangerous. A manager of a parts manufacturer who was also a board member of the automobile parts business association explained the business environment under Ahmadinejad's government: "[It's like] running on tops of waves in the sea and trying to keep your balance."[18] Many companies were faced with borrowing money from private banks at rates ranging from 15 to 20 percent. When the money dried up, they had difficulty in purchasing raw materials and in paying wages. To compensate for these losses, many automobile parts suppliers turned to imports of inexpensive parts. In general, the number of foreign automobile parts imported into Iran has increased steadily since the early 2000s: in 2001, Iran imported $700 million in automobile parts; by 2011, this amount had more than doubled to $1.78 billion a year.[19] The bulk of the increase is associated with the dramatic rise in automobile production in Iran and with the importation of higher value-added parts from European countries; even so, an increasing majority of the imports were lower-quality parts from China, Turkey, and India. Of these, China accounts for the largest increase: in 2000, Iran imported $380,000 in automobile parts and accessories from China; in 2011, the amount had risen to $189,000,000.

---

[17] The inflation rate in Iran has ranged from 15 to 25 percent per year for the past decade.
[18] Interview, manager at parts supplier company and business association, June 2011.
[19] From the United Nations Comtrade Dataset, http://comtrade.un.org/. Data from 2011.

Lower cost was not the only motivating factor behind sourcing parts from China. As the United States began to increase sanctions on Iran over its nuclear program, President Ahmadinejad incorporated a "go east" strategy in which China supported Iran over its nuclear program and, in return, Iran would increase the purchase of Chinese products.

The rise of China as a cheap source of automobile parts is currently the single largest threat to establishing local, indigenous technical capacity. When profits were squeezed due to price controls and high inflation, the automobile parts suppliers began incorporating cheap Chinese parts into automobile components to maintain profit margins. Tariffs on foreign parts in Iran are set at 15 to 20 percent, depending on the part, and have not changed since the early 1990s. These tariff rates forced local automobile companies in Iran to indigenize parts in the early 1990s through the early 2000s because most automobile parts at that time were manufactured in developed countries (Europe, North America, and Japan), where the cost of labor was much higher. However, by 2005 Chinese automobile parts of reasonable quality could be purchased on a global parts supply chain below the cost of parts manufactured locally in Iran.

Automobile parts companies in Iran incorporate Chinese parts in a few discreet ways. Most components produced by parts manufacturers contain several parts. For example, a company can source some parts in Iran and other parts (that are important to increasing profit margins) from China. Parts sourced from China are assembled together with the Iranian parts in Iranian factories. In this way, parts companies are able to claim high local content by hiding where the parts were made; in most cases, it is very difficult to determine whether the parts were manufactured in China or Iran.

A second method is to source components in batches. For instance, a company can source a certain portion (let's say 25 percent) from Iran and then purchase the same parts at much lower cost from Chinese companies. In this way, the company is able to maintain local manufacturing capabilities but with an increase in profit margins.

A third, more cynical way of sourcing parts from China is to import the parts and stamp "Made in Iran" on them at the port. A high-level manager working at a large parts company explained the dilemma parts companies are facing:

> We have been experiencing an attack from the Chinese economy in our market with low-priced, low-quality parts. Six years ago, a lot of spare parts manufacturers started importing parts from China, India, and Turkey; they repackage and re-label them and claim they are made in Iran. It is not economical anymore to buy only raw materials and manufacture [locally] because inflation is so high.

The two companies most responsible for manufacturing by sourcing components heavily from the global value chain are Ezam and Crouse, two of the largest parts companies in Iran. Both are private companies owned by young technocrats with strong connections to the Islamic leadership. They each produce between $1 and $2 billion a year in automobile parts for the industry. The manufacturing approach of these two companies is controversial. Leaders in the industry who are interested in seeing Iran become more integrated into the global economy view the owners of Ezam and Crouse as engaging in cutting-edge global manufacturing. The older industrial nationalists who worked hard to build the industry in the early 1990s, however, consider these companies to be shallow rent-seekers who are selling out national interests to global capitalism. The younger owners of the companies "don't have the big dreams" like the nationalists of the previous generation, who were the heavy lifters in the movement to build a self-sufficient industry.

One reason why imports of Chinese parts are attractive is that, compared to other global automobile industries, Iran's industry has not modernized its production system. The Iranian auto industry has more than 3 million square meters of factory space, but assembly operations incorporate dated techniques. For instance, few automobile factories in Iran have implemented just-in-time manufacturing techniques. In 2008, a group of automobile managers traveled to India and were surprised to discover that the Suzuki plant used one-third of the space used by Iran Khodro and Saipa. In addition, many parts suppliers face difficulties in obtaining the capital to invest in new machinery. For instance, Iran Tire struggles to supply tires to the industry because its machinery is too old. To make up for the low production volumes, Crouse has established a tire import business.

Impact of US Sanctions

As discussed in previous chapters, the US sanctions on Iran in the 1990s constrained the choices available to the industrialists in building an industry but did not prevent them from doing so. Several European and Asian countries refused to abide by the American sanctions and allowed their companies to establish relationships with Iranian automobile companies. The four most important countries to establish ties with the Iranians were France and Korea (multinational assemblers) and Germany and the United Kingdom (engineering-consulting firms). The sanctions, therefore, effectively became unilateral American sanctions.

In more recent years, the United States has been able to tighten economic sanctions on Iran relating to its nuclear program. In 2010 and 2011, the United States managed to obtain agreement on multilateral sanctions on foreign banks engaging in business transactions with Iran. Implementation of these sanctions brought mixed results. Many industrial managers with nationalist sentiments claimed that the sanctions helped Iran because this forced them to search for innovative ways to improve local, indigenous technical capacity. Other managers reported more difficulty in obtaining the materials needed to make automobile parts. Many of the companies were able to obtain the parts and raw materials but had to do so through intermediaries in countries that did not enforce the sanctions. Difficulties arose, however, when the automobile companies had to pay cash for raw materials or had to pay higher costs to intermediaries who took advantage of Iran's isolation by charging high transaction rates.

In February 2012, the sanction regime began to tighten when General Motors announced an alliance with Peugeot. It agreed to purchase a 7 percent stake in the French company and to engage in the development of joint vehicle platforms and automobile parts. Organizations opposed to American ties with companies doing business in Iran, such as United Against Nuclear Iran (UANI), began to pressure the American government to end Peugeot's exports to Iran. In the summer of 2013, Peugeot announced the end of its relationship with Iran Khodro, and Kia soon followed. As a result of these actions, automobile production in Iran dropped dramatically.

The aggregate of pressures on the Iranian automobile industry – outsourcing to China and sanctions – has *damaged* but *not destroyed* the Iranian automobile industry. Figure 6.1 shows the dramatic drop in

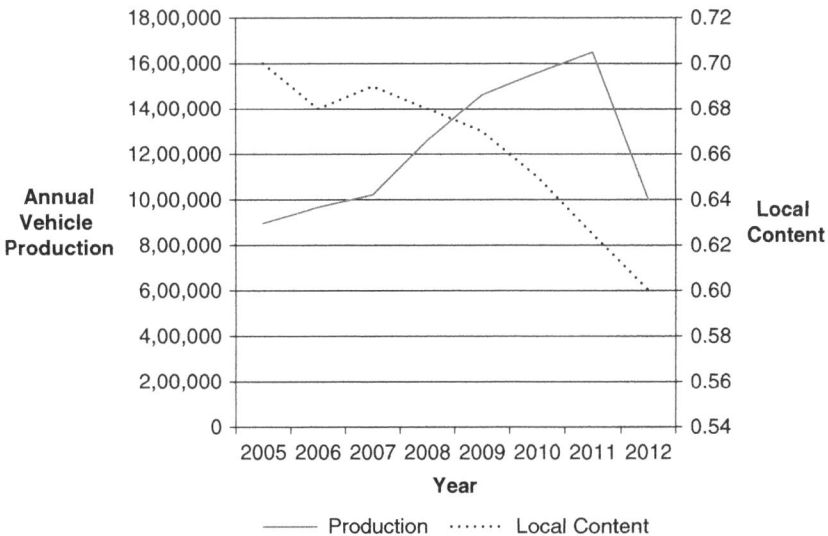

Figure 6.1 Automobile Production and Local Manufacturing Content, 2005–2012

production and local content from 2005 to 2012. In 2005, the Iranian automobile industry was producing 900,000 vehicles a year, and this output increased to just above 1.6 million by 2011. In 2012, however, production dropped to just over 1 million vehicles. Local content dropped from a weighted average of 70 percent in 2005 to approximately 60 percent in 2012. In addition, about 20 percent of the automobile parts manufacturers went out of business.

Is Iran Auto Successful? Comparing Postwar Automobile Industries

To determine the success of Iran's automobile industry, it's important and useful to compare it to that of other countries that have attempted to build national industries. Table 6.2 compares post–World War II automotive industries and those developed since the 1970s. The measures of success include a production volume of greater than 1 million (considered the minimum amount to achieve profitability); the ability to produce vehicles that meet global quality standards, as determined by J.D. Power and

Table 6.2 *Comparing Automobile Industries*

	Postwar		Post-1970s			
	East Asia (Japan, Korea)	Latin America (Mexico, Argentina)	China	India	Malaysia	Iran
Policies						
Infant Industry Protection	Yes	Yes	Yes	Yes	Yes	Yes
Foreign Direct Investment	No	Yes	Yes	Yes	Yes	No
Measures of Success						
Production (> 1 million)	Yes	No	Yes	Yes	No	Yes
Global Quality Standards	Yes	No	No	No	No	No
Exports ($US billions)[20]						
Vehicles	**	**	3.75	3.62	0.183	0.380
Parts	**	**	20.35	2.76	0.825	0.070

[20] Based on 2011 United Nations Comtrade Data, http://comtrade.un.org/. The years 2012 and 2013 are not available for some countries.

Associates; and exports to global markets (meaningful value set at greater than $1 billion).

As seen in the table, infant industry protection is the standard policy tool used by all nations intent on building an industry based on national brands. Its implementation has varied somewhat across nations. In the 1980s, both India and Iran banned imports; however, in the 1990s, both countries established a progressive tariff system similar to those of China and Malaysia.

Foreign direct investment shows interesting results. Japan, South Korea, and Iran are the only countries that have not relied on foreign direct investment as a policy tool. All of the remaining post-1970s countries have relied heavily on foreign direct investment. A developing country can use foreign direct investment in two ways. First, it can allow a multinational corporation access to its market by establishing local operations – but use infant industry protection to force it to transfer the technology. Second, it can engage in a joint venture with a multinational corporation in which each partner has an ownership stake in the venture. China, India, and Malaysia have relied heavily on joint ventures as a key strategy to create local technical capacity. India and Malaysia have relied heavily on Japanese automobile assemblers. And China has relied on a mix of automobile assemblers from the United States, Germany, and Japan.

Joint ventures are particularly important in an era when much of the technology incorporated into modern vehicles requires the transfer of high-level knowledge and skills, such as electronic controls and the manufacture of sophisticated materials. The automobiles produced through the 1980s incorporated technology that was less complicated; hence, much of the technology was developed through reverse engineering. Countries benefit the least in the transfer of technology when foreign-owned subsidiaries are allowed to establish a presence in developing countries and then source parts from their own network of tier 1 "follow-source" suppliers – instead of from local suppliers (Humphrey, 2003; Ivarsson & Alvstam, 2004; Rugraff, 2010).

Turning to measures of success: Iran, India, China, Japan, and South Korea were able to achieve high production volumes. A high production volume of at least 1 million vehicles a year is important for the profitability of a contemporary automobile industry. If production drops below this level, the industry is not profitable and cannot support a parts supply chain. The Malaysian automobile industry was not able to achieve high production volumes because of its low population and the inability to break into local markets dominated by the Japanese.

Interestingly, none of the post-1970 industries has been able to produce vehicles that meet global quality standards. The Japanese were able to achieve high quality by providing incentives for corporations to implement total quality control (TQC). This practice focuses on quality error prevention, making quality the responsibility of every employee and teaching production workers problem-solving tools. The Koreans were able achieve global quality standards by emulating the Japanese in implementing TQC techniques and relying on hiring retired Japanese automobile employees to transfer the tacit knowledge for quality control. It remains to be seen whether any of the newer-developing automobile industries will be able to produce vehicles that meet global quality standards.

Turning to exports of completely built up vehicles of the post-1970 industries: China exports the most, at $3.8 billion; India is second, at $3.6 billion; Iran is third, at $380 million; and Malaysia is last, at $183 million. With respect to parts exports, Iran ranks last, at a meager $70 million a year; and China leads the group at $20 billion a year. India also has a large auto parts exports industry valued at $2.7 billion a year, but Malaysia's industry is barely successful because it exports only $825 million a year. These data indicate that with respect to Iran's isolation from global institutions, the parts industry has suffered.

Even though Iran's isolation from the global economy has dramatically hurt its export capacity – particularly the automobile parts exports – the data should be evaluated with a few caveats. First, the Chinese and Indian automobile markets are much larger than those of Malaysia and Iran. In addition, compared to China and India, the already developed countries have much higher export volumes. For instance, Japan exported $87 billion worth of vehicles and $37 billion worth in parts in 2011. Second, foreign multinational corporations dominate the Chinese, Indian, and Malaysian automobile markets. For instance, domestic vehicle manufacturers control only 30 percent of the Chinese automobile market, so approximately 70 percent of the export value is produced by multinational corporations (Mitchel, 2014).

Conclusion

The classic studies of developmental states assume an alignment between political and industrial elites to implement effective industrial development. This case shows how those alignments can form even in political fields rife with political factions with opposing interests. In Iran, actors in the auto industry were able to form ties to the state apparatus to form political coalitions with key social groups and institutions, thereby enabling the implementation of nationalist policies that insulated the industry from social groups opposed to industrial development. Once sufficient state capacity is built, ties to engineering consulting firms and multinational automobile companies can provide the means to develop an industry with indigenous technical capacity.

This case shows how the construction of a pocket of efficiency in a politically fractious state relies on a higher degree of *agency* to create and sustain a coalition to support industrialization. Furthermore, it shows that the standard path toward building indigenous technical capacity for automobile industrial development does not need to privilege relations between global firms that dominate the end market for final products and national industries in less developed countries. In addition, this case shows how sequencing in the evolution of the state's role may be important in facilitating effective development. The construction of Iran's auto industry was the result of a process of collective action by elite managers of the industry at specific historical time periods where events and institutions helped shape positive development outcomes. However, by analyzing sequencing, this study reveals that a development project in an intermediate state is one that is "fragile." Once an industry is established, over time it can be weakened by unanticipated events, internal struggles, and social forces opposed to the vision of those who constructed it. The remainder of this section will focus on how this case study informs the current industrial development literature.

153

Development of the Iranian automobile industry passed through three main time periods: evolution from conflict to state capacity, coherent state-led development, and the defense of nationalist industrial policies. The first period was marked by a struggle between the leftists, who supported agriculture over industrial development, and the neoliberals, who supported imports over localization. The conflict with the agriculturalists resulted in a compromise, whereas the conflict with the neoliberals resulted in a crisis and the rise of industrial nationalists to dominate the automobile industry policy agenda. Strong lobbying ties among high-ranking automobile industrial managers, the development bureaucracy, and members of the parliament were key components in the establishment of a "pocket of efficiency" for the automobile sector. This argument builds on and extends the idea that "pockets of efficiency" within the state may be sufficient to achieve industrial transformation in a particular sector. It suggests that we should think about "autonomy" not just in relation to private interests but also in relation to parts of the state that do not share a developmental agenda.

Once the industrial nationalists dominated the automobile policy agenda, the automotive industry entered its second phase. Feedback was important in constructing coherent industrial policy and in coordinating the activities necessary for industrial development. The increase in the industry's profitability, the number of automobile parts companies, and the manufacture of higher value-added parts with the assistance of engineering consulting firms all worked to increase the embeddedness of the industry in Iranian society by increasing employment.

This embeddedness became important in the third phase, when social groups opposed to national development pushed to abandon infant industry protection and when the government implemented privatization. The Supreme Leader had an interest in protecting automobile manufacturing jobs, whereas the industrial nationalists wanted to protect the automobile market from foreign competition. Although the Islamic Leadership entered the automobile industry via Iran's Revolutionary Guard Corps, strong infant industry protection laws prevented that group from expanding its market share. As the industry became more successful, political coalitions became important in order to distribute the success more widely in return for industry support. The political coalition functioned as a protection pact to eliminate rivals perceived to be a danger to the industrial nationalists' privileges.

This study shows that strategic action to build coalitions for implementing nationalist industrial policies – and then to protect the policies – was an important factor in the rise of the Iranian automobile industry. This agency by industrial nationalists builds on the pockets of efficiency and the concept of sequencing in a few important ways. First, it shows that nationalists were able to decouple a key set of organizations sufficiently from other parts of the state apparatus to create a "pocket of efficiency" within the automotive sector. It differs from previous studies that argue that a pocket of efficiency is created largely through a top-down approach where a ranking state actor creates and protects the development organization from social groups seeking to undermine it. Second, this case shows that industrialists can build an industry through a middle-up lobbying process: they can use their ties to the state apparatus to construct a coalition to defeat opposition to the industry and thus realize their development goals.

This research also informs current scholarship concerning what embedded autonomy looks like in intermediate states. First, autonomy related to Weberian bureaucratic coherence attained through meritocracy is less important. Instead, autonomy is associated with the ability of pro-industry technocrats to engage in elite lobbying and to position the industry as a way to resolve economic problems. Once industrial nationalists gained control of the automotive industry, they were united by a shared industrial nationalist ideology. This research also adds insight into the concept of embeddedness and industrial development. In the case of Iran Auto, ties between the industrial nationalists and the development bureaucracy were key in providing feedback and monitoring to correct bad policy decisions. In addition, ties to form alliances with important social groups and institutions were key variables in the development of the industry. This case study shows that intermediate states can't rely solely on embeddedness between the development bureaucracy and the industry but instead must engage in strategic action to build alliances and coalitions apart from the development project to protect the integrity of industrial policy.

This research also highlights the concept of sequencing in the development of state capacity. Successful lobbying by industrialists confirms recent findings that coherence from exclusionary (instead of obligatory) business associations is effective in implementing coherent policies. However, it also shows that the historical time period and the network position of elites within the industrial hierarchy were important factors. Industrialists in the automobile committee were effective: they were well positioned during economic crises to defeat opposition to automobile development by voicing their opinions to high-level bureaucrats in the Ministry of Heavy Industry. Settlement of political conflicts and implementation of infant industry protection were key factors in constructing coherent policies. Later, after the Iran Automobile Manufacturers' Association had been founded and had developed into a large association, the industrial elites were effective: they represented a constituency of large manufacturers and parts companies that became ever more important to Iran's economy as the industry rapidly developed.

Later, the coalition became a protection pact when social groups pushed to abandon infant industry protection and the government implemented privatization. The Supreme Leader had an interest in protecting automobile manufacturing jobs, whereas industrial nationalists wanted to protect the automobile market from outside competition. Although the Islamic leadership entered the automobile industry via Iran's Revolutionary Guard Corps, strong infant industry protection laws prevented that group from expanding its market share. As the industry became more successful, elite alliances gained importance by distributing the success more widely in return for industry support. The elite alliances functioned as a protection pact to eliminate rivals perceived to threaten the elites' privileges. This research differs from previous studies, however, in that the coalition was localized within the automobile sector and relied on agreements among factions supporting national industrial policies in exchange for distributing its success to constituents.

This research also informs development network state theory by showing that pockets of development can exist in countries with fragmented institutions. Once the industrial nationalists had dominated the automobile policy agenda, they facilitated and coordinated the activities necessary for deep industrial development. The increase in the industry's profitability, the number of automobile parts companies, and the manufacture of higher value-added parts with the assistance of engineering consulting firms all worked to increase the technical and organizational capacity of the industry and to increase embeddedness of the industry in Iranian society by improving employment. Moreover, business-state relationships for the automobile project became highly legitimate because it was able to achieve long-term national development goals.

The application of neo-institutional theory was important in analyzing the cultural framing used to create a pocket of efficiency in the automobile industry. Field theory and social skill were particularly important for understanding industry outcomes during the critical juncture years (1988–1992). The reform period was a critical turning point because changes in the political and economic field led to the creation of different institutions and political alliances that shaped the long-term development of the industry.

These changes inform our understanding of social field theory and industrial development in a couple of important ways. First, it is understood that successful outcomes can be achieved when strategic actors provide cultural frames for motivating others to engage in collective action. Rafsanjani contributed to building state capacity by reframing Islam away from a populist-leftist agenda and by appointing technocrats over religious ideologues into positions within the state apparatus. The reframing away from leftist economic policies to a pro-business agenda also helped legitimize entrepreneurship. Rafsanjani's neoliberal policies, however, undermined industrial development because they favored importers over local manufacturing. The action of Rafsanjani opened up a space for the industrial nationalists to use their ties to the political apparatus to build a coalition to create a relatively successful industry. They used the cultural framing of building a "national" industry to legitimize support for it.

The events that occurred at the intersection of the political and economic field proved important for positive development outcomes. The field of the automotive industry is partially constituted by its relationship to the state (the political field), but an important part of the story is how the industrial nationalists, through middle-up collective action and lobbying, carved out the autonomy from the state. Here, Iran Auto operated in two sorts of ways: it had to manage its relationship to the state, but it also had to manage its economic field of suppliers and customers. This arrangement suggests that the industrial managers were using even more social skill compared to Rafsanjani because they were balancing two games, not one. In the long run the relationship between the political and economic field remained relatively stable because key actors in both fields benefited from the success of the automobile industry. Rafsanjani and the political leaders who succeeded him could claim success of supplying jobs and needed goods to an economy based on oil, and the industrial nationalists and their firms profited from high rates of entrepreneurship, local manufacturing, and indigenous technical capacity.

The case of Iran Auto shows that scholars who study intermediate states can enhance their understanding of positive development outcomes by incorporating the field theoretic approach. From the embedded autonomy perspective, the political project of states and bureaucrats are potentially separate from the economic projects of business elites. The "right" amount of autonomy between them can lead to positive development outcomes. So, if the state is too dominant, the result is patrimonialism, and if business is not connected to the state, there can be rent-seeking and crony capitalism where economic actors buy off state officials producing suboptimal outcomes. Development is optimized when states create space for entrepreneurs but remain in control of regulation and the rule of law. Field theory helps us analyze the relationship between states and industries by providing the notion that a sector of the economy can be conceived of as a place where firms face off with similar firms and states contain multiple fields that are organized to interact with societal actors, including firms. There are three sorts of relationships: one field can dominate another, the fields can exist symbiotically (i.e., interdependence), or no relationship at all. Embedded autonomy is weak when one field has too much power over the other: too much state is patrimonialism; too much market is crony capitalism. Getting a more symbiotic relation produces more optimal outcomes. In the case of Iran Auto, the industrial nationalists carving out autonomy for the auto industry by using their influence in the political field is half of the story, but the other half is that the firms in the sector form a coalition to defend the autonomy of the sector. The field concept therefore helps the embedded autonomy argument by providing a social structural way to understand how two fields relate and what can cause good or bad outcomes.

The second contribution of this case study to field theory is in understanding the factors behind the formation of state capacity. The industry began under the Shah's rule, after he used the state apparatus and his relationship with the United States to suppress or crush groups opposed to industrial development. State entrepreneurs were then granted the autonomy to establish the industry while import substitution protected it. After the revolution, crushing of opposition groups was not an option. Many of the social groups and factions that had formed had powerful constituencies that could not be suppressed. Instead, political action that led to coalitions became the way to establish autonomy. The political action by the industrial nationalists to build an industry was particularly effective because of strong within-group coherence held together by a shared nationalist ideology. In later years when this coherence began to fray because of conflict among those who supported building a global parts supplier network over local assembly, the industrial nationalists were united in opposing liberalization of the industry. This fracturing of the industrial nationalists therefore did not undermine the goal of building a national industry. An important factor that could have produced enough power for the industrialists to achieve their goal of opposing liberalization was that both the parts suppliers and assemblers had network-based ties of economic interdependence: as manufacturers their ability to produce profits relied on protecting the market from outside social groups.

Although this research argues that the formation of specific state structures was instrumental in positive development outcomes, the development path of the auto industry has been shaped largely by institutional structures created both by the Iranian revolution and, earlier, by the Shah. It is important to note that no other industry in Iran has dealt with such strict infant industry protection laws. During the Shah's reign, the automobile industry was successful (compared to other industries), and a critical number of companies were founded. Top managers of these companies were on the Automobile Committee established by the Ministry of Industry during the Rafsanjani presidency. During the critical juncture years of the early 1990s, the automobile industry was still relatively large compared to other industries, and its leaders therefore had the power to implement their policy preferences in the Automobile Committee and through political connections in the parliament. Most other industries had – and continue to have – weak connections to the state apparatus because they are not government-owned (i.e., are entirely private) or are dominated by small and medium-sized enterprises instead of large manufacturers. Hence they have business associations where political power is too fragmented.[1]

In addition, the unique organizational form of the Islamic cooperative established after the revolution helped preserve development outcomes consistent with the industrial nationalist agenda. During the privatization movement of the 1990s, the business associations and the automobile companies formed a coalition to found cooperatives for purchasing major shares in the large automobile companies. This was done in order to avoid transferring ownership to organizations and companies that did not share the same industrial-nationalist ideological agenda. This maneuver helped keep ownership of the industry away from social groups with interests in dismantling the industry. In addition, the stakeholder arrangement of minor shareholders provided further insulation from these groups because ownership was dispersed mostly among organizations within the same group who shared similar interests.

This shift in industry ownership resulted from the formation of a coalition between government and industrialists to support mutual interests. The coalition informs our understanding of what industries look like in intermediate states. The Iranian government was reluctant to give up control of large industrial organizations because the social groups with sufficient capital to purchase the industry were not aligned with its domestic and geopolitical goals. These goals, considered important for Iran's "national security," included providing the country with high-quality industry jobs, expansion of the industry abroad, and prevention of another currency crisis caused by foreign automobile imports. The industrial nationalists supported government ownership of the industry because losing control would have undermined their profits. One can argue that this is a case of crony capitalism, where industrialists use their ties to the government to maintain ownership control and protection of the industry to enrich themselves. However, I argue that in an intermediate state where political factionalism and patrimony are deeply embedded in social institutions and social groups, an industry dominated by engineers and technocrats, even if they are rent-seeking, is perhaps the best possible outcome. For instance, had the industry fallen into the hands of neoliberals or left-wing agriculturalists during its development trajectory, it is likely Iran would not have a significant automobile industry.

Finally, historical contingencies played a large role in shaping development outcomes. In the early 1990s, infant industry protection in automobile manufacturing was viewed as a legitimate long-term policy to deal

---

[1] Interview with board member of non-automobile business association, December 2013.

with Iran's currency problems. The use of infant industry protection would not have been legitimate, had the left (which dominated the political field in the 1980s) banned automobile imports. Thus by the late 1980s, the pent-up demand, together with the liberalization of trade, resulted in a sharp increase in imports for automobiles – an important factor that led to the economic crisis. Had the left not banned automobiles, it would have been more difficult for the industrial nationalists to make a case for promoting policies that supported local manufacturing.

The case of Iran Auto builds on network-centered theory by illustrating that the global reconfiguration of industrial production has created a diversity of global networks in whose construction the state can play a role. Most important, it shows how small firms can collaborate with the state in finding ways to help break a multinational assembler's control over intellectual property rights. In addition to technology transfer, the consulting firms worked with the state to build the financial and organizational capacity to help achieve project success. This collaboration is particularly important in countries where conventional forms of technology transfer – those accessible to globally more integrated countries – are not available. Whereas globally more integrated countries can rely more heavily on ties to global technology through foreign direct investment and joint ventures to create a synergy that can lead to new innovations, Iran's global isolation meant that it had to rely on engineering consultancies to replicate the synergy important for its industrial development project.

The case of Iran Auto highlights both the strengths and weaknesses of unilateral versus multilateral sanctions. The global reconfiguration of industrial production is the most important variable in understanding the limits of sanctions. Through 2011, the United States' unilateral sanctions, designed to punish Iran over its nuclear program, were not effective because European and Asian countries refused to abide by the sanctions. While American companies were barred from doing business with Iran, French, German, and Korean companies were not. Iranian automobile companies could therefore access a diverse global network of ties to companies to obtain the technology and resources for the project. Most importantly, since most of the high-powered engineering consultancies are located in Europe, Iran was able to deepen its indigenous technical capacity despite the American sanctions regime. When multilateral sanctions were applied in 2012, preventing European and Asian companies from doing business with Iran, the industry began to decline. This case therefore shows that multilateral as opposed to unilateral sanctions are far more effective in influencing a state's behavior.

This research also deepens the understanding of how development of global value chains has shaped current possibilities for automobile industrial upgrading. An important point about current possibilities is that the use of global corporate networks to develop an industry shows that they are not homogeneous. Different sorts of global corporate networks have very different properties and very different implications for national industrial development. For instance, engineering consulting firms not only help the state to create an innovation system with greater indigenous technical capacity, they can do it more quickly than if the developing country had to rely on the step-by-step process of industrial upgrading during an era of vertical integration. Whereas any country can hire consulting firms, the rise of global value chains has led to greater opportunities for developing countries to create more independent automobile industries. Once the ability to design vehicles and engines is transferred, developing countries can use the ties to global parts suppliers to redesign the products or create new brands independent of multinational assemblers. For a country not so globally isolated as Iran, a sound strategy might be to establish ties with engineering consulting firms to obtain value-added technology. Similarly, it might be strategically advantageous to form joint-venture ties with multinational firms to obtain organizational techniques (such as quality control) and to use their global ties to sell locally manufactured products on a global supply chain.

Although the role of engineering consulting firms proposed in this book is based on a single case study, these firms are currently being used in other developing countries. China recently developed into the most important market for the consultancies. Here, Ricardo is currently developing in-house R&D capabilities for Shanghai Automotive Industrial Corporation.[2] FEV's recently opened China Technical Center in Dalian is managed by its engine experts and staffed with 100 German and Chinese engineers.[3] Since the mid-1990s, Pininfarina has created more than two dozen automobile designs for a variety of Chinese companies.[4]

This research also confirms certain propositions of the developmental state perspective while contradicting others. It confirms the developmental state perspective – that rejecting global rules helps open up a policy space to implement infant industry protection and reverse engineering for meaningful industrial development. For instance, Iran is not a World Trade Organization member and so does not need to follow the rules stipulated by the Agreement of Trade-Related Aspects of Intellectual Property Rights (TRIPS). However, the research contradicts this perspective by showing that less developed countries can gain access to high technology through global corporate networks.

Despite the relative success of the automobile industry, the pockets of efficiency and technology transfer model presented here is "fragile."

[2] Economic Intelligence Unit, *Driven: Are Chinese Car Manufacturers Ready to Compete in the US and Europe?* 2006.
[3] China Technical Center, www.fev.com/content/public/default.aspx?id=571.
[4] www.businessweek.com/ap/financialnews/D9FT95EO0.htm.

Managing directors of the automobile companies and members of the development bureaucracies are political appointees, so the political will to engage in nationalist development can be weakened if those appointed do not share the same ideological orientation. In addition, nationalistic policies are only as strong as the alliance that holds them together. It is widely held that years of protection have resulted in an industry that still cannot succeed against foreign competition. For instance, automobile quality has become a major issue because the industry enjoys a near-monopoly. If the industry loses its legitimacy due to continuing problems with quality, the alliance may collapse. In addition, in recent years the Ahmadinejad government has undermined development through incoherent policies, such as price controls. Furthermore, the government's anti-American rhetoric and the unresolved nuclear issue resulted in strict sanctions that damaged production capacity and profitability. All of these factors precipitated a more recent downturn in the industry.

President Rouhani's government has recently reversed price control policies, and the recent nuclear agreement has helped revive the industry. European engineering consulting firms and large automobile producers are now allowed to resume business with Iranian companies. Production is reaching pre-sanctions level, and Iranian automobile companies are establishing new relationships with multinational automobile companies and strengthening old ones. The case of Iran Auto, therefore, shows that in intermediate states, a development project is highly influenced by internal and external social forces and events at specific historical time periods, phenomena that may open up opportunities for its success or, conversely, may precipitate its downturn. These swings in social forces outside the development project, as well as internal politics that can lead to an increase or decrease in state capacity, may result in automobile industries with mixed outcomes. Still, compared to the success of automobile development in other developing countries, the capacity to produce 1.6 million vehicles with an average local content of 60 percent is a significant accomplishment.

In addition to this fragility, the use of engineering consulting firms is not without risks. With the Samand, Iran Khodro's first national project, the consultancies did not transfer target-pricing techniques; therefore, the final cost of the vehicle was above the target price. Consequently, its manufacture did not reach the economies of scale to make it a financially lucrative project. In addition, to ensure success, a country needs to have sufficient infrastructure and political stability to absorb the technology and keep it within its borders. A turnkey project, where the consulting firm designs the product based on client specifications and delivers it to the client, can help remedy this problem. Turnkey projects, however, do not help build technical capacity because they do not involve technology transfer.

Since engineering firms occupy a niche in vehicle or engine design, no engineering consultancy offers one-stop shopping for all technology. Even though consulting firms can transfer the knowledge to integrate technologies to a high level of fit and finish for certain components, such as engines, no single firm can integrate all the technologies and components for the entire vehicle. Furthermore, although Iran has not been able to fully achieve manufacturing independence, approximately 30 percent of the parts for vehicles with the highest local content are still purchased from abroad.

Finally, this case study applies to an industry in its advanced stages and in which the market for technology is highly mature. The same may not hold true for higher-tech industries, where technology is moving at a much quicker rate and the technology is more highly protected.

Bibliography

Abbott, J. P. (2003). *Developmentalism and Dependency in Southeast Asia: The Case of the Automotive Industry*. London: RoutledgeCurzon.

Abrahamian, E. (1982). *Iran between Two Revolutions*. Princeton: Princeton University Press.

(1993). *Khomeinism: Essays on the Islamic Republic*. Berkeley: University of California Press.

Akhavi-pour, H. (1992). Barriers to Private Entrepreneurship in Iran. *Middle East Critique*, 54–63.

Alizadeh, P. (1984). *The Process of Import Substitution Industrialization in Iran (1960–1978)*. University of Sussex (unpublished dissertation).

Amirahmadi, H. (1990). *Revolution and Economic Transition: The Iranian Experience*. Albany: State University of New York Press.

Amsden, A. (1989). *Asia's Next Giant*. New York, Oxford: Oxford University Press.

Amuzegar, J. (1997a). Adjusting to Sanctions. *Foreign Affairs*, 76 (3), 31–41.

(1977). *Iran: An Economic Profile*. Washington, DC: Middle East Institute.

(1997b). *Iran's Economy under the Islamic Republic*. London: I.B. Taurus.

(2005). Iran's Third Development Plan: An Appraisal. *Middle East Policy*, 12 (3).

Arndt, S. W., & Kierzkowski, H. (2001). *Fragmentation: New Production Patterns in the World Economy*. Oxford: Oxford University Press.

Baktiari, B. (1996). *Parliamentary Politics in Revolutionary Iran: The Institutionalization of Factional Politics*. Gainesville: University Press Florida.

Bessant, J., & Rush, H. (1995). Building Bridges for Innovation: The Role of Consultants in Technology Transfer. *Research Policy*, 24, 97–114.

Bhagwati, J. (2004). *In Defense of Globalization*. Oxford: Oxford University Press.

Biggart, N. W., & Guillen, M. F. (1999). Developing Differences: Social Organization and the Rise of Auto Industries of South Korea, Taiwan, Spain, and Argentina. *American Sociological Review*, 722–747.

Block, F. (2008). Swimming against the Current: The Rise of the Hidden Development State in the United States. *Politics and Society*, 36 (2), 169–206.

Block, F., & Keller, M. (2011). *State of Innovation: The U.S. Government Role in Technological Development*. Oxfordshire: Paradigm Publishers.

Breznitz, D. (2007). *Innovation and the State: Political Choices and Strategies for Growth in Israel, Taiwan and Ireland*. New Haven: Yale University Press.

Breznitz, D., & Murphree, M. (2011). *Run of the Red Queen: Government, Innovation, Globalization, and Economic Growth in China*. New Haven: Yale University Press.

Breznitz, D., & Ornston, D. (2013). The Revolutionary Power of Peripheral Agencies: Explaining Radical Policy Innovation in Finland and Israel. *Comparative Political Studies*, 1–27.

Brumberg, D. (2001). *Reinventing Khomeini*. Chicago: University of Chicago Press.

Brzezinski, Z., Scowcroft, B., & Murphy, R. (1997). Differentiated Containment. *Foreign Affairs*, 76 (3), 20–30.

Carlos, W. C., Sine, W. D., Lee, B., & Haveman, H. (2011). Gone with the Wind: Industry Development and the Evolution of Social Movement Influence. *Johnson School of Business Working Paper*.

Carroll, G., & Swaminathan, A. (2000). Why the Microbrewery Movement? Organizational Dynamics and Resource Partitioning in the U.S. Brewing Industry. *American Journal of Sociology*, 106, 715–767.

Chang, H.-J. (2002). *Kicking Away the Ladder: Development Strategy in Historical Perspective*. London: Anthem Press.

Cheng, T.-J., Haggard, S., & Kang, D. (1998). Institutions and Growth in Korea and Taiwan: The Bureaucracy. *Journal of Development Studies*, 36 (4), 87–111.

Chibber, V. (2002). Bureaucratic Rationality and the Developmental State. *American Journal of Sociology*, 107 (4), 951–989.

(2006). *Locked in Place: State-Building and Late Industrialization in India*. Princeton: Princeton University Press.

Cole, R. E., & Flynn, M. (2009). Automotive Quality Reputation: Hard to Achieve, Hard to Lose, Still Harder to Win Back. *California Management Review*, 52 (1).

Collier, R. B., & Collier, D. (2002). *Shaping the Political Arena: Critical Junctures, the Labor Movement and Regime Dynamics in Latin America*. Notre Dame: University of Notre Dame Press.

Creswell, J. (2013). *Research Design: Qualitative, Quantitative and Mixed Methods Approaches*. Thousand Oaks: SAGE Publications.

D'Costa, A. P. (1995). The Restructuring of the Indian Automobile Industry: Indian State and Japanese Capital. *World Development*, 23 (3), 485–502.

Dexter, L. (2008). *Elite and Specialized Interviewing*. Colchester: European Consortium for Political Research Press.

Doner, R. F. (1991). *Driving a Bargain: Automobile Industrialization and Japanese Firms in Southeast Asia*. Berkeley: University of California Press.

Doner, R. F., Ritchie, B. K., & Slater, D. (2005). Systematic Vulnerability and the Origins of Developmental States: Northeast and Southeast Asia in Comparative Perspective. *International Organization*, 59 (2), 327–361.

Ernst & Young. (2010). *Hitting the Sweet Spot: The Growth of the Middle Class in Emerging Markets*. New York: Ernst & Young.

Evans, P. B. (1979). *Dependent Development: The Alliance of Multinational, State and Local Capital in Brazil*. Princeton: Princeton University Press.

(1997). The Eclipse of the State? Reflections on Stateness in the Era of Globalization. *World Politics*, 50 (1), 62–87.

(1995). *Embedded Autonomy: States and Industrial Transformation*. Princeton: Princeton University Press.

(1998). Transferable Lessons? Re-examining the Institutional Prerequisites of East Asian Economic Policies. *Journal of Development Studies*, 34 (6), 66–86.

Evans, P., Reuschemeyer, D., & Skocpol, T. (1985). *Bringing the State Back In*. Cambridge: Cambridge University Press.

Fayazmanesh, S. (2010). *The United States and Iran: Sanctions, Wars and the Policy of Dual Containment*. London: Routledge.

Fligstein, N. (1996). The Economic Sociology of the Transition from Socialism. *American Journal of Sociology*, 101 (4), 1074–1081.

(2001). Social Skill and the Theory of Fields. *Sociological Theory*, 19 (2), 105–125.

(1993). *The Transformation of Corporate Control*. Cambridge, MA: Harvard University Press.

Fligstein, N., & McAdam, D. (2012). *A Theory of Fields*. Oxford: Oxford University Press.

(2011). Toward a General Theory of Strategic Action Fields. *Sociological Theory*, 29 (1), 1–26.

Foran, J. (1993). *Fragile Resistance: Social Transformation in Iran from 1500 to the Revolution*. Boulder: Westview.

Freyssenet, M. (2009). *The Second Automobile Revolution: Trajectories of the World Carmakers in the 21st Century*. New York: Palgrave Macmillan.

Gasiorowski, M. J., & Byrne, M. (2004). *Mohammad Mosaddeq and the 1953 Coup in Iran*. Syracuse: Syracuse University Press.

Gasiorowski, M. (1991). *U.S. Foreign Policy and the Shah: Building a Client State in Iran*. Ithaca: Cornell University Press.

Geddes, B. (1990). Building "State" Autonomy in Brazil. *Comparative Politics*, 22 (2).

(1994). *Politician's Dilemma: Building State Capacity in Latin America*. Berkeley: University of California Press.

Gereffi, G., & Korzeniewicz, M. (1994). *Commodity Chains and Global Capitalism*. Westport, CT: Praeger.

Gerlach, M. (1997). *Alliance Capitalism: The Social Organization of Japanese Business*. Berkeley: University of California Press.

Gerschenkron, A. (1962). *Economic Backwardness in Historical Perspective*. Cambridge: Belknap.

Greve, H., Pozner, J.-E., & Rao, H. (2006). Vox Populi: Resource Partitioning, Organizational Proliferation, and the Cultural Impact of the Insurgent Microradio Movement. *American Journal of Sociology*, 112 (3), 802–837.

Guthrie, D. (2001). *Dragon in a Three-Piece Suite: The Emergence of Capitalism in China*. Princeton: Princeton University Press.

Halliday, F. (1979). *Iran: Dictatorship and Development*. London: Penguin Books.

Hamdhaidari, S., Agahi, H., & Papzan, A. (2008). Higher Education during the Islamic Government of Iran, 1979–2004. *International Journal of Education Development*, 28 (3).

Hargadon, A., & Sutton, R. I. (1997). Technology Brokering and Innovation in a Product Development Firm. *Administrative Science Quarterly*, 42, 716–749.

Harris, K. (2010). Lineages of the Iranian Welfare State: Dual Institutionalism and Social Policy in the Islamic Republic of Iran. *Social Policy and Administration*, 44 (6), 727–745.

(2013). The Rise of the Subcontractor State: Politics of Pseudo-Privatization in the Islamic Republic of Iran. *International Journal of Middle East Studies*.

Harvey, D. (2007). *A Brief History of Neo-liberalism*. Oxford: Oxford University Press.

Harwit, E. (1995). *China's Automobile Industry: Policies, Problems and Prospects*. London: Routledge.

(2001). The Impact of WTO Membership on the Automobile Industry in China. *China Quarterly*.

Hau, M. v. (2013). *Beyond Good Governance: New Perspectives on State Capacity and Development*. Paper presented at the American Sociological Association. New York.

Hertog, S. (2010). Defying the Resource Curse: Explaining Successful State-Owned Enterprises in Rentier States. *World Politics*, 62 (2), 261–301.

Holland, S. (1972). State Entrepreneurship and State Intervention. In S. Holland, *The State and Entrepreneur: New Dimensions in Public Enterprise*. London: Weidenfeld and Nicolson.

Hout, W. (2007). Development under Patrimonial Conditions: Suriname's State Oil Company as a Development Agent. *Journal of Development Studies*, 43 (8), 1331–1350.

Humphrey, J. (2003). Globalization and Supply Chain Networks: The Auto Industry in Brazil and India. *Global Networks*, 2, 212–241.

Ivarsson, I., & Alvstam, C. G. (2004). International Technology Transfer through Local Business Linkages: The Case of Volvo Trucks and Their Domestic Suppliers in India. *Oxford Development Studies*, 32 (2), 241–260.

Jenkins, R. (1987). *Transnational Corporations and the Latin American Automobile Industry*. Pittsburgh: University of Pittsburgh Press.

Johnson, C. (1982). *MITI and the Japanese Miracle: The Growth of Industrial Policy, 1925–1975*. Stanford: Stanford University Press.

Jonathan, D., & Putzel, J. (2009). *Political Settlements*. Discussion Paper. Birmingham: University of Birmingham.

Karl, T. L. (1997). *The Paradox of Plenty: Oil Booms and Petro States*. Berkeley: University of California Press.

Katouzian, H. (1981). *The Political Economy of Modern Iran: Despotism and Pseudo-Modernism, 1926–1979*. New York: New York University Press.

Keddie, N. (2006). *Modern Iran: Roots and Results of Revolution*. New Haven: Yale University Press.

Keller, M., & Block, F. (2012). Explaining the Transformation in the US innovation System: The Impact of a Small Government Program. *Socio-Economic Review*, 1–28.

Keshavarzian, A. (2009). *Bazaar and State in Iran: The Politics of the Tehran Marketplace*. Cambridge: Cambridge University Press.

Khajehpour, B. (2014, 7 January). Can Rouhani reverse Iran's brain drain? *Al-Monitor*.

Khan, M. H. (2010). *Political Settlements and the Governance of Growth-Enhancing Institutions*. London: SOAS Mimeo.

Khan, M. (2004). State Failure in Developing Countries and Institutional Reform Strategy. In B. Tungodden, N. H. Stern, & I. Kolstad, *Toward Pro-Poor Policies: Aid, Institutions and Globalization* (pp. 165–196). Oxford: Oxford University Press.

Kim, L. (2004). The Multifaceted Evolution of Korean Technical Capabilities and Its Implications for Technical Policy. *Oxford Development Studies*, 32 (3), 341–363.

Kohli, A. (2010). *Democracy and Development in India: From Socialism to Pro-Business*. Oxford: Oxford University Press.

(2004). *State-Directed Development: Political Power and Industrialization in the Global South*. Cambridge: Cambridge University Press.

Kronish, R., & Mericle, K. (1984). *The Political Economy of the Latin American Motor Vehicle Industry*. Cambridge, MA: MIT Press.

Lall, S. (1992). Technological Capabilities and Industrialization. *World Development*, 20 (2), 165–186.

La Porta, R., Lopez-De-Salinas, F., Shleifer, A., & Vishny, R. (1998). Law and Finance. *Journal of Political Economy*, 1113–1155.

(1999, March). The Quality of Government. *Journal of Law, Economics and Organization*, 222–279.

Levi-Faur, D., & Jordana, J. (2005, March). Regulatory Capitalism: Policy Irritants and Convergent Divergence. *The Annals of the American Academy*, 191–197.

MacKenzie, D. (2010, 18 February). Iran Showing Fastest Scientific Growth of Any Country. *New Scientist*.

Mahoney, J. (2000). Path Dependence in Historical Sociology. *Theory and Society*, 29, 507–548.

Mahoney, J. (2001). Radical, Reformist and Aborted Liberalism: Origins of National Regimes in Central America. *Journal of Latin America Studies*, 33 (2), 221–256.

Maloney, S. (2000). Agents or Obstacles? Parastatal Foundations and Challenges for Iranian Development. In P. Alizadeh, *The Economy of Iran: Dilemmas of an Islamic State*. London: I.B. Tauris.

Milani, A. (2008). *Eminent Persians: The Men and Women Who Made Modern Iran, 1941–1979*. Syracuse: Syracuse University Press.

Mitchel, T. (2014, 5 May). China's Indigenous Brand Policy Backfires. *Financial Times*.

Mizruchi, M. (1992). *The Structure of Corporate Political Action: Interfirm Relations and Their Consequences*. Cambridge, MA: Harvard University Press.

Moore, P. W. (2004). *Doing Business in the Middle East: Politics and Economic Crisis in Jordon and Kuwait*. Cambridge: Cambridge University Press.

(2001). What Makes Successful Business Lobbies? Business Associations and the Rentier State in Jordon and Kuwait. *Comparative Politics*, 33 (2), 127–147.

Moslem, M. (2002). *Factional Politics in Post-Khomeini Iran.* Syracuse: Syracuse University Press.

Moyser, G. (2006). Elite Interviewing. In V. Jupp, *The SAGE Dictionary of Social Research Methods* (pp. 85–87). London: Sage Publications.

Negoita, M., & Block, F. (2012). Networks and Public Policies in the Global South: The Chilean Case and the Future of the Developmental Network State. *Studies in Comparative International Development, 47*, 1–22.

Noble, G. W. (2013). The Chinese Auto Industry as Challenge, Opportunity and Partner. In D. Breznitz & J. Zysman, *The Third Globalization? Can Wealthy Nations Stay Rich in the Twenty-first Century.* Oxford: Oxford University Press.

Nohria, N., & Garcia-Pont, C. (1991). Global Strategic Linkages and Industry Structure. *Strategic Management Journal, 12*, 105–124.

North, D., Wallis, J. J., & Weingast, B. (2009). *Violence and Social Orders: A Conceptual Framework for Interpreting Recorded Human History.* New York: Cambridge University Press.

O'Riain, S. (2000). The Flexible Developmental State: Globalization, Information Technology and the "Celtic Tiger." *Politics and Society*, 28 (2), 157–193.

(2004). *The Politics of High-Tech growth: Developmental Network States and the Global Economy.* Cambridge: Cambridge University Press.

Perrow, C. (1984). *Normal Accidents: Living with High-Risk Technologies.* New York: Basic Books.

Peters, A. M., & Moore, P. W. (2009). Beyond Boom and Bust: External Rents, Durable Authoritarianism, and Institutional Adaptation in the Hasemite Kingdom of Jordon. *Studies in Comparative International Development, 44*, 256–285.

Pierson, P. (2004). *Politics in Time: History, Institutions and Social Analysis.* Princeton: Princeton University Press.

Pozner, M. V., & Woolf, S. J. (1967). *Italian Public Enterprise.* Cambridge, MA: Harvard University Press.

Robinson, A. (1998, 8 June). Roar for the Door. *Automotive News.*

Rugraff, E. (2010). Foreign Direct Investment (FDI) and Supplier Oriented Upgrading in the Czech Motor Vehicle Industry. *Regional Studies*, 44 (5), 627–638.

Saeidi, A. A. (2004). The Accountability of Para-governmental Organizations: The Case of Iranian Foundations. *Iranian Studies, 37.*

Salami, G. E. (2004). *The State in the Auto Industry: A Comparative Analysis between Iran, South Korea and Germany.* Tehran: University of Tehran (unpublished dissertation).

Saylor, R. (2012). Sources of State Capacity in Latin America: Commodity Booms and State Building Motives in Chile. *Theory and Society*, 41 (3), 301–324.

Schirazi, A. (1993). *Islamic Development Policy: The Agrarian Question in Iran.* Boulder: Lynne Rienner.

Schrank, A., & Whitford, J. (2011). The Anatomy of Network Failure. *Sociological Theory*, 29 (3).

Siavoshi, S. (1992). Factionalism and Iranian Politics: The Post-Khomeini Experience. *Iranian Studies*, 25 (3/4), 27–49.

Sit, V., & Liu, W. (2000). Restructuring and Spatial Change of China's Auto Industry under Institutional Reform and Globalization. *Annals of the Association of American Geographers*, 90 (4), 653–673.

Skocpol, T. (1982). Rentier State and Shi'a Islam in the Iranian Revolution. *Theory and Society*, 11 (3), 265–283.

Slater, D. (2010). *Ordering Power: Contentious Politics and Authoritarian Leviathans in Southeast Asia*. New York: Cambridge University Press.

Small, M. L. (2009). How Many Cases Do I Need?: On Science and the Logic of Case Selection in Field-Based Research. *Ethnography*, 10 (5), 5–38.

Soifer, H., & Hau, M. V. (2008). Unpacking the Strength of the State: The Utility of State Infrastructural Power. *Studies in Comparative International Development*, 43, 219–230.

Stark, D. (1991). Path Dependence and Privatization Strategies in East Central Europe. *East European Politics and Society*, 6 (1).

(1996). Recombinant Property in Eastern European Capitalism. *American Journal of Sociology*, 101 (4), 993–1027.

Sturgeon, T. J. (2002). Modular Production Networks: A New American Model of Industrial Organization. *Industrial and Corporate Change*, 11 (3), 451–496.

Sturgeon, T., Biesebroeck, J. V., & Gereffi, G. (2008). Value Chains, Networks and Clusters: Reframing the Global Automotive Industry. *Journal of Economic Geography*, 8, 297–321.

Thun, E. (2006). *Changing Lanes in China: Foreign Direct Investment, Local Governments and Auto Sector Development*. Cambridge: Cambridge University Press.

(2004). Keeping Up with the Jones': Decentralization, Policy Imitation and Industrial Development in China. *World Development*, 32 (8), 1289–1308.

Turner, R. (1996, 12 August). Faster Product Development Revolutionalizes Design Sector. *Automotive News*.

UNIDO. (2003). *United Nations Industrial Development Organization Strategy Document to Enhance the Contribution of an Efficient and Effective Small and Medium-Sized Enterprise Sector*. Vienna: United Nations Industrial Development Organization.

Wade, R. (2004). *Governing the Market*. Princeton: Princeton University Press.

(2003). What Strategies Are Viable for Developing Countries Today? The World Trade Organization and the Shrinking of "Development Space." *Review of International Political Economy*, 10 (4), 621–644.

Walder, A. (1995). Local Governments as Industrial Firms: An Organizational Analysis of China's Transitional Economy. *American Journal of Sociology*, 101 (2), 263–301.

Waldner, D. (1999). *State Building and Late Development*. Ithaca: Cornell University Press.

Waterbury, J. (1993). *Exposed to Innumerable Delusions: Public Enterprise and State Power in Egypt, India, Mexico and Turkey*. Cambridge: Cambridge University Press.

Weber, M. (2013, orig. published 1922). *Economy and Society*. Berkeley: University of California Press.

White, H. (2008). *Identity and Control: How Social Formations Emerge*. Princeton: Princeton University Press.

Whitford, J., & Potter, C. (2007). Regional Economies, Open Networks and the Spatial Fragmentation of Production. *Socio-Economic Review*, 5, 497–526.

Whittaker, H. D., Zhu, T., Sturgeon, T., Tsai, M. H., & Okita, T. (2010). Compressed Development. *Studies in Comparative International Development*, 45, 439–467.

Williams, M. (2014). *The End of the Development State?* London: Routledge Studies in Development and Society.

Wolfe, J. (2010). *Autos and Progress: The Brazilian Search for Modernity*. Oxford: Oxford University Press.

Wolfe, M. (2005). *Why Globalization Works*. New Haven: Yale University Press.

Wong, J. (2005). Re-making the Development State in Taiwan: The Challenges of Biotechnology. *International Political Science Review*, 25 (2), 169–191.

Woo-Cumings, M. (1999). *The Developmental State*. Ithaca: Cornell University Press.

Woods, N. (2006). *The Globalizers: The IMF, the World Bank and Their Borrowers*. Ithaca: Cornell University Press.

Wright, E. O. (1996). Embedded Autonomy Book Review. *Contemporary Sociology*, 25 (2), 176–179.

Appendix A   Methodology

Very little is known about the Iranian automobile industry. One unpublished Ph.D. dissertation from the 1970s provided background analysis before the revolution. Since the revolution, there have been no scholarly publications on the industry. Given that there is very little known about the industry, to ensure that I collected robust data and that the conclusions were accurate, I used the exploratory sequential mixed-methods approach (Creswell, 2013). In this approach, the researcher first begins with a qualitative research phase to explore the views of the participants. The data are then analyzed, and the information is used to build into the research agenda a second, quantitative phase. For this research, I employed the exploratory sequential method by starting with in-depth interviews and then analyzed archival data and reports to understand what important variables had led to the rise of the industry. I then used social-network analysis and the analysis of organizational and economic/statistical datasets to validate the variables obtained during the qualitative phase. Following is an overview of the methods used in the book and the techniques used to ensure accurate results.

In-Depth Interviews

The seventy-four interviews conducted for this book were important in shedding light on the policies of the industry, who the key actors were, and why they made policy decisions at specific points in time. Interviews allowed me to add detail in answering specific questions – detail that could not be achieved through content or quantitative analysis.

The majority of the interviews were conducted with current and former managers in the Iranian automobile industry and took place in their offices in Tehran in 2010–2011. Those interviewed were managers at Iranian automobile assembly plants, managers at parts-supplying companies, government employees of industrial development organizations, members of automobile business associations, Iranian politicians, and engineering consultants in Europe and Iran. Most of those interviewed had several years' work experience in the industry and could provide insight into the progress of the industry from 1980s through the 2000s. A few interviews with Western consultants took place via Skype or email correspondence. The duration of the interviews ranged between forty-five minutes and three hours. The interviews contained both structured and unstructured questions.

Snowball sampling was used for the interviews. There are two main reasons for using this method. The first is that Iran is a very closed society, and only through contacts can one develop trust to conduct an interview. The second is that the political situation made it difficult to implement random sampling by cold-calling potential participants.

To ensure that the interviews produced accurate data, I implemented error-reduction methods. First, snowball sampling has the disadvantage of causing the results to be biased, but I attempted to reduce the bias effects by increasing social contacts in the industry. Fortunately, I was able to interview all of the key actors in the industry except for a few who were not available because of political reasons. Second, an issue with interviewing past managers of the development project is recall bias, since memory can fade or create distortions of events. I attempted to reduce recall bias by relying on multiple sources such as archival data, newspaper articles, and previous interviews – using these sources to validate the accuracy of the interviews. Third, I focused on validating data that was politically sensitive. For instance, I relied on multiple sources to validate the accuracy of the role of engineering consultancies in transforming the technical capacity in the industry. Many of the informants were helpful in fleshing out inaccuracies on the part of industry insiders who wanted to portray a positive image of the industry. These informants were particularly useful in validating local manufacturing content. For instance, I discovered through multiple interviews that even though some high-ranking managers disagreed with Iran's industrial development policies, no one denied that the policies were instrumental in producing high local manufacturing content. However, critics of the industry were key in pointing out ways in which the numbers were inflated, and they provided insight into how to correct them to reflect the real local manufacturing content.

For interview methods, I used the case selection (Small, 2009) and elite interviewing methods (Moyser, 2006; Dexter, 2008). I developed an initial set of research questions based on the theoretical framing of the book. Consistent with elite interview methods, I allowed the interviewee the space to speak in an unstructured way without interruption before asking the next question. Elites are not accustomed to interruption while speaking, so the space to voice their experiences and opinions about the industry was key in gathering relevant data. Since most of the informants were high-status managers, they were often gatekeepers to other key managers in the industry; therefore, at the end of the interviews I asked them to provide contacts for others whom I could interview. After a critical number of initial interviews were conducted, I analyzed the data and generated new questions to probe deeper into new facts and events for a new round of interviews.

Archival Data

Archival data was retrieved from industrial trade magazines, newspapers and publications, annual reports, websites, popular newspaper articles, and the American publication titled the Foreign Broadcast Information Service (FBIS). Included among key trade magazines were the *Message* of Iran Khodro, the *SAPCO Magazine*, the *World of Automobiles*, Industrial Development and Renovation (IDRO) publications, *Iran International Trade Magazine*, and *World of Finance*. Some of the articles were originally published in English, while many were originally published in Farsi. Professional translators hired in Iran translated the Farsi articles. Archival analysis of newspaper articles was particularly important in uncovering the success and failure of industrial policies and the influence of political Islam on the transformation of the industry.

Social-Network and Statistical Analysis

The statistical data collected include complete production information from 1969 to 2009, prices of automobiles, quality data, a complete list of all current auto manufacturing companies in Iran (and what they manufacture), the number of auto companies and manufacturing companies founded per year, and the number of workers in the manufacturing sector.

I obtained two social-network datasets. The first is a dataset of technology transfer with 186 observations. The data relate to ties between foreign and Iranian parts companies, types of technology transferred, types of technical cooperation, and the year in which the cooperation was established. Ties between engineering consulting firms and multinational corporations on the one hand and between consulting firms and Iranian auto companies on the other hand were obtained through press releases, websites, trade press articles, and in-depth interviews.

The second dataset shows ownership ties in the Iranian automobile industry. The data for the social network analysis were obtained from a large, reputable Iranian business-consulting firm that conducted shareholder-mapping research of Iran Khodro and Iran Khodro Diesel for a foreign automobile client. The data contained a detailed mapping of all major and minor shareholders of Iran Khodro and Iran Khodro Diesel plus the percentage of shares owned by government ministries and financial firms and by Islamic state agencies such as the bonyads and various financial firms owned by the Islamic leadership.

Appendix B Timeline of Automobile Industrial Development

1949 – First Development Plan, Westernization of institutions.

1952 – 1953 – Fiat and Jeep begin assembling vehicles in Iran.

1953 – CIA overthrow of Prime Minister Mohammed Mossadegh.

1956 – Shah implements Second Development Plan.

1960 – Economic crisis: Iran and United States establish patron-client relationship. Iran becomes autonomous and implements infant industry protection.

1963 – Shah merges development agencies into the Ministry of Economy to manage industrial development.

1963 – Automobile industry is founded with the assembly of Hillman Hunter under the name of the Peykan.

1967 – Industrial Development and Renovation organization is established to speed up the pace of industrial development.

1974 – Shah lifts import substitution industrial policies and liberalizes the automobile industry.

1979 – Shah is deposed in the Iranian Revolution.

1980–1981 – Automobile industry is nationalized and foreign automobile imports are banned.

1980 – Iran-Iraq war begins.

1980–1988 – Era of incoherent automobile industrial development.

1988 – Iran-Iraq war ends.

1988 – Talbot goes bankrupt and Minister Behzan Nabavi purchases Peykan manufacturing equipment.

1989 – War related damage leads to economic crisis. Rafsanjani elected president and begins restructuring of the executive branch of government, institutional restructuring, legitimizing industrial development, rebuilding state capacity.

1989 – Rafsanjani Appoints Nejat Hossenian as Minister of Industry. He establishes Automobile Committee.

1989–1990 – Industrialists have conflict with left over manufacturing the Peugeot 405, compromise focus on Peykan.

1990 – Industrialists start conflict with neoliberals.

1990 – Saipa's parts supplier company Saze Ghostar founded.

1992 – Rafsanjani's economic policies create economic crisis, industrialists win against neoliberals and form national alliance to implement infant industry protection.

1992 – Nejat Hosseinian establishes automobile business associations.

1992 – Beginning of era of coherence and deepening of modern automobile manufacturing and founding of parts companies.

1992–1996 – Rafsanjani's privatization failure – sells companies to his cronies, economic crisis so privatization abandoned.

1993 – Iran Khodro's parts supplier company SAPCO founded.

1990–1995 – Large multinational automobile companies create independent automobile companies.

1995 – Samand project begins, Iran Khodro establishes ties with British engineering consultancy CGI.

1996 – Khatami does not prioritize privatization.

2001 – Conflict over globalization and conflict between Veyseh and Gharavi begins.

2004 – Iran Powertrain Company established to transfer technology.

2005 – Attacks on infant industry protection begin.

2005 – Ahmedenijad begins to implement privatization.

2006 – Government provides incentive for Iran Khodro and Saipa to open factories in rural areas.

2011 – Iran Khodro lobbies Supreme Leader to protect industry.

2011 – Ahmedenijad begins stronger push toward privatization.

2011 – Stakeholder model develops as result of privatization.

Index